'This timely and important book provides a critical look at borders and belonging. It illuminates the tensions and contradictions that often exist within the logic of legal and political mechanisms that define regional and national boundaries and the reality of the lives lived within these constructions. The resulting essays are instructive, thought-provoking and sometimes very moving explorations of the making and meaning of historical and contemporary borderlands.'

– Roisín Higgins, Professor of History,
National University of Ireland Maynooth

'This volume is a masterful combination of analyses of feelings of belonging and identities following from changing state and cultural borders in the past and present and their challenges for living together. Its chapters analyse the intersections of people, territory, institutions and law from theoretical perspectives as well as through reflexive individual experience of social identity formation from below, often with a focus on their contestation in (re-)territorialized sub-state regions.'

– Josef Marko, Professor of Comparative Public Law and Political Sciences,
University of Graz

Changing Borders and Challenging Belonging

Changing Borders and Challenging Belonging

Policy Change and Private Experience

Georg Grote and Andrea Carlà (eds)

PETER LANG

Oxford - Berlin - Bruxelles - Chennai - Lausanne - New York

Bibliographic information published by the Deutsche Nationalbibliothek. The German National Library lists this publication in the German National Bibliography; detailed bibliographic data is available on the Internet at http://dnb.d-nb.de.

A catalogue record for this book is available from the British Library.

Library of Congress Cataloging-in-Publication Data

Names: Grote, Georg, 1966- editor. | Carlà, Andrea, 1975- editor.
Title: Changing borders and challenging belonging : policy change and
    private experience / [edited by] Georg Grote and Andrea Carlà.
Description: New York : Peter Lang, 2024. | Includes bibliographical
    references and index.
Identifiers: LCCN 2023022286 (print) | LCCN 2023022287 (ebook) |
    ISBN 9781800796645 (paperback) | ISBN 9781800796652 (ebook) |
    ISBN 9781800796669 (epub)
Subjects: LCSH: Europe—Boundaries. | Minorities—Government
    policy—Europe. | Group identity—Europe. | Place attachment—Europe.
Classification: LCC D1058 .C495 2024 (print) | LCC D1058 (ebook) | DDC
    305.80094—dc23/eng/20230710
LC record available at https://lccn.loc.gov/2023022286
LC ebook record available at https://lccn.loc.gov/2023022287

This is a Gold Open Access title, with funding from EURAC.

Cover image: An original drawing by Ellen Earner.
Cover design by Peter Lang Group AG

ISBN 978-1-80079-664-5 (print)
ISBN 978-1-80079-665-2 (ePDF)
ISBN 978-1-80079-666-9 (ePub)
DOI 10.3726/b18969

PETER LANG
Open CC BY

© 2024 Georg Grote and Andrea Carlà
Published by Peter Lang Ltd, Oxford, United Kingdom
info@peterlang.com - www.peterlang.com

Contents

GEORG GROTE AND ANDREA CARLÀ

Changing Borders and Challenging Belonging: Policy Change and Private Experience

Introduction

The term *Zeitenwende* has, in recent months, once again become a household trope referring to drastic political events which shape a multitude of countries and regions and have repercussions across the globe. The Russian invasion of Ukraine and the atrocities committed by Russian soldiers have popularized this concept of disruption and existential angst as well as major political and military upheaval that uproot an entire population and create havoc with the world order – to some extent comparable to 1914, 1939, 2001 and other shocks to the global system. Global political upheavals of this sort always result in human catastrophe – ordinary people trying to cope with the magnitude of disruption and accommodate their lives within the maelstrom of change. In particular – and among the consequences of *Zeitenwenden* – such dramatic events impact borders as well as their definition and affect people's feelings of belonging and identities, posing both threats and/or opportunities for individuals and collectives alike.

Against this background, this volume has a two-fold focus: investigating the repercussions of major political events relating to changing borders and challenging belonging both 'from above' and 'from below'. From above, it explores legal and policy measures, institutional mechanisms and theoretical approaches addressing issues of borders and belonging across the globe following the alterations of legal and cultural frameworks, such as new borders, regime change, (de)colonization and violent upheavals. From below, it explores personal views on and responses to significant changes in addition to repercussions of major political events on private lives and feelings of belonging, principally in border regions and/or colonial and post-colonial contexts.

Across academic disciplines, social research has tended to be divided between research on the macro-level, focusing on large-scale political and social processes and developments, and on micro-level analysis, highlighting small-scale actions and interactions among individuals. This volume bridges this divide, comprising legal analysis, political science research on institutions and political processes as well as theoretical reflections and historical approaches focusing on a history from below and personal responses to changing political landscapes and new boundaries.

Our starting assumption is that both borders and identities are social constructions. Indeed, borders do not exist as they appear on maps. Political borders are not drawn in nature; rather they are 'imagined line(s)',[1] created by humans by 'connecting materiality and symbolic meaning'.[2] Performative discourses and practices transform geographical elements into borders.[3] Thus borders are not fixed and static entities, but they can change, move and be redrawn, gaining and losing importance. Moreover, processes of de- and reterritorialization as well as externalization of borders might be in place. As human artefacts constructed though narratives and practices, political borders have the potential to be sites of contestation, conflicts and tensions. In this context, concepts such as 'borderscape' aim at capturing the politics, fluidity and fluctuation of borders and their surrounding areas,[4]

1   Andrea Carlà, 'Securitizing Borders: The Case of South Tyrol', *Nationalities Papers* 50/1 (2022), 166–84, 168.

2   Paul Reuber, *Politische Geographie* (Paderborn: Ferdinand Schöningh, 2012), 67.

3   Petra Wlasak, 'Grenzen im Spannungsfeld von staatlichem Flüchtlingsmanagement, gesellschaftlichem Diskurs und migrantischer Selbstbestimmung', in Elisabeth Alber, Alice Engl and Günther Pallaver (eds), *Politika 2017* (Bozen: Edition Raetia, 2017), 53–63.

4   Chiara Brambilla, 'Il confine come borderscape', *Intrasformazione* 4/2 (2015), 5–9.

while Burridge et al. use the term 'polymorphic borders' to highlight their complexity and intersections with people, law, territory and institutions.[5]

Although artificially created, borders have real effects and consequences, moulding people's lives, since they are 'a manifestation of power that demarcates and organizes a space and articulates its limits, ordering as well the people that are located within' it.[6] In particular, they are markers of belonging that delimit people's identities and define membership in the community, and thereby people's rights and opportunities.[7] Usually, the term border is used in relation to borders between states, but different types of borders exist – from political borders delimiting states to administrative borders between regions and provinces or cultural borders, like linguistic and religious ones. We can find such power dynamics and processes of inclusion and exclusion in all types of borders.

Like borders, identities are social constructions, though at times primordial understandings are put forward, where national and ethnic/cultural identities are considered as fixed givens based on affiliations that are ascriptive and difficult to change.[8] The so-called instrumentalist approach highlights the strategic manipulation of identities by pointing out that people continually framed and reframed their identities for economic and political benefits. For example, in defining ethnic groups, Robert Bates emphasizes the fact that they 'are organized about a set of common activities', that their members 'share a conviction that they have common interests and common fate' and that they have 'a cultural symbolism expressing their cohesiveness'.[9] In his account, ethnic groups and identities are the fruit

---

5   Andrew Burridge, Nick Gill, Austin Kocher and Lauren Martin, 'Polymorphic Borders', *Territory, Politics, Governance* 5/3 (2017), 239–51.

6   Carlà, 'Securitizing Borders', 168.

7   David H. Kaplan, 'Conflict and Compromise among Borderland Identities in Northern Italy', *Tijdschrift voor Economische en Sociale Geografie* 91/1 (2000), 44–60; Wlasak, 'Grenzen im Spannungsfeld'.

8   See Donald Horowitz, *Ethnic Groups in Conflict* (Berkeley: University of California Press, 1985); Samuel P. Huntington, *The Clash of Civilizations and the Remaking of World Order* (New York: Simon and Schuster, 1996).

9   Robert Bates, 'Modernization, Ethnic Competition, and the Rationality of Politics in Contemporary Africa', in Donald Rothchild and Victor Olorunsola (eds), *The*

of rational efforts to create coalitions in order to secure material benefits created by social economic transformations. Identities are thus situational and 'dynamic;' their politicization is the result of rational decisions, made mostly by strategic political entrepreneurs.[10]

However, in this instrumentalist view, it is not clear why identities persist and why some identity groups mobilize while others do not. Furthermore, it does not address the contradiction of individuals considered rational calculators, who believe that their identity is a biological given. Addressing these issues, constructivist scholars of identity politics point out that social structures determine which social-cultural divisions become politicized. As pointed out by David Laitin, government activity 'structures opportunities in such a way as to determine the nature of social cleavage'.[11] By legitimizing some group identities to the detriment of others and creating common-sense thinking about these collectives, governments forge these identities politically, which, once forged, 'become commonsensically real'.[12] Such a constructivist perspective focuses on the source of the institutionalization of identities, emphasizing the importance of the structural context and the state in shaping identities and societal cleavages.

Within the constructivist tradition, this volume recognizes that any groupings of people are communities based on fictitious constructions and narratives. From this perspective, using Anderson's definition, nations are 'imagined communities' resulting from the 'social construction of reality'.[13] Similarly, as pointed out by Brubaker, ethnic groups are 'collective cultural representation [...] that sustain the vision and division of the social world in racial, ethnic, or national terms'. However, two clarifications are

---

    State Versus Ethnic Claims: African Policy Dilemmas (Boulder, CO: Westview Press, 1983), 153.

10 Bates, 'Modernization', 165; see also David Laitin, 'Hegemony and Religious Conflict: British Imperial Control and Political Cleavages in Yorubaland', in Peter B. Evans, Dietrich Rueschemeyer and Theda Skocpol (eds), *Bringing the State Back In* (New York: Cambridge University Press, 1985), 285–316, 300.

11 Laitin, 'Hegemony', 287.

12 Laitin, 'Hegemony', 308.

13 Benedict Anderson, *Imagined Communities* (London: Verso, 1983).

necessary.[14] First, as Joseph Marko clarifies, 'whenever people define this situation as "real" the consequences following from their actions are no less "real" than the "existence" of things'.[15] Thus, we cannot supersede the role that identities play in human society. Second, this volume builds on the notion that in processes of identity construction, people are not passive objects of broader social forces and dynamics; rather they are active subjects that interact with the social and institutional structures and negotiate and renegotiate their identities. In this regard, it is necessary to highlight the role that individuals' emotions, such as hatred, fear and resentment, might play in shaping identities.[16] Indeed, the concept of emotion can help explain why and how institutionally constructed identities become essentialized and crystallized and then become dominant. Thereby our aim is to combine and bring together top-down structural approaches and bottom-up analysis of personal experiences, with their weight of emotional baggage.

Within this constructivist framework, the volume explores issues surrounding changing boundaries and challenging belonging, addressing the tensions and contestations in the concepts of borders and identities. In this introduction, we start providing some in-depth reflections on the process of regionalization which has taken place within the European Union (EU) in the past decades. In the fallacy of Herderian understanding of nationalism, (state) borders and (national) identities are in symbiosis. However, in reality, the idea of a homogeneous nation-state is a myth. Human society is indeed based on the social facts of diversity and people's multiple identities. Regionalization is used as a tool to go beyond a 'nation-cum-state paradigm,' based on the slogan 'one nation, one culture, one

---

14   Roger Brubaker, *Ethnicity without Groups* (Boston, MA: Harvard University Press, 2004), 79.

15   Joseph Marko (ed.), *Minority Protection by Multiple Diversity Governance. Law, Ideology, and Politics in European Perspective* (London: Routledge, 2019).

16   Stuart J. Kaufman, *Modern Hatreds* (Ithaca, NY: Cornell University Press, 2001); David Lake and Donald Rothchild, 'Containing Fear: The Origins and Management of Ethnic Conflict', *International Security* 21/2 (1996), 41–75; Roger D. Petersen, *Understanding Ethnic Violence* (Cambridge: Cambridge University Press, 2002).

state',[17] recognizing simultaneously sub-state entities and state borders. In this regard, following a symposium in February 2012 in Bozen where academics investigated the role of borders in modern Europe, the proceedings were published in a volume titled 'Un mondo senza stati è un mondo senza guerre' – Politically Motivated Violence in Regional Contexts,[18] which dwelled on the somewhat naive notion that a limitless and timeless peace among people can be achieved through the rejection of the notion of statehood and its borders. At the time, the EU as a peace project appeared to many to be too reluctant to give up state boundaries in favour of a stronger role of the Unions' regions which were striving for greater political participation within the conglomerate of European states.

In 1984, historian Hans Mommsen proclaimed 'Die Nation ist tot, es lebe die Region' (The Nation is dead, long live the Region),[19] thus summarizing a widely felt notion that the nation, the decisive marker of collective belonging in Europe, had become an outdated model and was going to be replaced by regions, that is, sub-state geographic entities which were not associated with similar historic burdens. In 1998, Michael Keating published a comprehensive analysis of this new European order – *The New Regionalism in Western Europe. Territorial Restructuring and Political Change*[20] – which outlined both the major advantages of this regional focus for peacekeeping and the organization of collective identities and its potential threats to the existing order of Europe, the hollowing out of

17   On the nation-cum-state paradigm, see Joseph Marko et al. 'The Historical-Sociological Foundations: State Formation and Nation Building in Europe and the Construction of the Identarian Nation-cum-State Paradigm', in Joseph Marko (ed.), *Human and Minority Rights Protection by Multiple Diversity Governance. History, Law, Ideology and Politics in European Perspective* (London: Routledge, 2019), 33–95.

18   Georg Grote, Hannes Obermair and Günther Rautz (eds), *'Un mondo senza stati è un mondo senza guerre' – Politically Motivated Violence in Regional Contexts* (Bozen: Eurac Research, 2012).

19   Hans Mommsen, 'Die Nation ist tot, es lebe die Region', in Guido Knopp, Siegfriedt Quandt Herbert Scheffler (eds), *Nation Deutschland?* (Munich: Schöningh, 1984), 35.

20   Michael Keating, *The New Regionalism in Western Europe. Territorial Restructuring and Political Change* (Cheltenham: Edward Elgar, 1998).

the competencies of the nation-states through super state European institutions and sub-state regionalization.

Regional reorganization and increased political participation of the
regions seemed, at the time, to be a realistic option for the future of
the EU; after all, the Union had invited the regions as early as 1980 – in
the so-called Madrid Treaty – to embark on cross-border trade and political decision-making, thus following its own principle of subsidiarity.
The introduction of the European Groupings of Territorial Cooperation
(EGTCs) in the new millennium strengthened the role of regions once
again, and this at a time when the regions had already taken quite a bat-
tering in their political standing within the EU.

Nowhere in Europe and among the European regions has the pacifying
and prosperity-creating character of regionalization been more manifest
than in South Tyrol, the so-called German-speaking part of Italy. In this
province, which had, since its annexation by Italy in 1918, been a trouble-
some region in Europe for large parts of the twentieth century and a 'messy'
borderland and 'zone of confusion', a far-reaching geographical, political
and cultural autonomy for the German-speaking population (and a Ladin-
speaking minority) and its Italian fellow citizens has been instrumental in
creating a prosperous and peaceful area in the north of Italy.[21]

If the process of regionalization as a path to right historical wrongs
and to create peace and stability in a minority conflict scenario needed
any successful advocate, it was the case of South Tyrol. After achieving her
autonomy in Italy in 1972, the province made full use of any instruments
provided by the EU to emancipate from Italy – the one-time colonizer of
the area – and, somewhat more surprisingly, also from the old fatherland
Austria. South Tyrol, through the process of regionalization, has come as
close as possible to the idea of internal self-determination in the era of classic
nation-building processes of the nineteenth- and early-twentieth-century
period.[22] The autonomy, however, manifests itself within the confines of

21   Kaplan, 'Conflict and Compromise', 46.
22   See the detailed analyses of the South Tyrol issue by Georg Grote, *'I bin a*
      Südtiroler'. Kollektive Identität zwischen Nation und Region im 20. Jahrhundert
      (Bozen: Athesia, 2009) and *The South Tyrol Question, 1866–2010. From National*
      Rage to Regional State (Oxford: Peter Lang, 2012).

the Italian state and within a European framework in which state borders are guaranteed by fellow union states. While, at the same time, it has been a clear policy within the EU to reduce the significance of national boundaries both for its citizens and for international decision-making in Brussels.

At the end of the 1990s, the region seemed to be the key to solving most problems of citizens' political participation and the democratic deficits in the EU, which were rooted in the creation of its member states.

Designed to be a manifestation of collective identities on the sub-state level and thus well-equipped to solve regional trouble spots, created in the process of building the European nation-states, regions proved to be incapable, however, of responding to some of the major challenges of the new millennium. In fact, it was the reaction of the nation-states globally – and superstructures such as the EU – that defined the response to the terrorist attacks on the US in September 2001. Equally, regions had neither the tools nor the means to confront the fiscal and banking crisis in the EU from 2007–8 onwards, which required multinational responses.

The so-called migration crisis of 2015 saw regions as onlookers rather than actors, and the powerlessness of some of the UK's constituent territories in light of the 2016 Brexit referendum was yet another brick in the wall highlighting the impotence of regions. A similar situation arose with the Covid-19 pandemic, which was particularly drastic for those regions that had embarked on cross-border co-operation and the founding of cross-border bodies, such as the EGTC comprising Italian South Tyrol, Trentino and Austrian Tyrol. National borders, re-erected to stem the spread of the virus, now prevented free access from one part of the EGTC to the other. The Ukraine war presented its specific challenges, and once again the EU regions were in no position to respond, quite the opposite: the Russian threat made EU regions take shelter behind the boundaries of the EU and its individual building blocks, the nation-states. If anything, rather than re-gionalization, these dramatic events proved the need in a globalized world for proper coordination among levels of governance, regions, nations, the EU and other supranational institutions.

All of a sudden, the EU's core principle – whereby the EU guaranteed the existence of the national boundaries to all its member states – was no longer seen as a threat to the EU's collective identities, both large and small, but turned into a peace-keeping and peace-protecting means on the European continent, which was experiencing a real and existential threat of a brutal invader from the East. It has, to date, been the EU's strength that it confronts the external military, economic and political pressure created by Russia through its common and united stance and repeated declarations that its boundaries – that is, the individual state borders of its constituents – will be defended. This decisive stance also protects the European regions, and it is closely associated with the EU's most essential quality: the EU is first and foremost a peace project built on the destruction of the Second World War.

Thus, the question may be asked: are we looking at this particular *Zeitenwende* as a revitalizer and a guarantor of the peace-creating and peace-maintaining idea which has been at the core of the EU since its inception in the late 1950s? And are we living in a time where we witness new dynamics changing established borders and challenging belonging?

To explore macro-political processes and their consequences on the micro-level is at the core of this volume. Long before war was hoisted on Ukraine by Russia, we had planned a symposium at Eurac Research in South Tyrol, which, due to the Covid-19 pandemic, had to be first postponed and then abandoned. However, this volume bundles some of the contributions which would have formed the symposium in 2020, in order to make them accessible to a wider academic community.

Changing Borders and Challenging Belonging is therefore a multi-disciplinary investigation into issues of borders and belonging in general and in particular – both yesterday and today. This volume comprises, therefore, a range of analyses into the creation of borders and identities, both within given territorial entities and between them, and the effects of border creation on ordinary people. We do not understand borders purely in the post-Second World War context but aim beyond the realities of post-war Europe. Thus, *Changing Borders and Challenging Belonging* investigates scenarios prior to 1945 as well. While paying attention to South Tyrol, it also moves its focus to other parts of Europe and the world, from the UK to Australia.

Borders, in this context, can be defined as traditional borders between states, but also the newly erected boundaries within states to include one group and exclude others; they can mean state policy and they can be societal exclusion. We are including internal and external boundaries, physical and psychological demarcations into groups of those who belong and those who are excluded. Yet, whatever the nature of border creation might be, they trigger responses by those affected, which is the other main focus of this volume. Boundary changes have had massive consequences for people everywhere and at any time. It did not need the Ukraine war to demonstrate to us how so-called ordinary people have been affected by administrative changes, by domestic and international power politics and by wars.

The contributions in this volume range from theoretical approaches towards the topic to historical analyses, comprising micro-historical approaches and system analysis, to contemporary scenarios such as Brexit, just shy of the Ukraine war. The volume is organized according to approaches both from above and from below. It starts with analyses from above, presenting theoretical contributions by first JUSSI P. LAINE and then ROBERTA MEDDA-WINDISCHER and KARL KÖSSLER. LAINE provides theoretical insights that touch upon the core topic of the volume, highlighting the continuous misrepresentation of the real volume and value of migration and human mobility and the role of borders in processes of categorization. The author, furthermore, questions a nationalistic understanding of the concept of integration in light of multi-layered aspects of belonging that challenge the boundaries of nations and states. Connected to LAINE's appeal to turn inclusive egalitarian principles into concrete actions, MEDDA-WINDISCHER and KÖSSLER challenge the traditional understanding of citizenship, discussing the concept of regional citizenship and residence-based civic citizenship as a tool of social inclusion and participation at the sub-national level. Referring to a variety of examples mostly within the EU, the authors build theoretical arguments in favour of regional/residence-based practices of citizenship.

Moving from theory to empirical case studies, LEAH SIMMONS WOOD explores the slogan of taking back control implicit in the Brexit leave campaign, pointing out its fallacies – since the UK has never lost control of its borders within the EU framework – and its links with a nostalgia for the British Empire, where British identity has been built on racial exclusion. UK policies towards migrants and especially asylum seekers expose this desire to reinforce external and internal bordering, which has dramatic humanitarian consequences. ANDREA CARLÀ switches attention to the role of institutions for divided societies on the relationship between different communities and their identities. Using a securitization framework, the author compares Northern Ireland and South Tyrol, and analyses how their consociational power-sharing system affects the perception of others, fostering inclusive or exclusive understanding of the community.

Both ALEXANDRA TOMASELLI and TOBIAS WEGER draw attention instead to the impact of the process of state formation. TOMASELLI highlights its consequences for the Sámi people in Northern Europe and Russia, focusing and comparing the limited political powers of Sámi communities across countries (Norway, Sweden, Finland and to a lesser extent Russian Federation), as well as issues of discrimination and cross-border co-operation. Her analysis reveals a persistent colonial structure vis-à-vis Indigenous Peoples. Bridging from-above and from-below approaches, WEGER looks at the case of the contested border area of Dobrudja, divided between Romania and Bulgaria. Adopting a top-down perspective, the author traces the reconfiguration of state borders and state policies affecting the region and its diverse communities since 1878 to today, while exploring with a bottom-up approach the everyday pragmatic choices made by Dobrudja's inhabitants to face these political changes.

The remaining contributors apply the view from the bottom up as they investigate how government policies, national ideologies and state persecution affected individuals and groups inside and outside the defined frameworks. ENIKŐ DÁCZ discusses the autobiographical challenges of the ideological turbulences associated with the Second World War faced by three South-Eastern European writers, and particularly how they reworked their autobiographical narratives in an effort to come to terms with their own experiences and contacts with dictatorial regimes in the war period, while WINFRIED R. GARSCHA outlines the devastating effects of the National Socialist racial ideology on a young liberal Jewish woman, who, originating from a modern liberal identity perspective, got trapped in the binary Jewish/non-Jewish scenario created by the Nazis and who eventually falls victim to this pseudo-ideology.

KATIE HOLMES focuses on a different aspect of policy enforcement in the Australian context, the ill-fated settlement scheme of war veterans and their individual plight in the Australian outback. This example demonstrates that a policy which originated in the idea that the state would create a kind of welfare system for its veteran soldiers while, at the same time, continue to colonize the Australian continent could nevertheless have severe consequences on these individuals due to the shortcomings of the plan.

Finally, both MARKUS WURZER and GEORG GROTE focus on the central Alpine area. WURZER's contribution highlights the involvement of local German-speaking South Tyrolean soldiers in Italian colonial warfare – representatives of a recently colonized people in the north of Italy who now gained the opportunity to join the Italian army on its occupation of Abyssinia and who fell very much in line with the colonial narrative of Italy. GROTE's chapter is on the devastating impact of the Hitler-Mussolini agreement of 1939 on the identity of one South Tyrolean family. He demonstrates how the two dictators' dictum – if you cannot change the landscape you may exchange the populations – threw the relationship between five siblings into turmoil and how they tortured themselves and each other over the question to stay or to go in the run-up to the deadline of December 1939.

JUSSI P. LAINE

On Unbounded Belongingness: An Exploration into Reconfiguring Borders beyond Dualisms and Detachment

Introduction

This chapter advances the notion that people are not from a particular place. It argues that the politics of belonging cannot be reduced to a geographically placed and bounded community. Social, political and territorial demarcations persist, largely because of the collective reproduction of their underlying essentialist conception and logic, yet belonging and the conception of home are increasingly formed in relationship to movement. In a world increasingly on the move, it is necessary to acknowledge the multi-layered aspects of belonging that often straddle the boundaries of a state and nation. This necessitates a transition from the confines of methodological nationalism, social naturalization and political fixations to the empowering acts of belonging. Such a move also enables an integration of spatial socialization amid the multiplicity and situatedness of individual attachments, participation and the need for representation.

The chapter begins with a brief description of the recent migration patterns to demonstrate that migration continues to be largely misconstrued and misrepresented: it is often exaggerated yet it is less expectational than is often claimed. Migration – and its commonplace associated fears – has become effectively politicized. Such politicized migration is a global phenomenon but has been especially evident in the case of Europe.[1] The chapter elaborates on the role of borders in constructing and reconfirming the category of 'international migrant' in explaining how territorial state-centric imaginaries foster exclusionary policies, whereby the policies of nation-states often result in migration and harm. It thus seeks to contribute to and provide further grounds for the premise already stated in this volume's introduction that both borders and identities are social constructions rather than fixed, permanent and axiomatic lines of division. As human artefacts constructed through narratives, practices and performances, political borders can be conceptualized sites of both encounter and contestation,[2] open to some, yet closed to others.[3]

Before concluding with discussions of belonging in a globalized world, the chapter offers critical remarks on the normative aspects of integration.[4] Used as a yardstick, integration continues to be assessed predominantly with quantitative measures of migrants' socioeconomic performance, commonly in contrast with the 'non-migrant' 'native' population. Less attention is paid to who and what constitute the host population and society to

1   Mathias Czaika and Hein de Haas, 'The Effect of Visas on Migration Processes', *International Migration Review* 51/4 (2017), 894.

2   C. Brambilla, J. Laine, J. W. Scott and G. Bocchi, 'Introduction: Thinking, Mapping, Acting and Living Borders under Contemporary Globalisation', in C. Brambilla, J. Laine, J. W. Scott and G. Bocchi (eds), *Borderscaping: Imaginations and Practices of Border Making* (London: Ashgate, 2015), 1–9; Jussi P. Laine, Innocent Moyo and Christopher Changwe Nshimbi, 'Borders as Sites of Encounter and Contestation', in Christopher Changwe Nshimbi, Innocent Moyo and Jussi P. Laine (eds), *Borders, Sociocultural Encounters and Contestations: Southern African Experiences in Global View* (London: Routledge, 2020), 7–14; Chiara Brambilla and Reece Jones, 'Rethinking Borders, Violence, and Conflict: From Sovereign Power to Borderscapes as Sites of Struggles', *Environment and Planning D: Society and Space* 38/2 (2020), 287–305.

3   Jussi P. Laine, 'Exploring Links between Borders and Ethics', in J. W. Scott (ed.), *A Research Agenda for Border Studies* (Camberley: Edward Elgar, 2020), 177–8.

4   Jussi P. Laine, 'Thesis 6 – Inclusion of Migrants in Rural and Mountain Territories Is a Multilevel and Multidimensional Process', in A. Membretti, T. Dax and A. Krasteva (eds), *The Renaissance of Remote Places*. MATILDE Manifesto (London: Routledge, 2022), 60–7.

which a migrant is expected to aspire. Instead of continuing to fine-tune the analytical approach or fashioning yet another conceptualization of integration, this chapter claims that the entire premise from which the key postulation guiding our thinking stems needs to be re-evaluated. In an increasingly mobile world, it is necessary to acknowledge the multi-layered aspects of belonging, which often straddle the boundaries of nation and state. This chapter argues that a new understanding of being local, of belonging, should be sought through processes of inclusion and mutual recognition. These require continuous negotiation, but they fuel a social innovation in which the focus can be shifted from integration and assimilation to the co-creation of new transcultural spaces through embedding and of emplacement to allow everyone to feel at home.

Misleading migration patterns

The governance of human mobility can undoubtedly be seen as the most important challenge of the twenty-first century.[5] The challenge is not alleviated by the observation that much migration governance occurs in the shadow of an uncertainty in which facts, values and beliefs blur.[6] Rational assessments tend to be overshadowed by emotional outbursts, short-sighted stances and crisis-oriented framings. These not only obscure the matter at hand but also diminish the potential to understand and thus seek to properly address the challenge. Migration has become a field in which estimations often outweigh researched actualities, and hearsay

5   Achille Mbembe, 'Thoughts on the Planetary: An Interview with Achille Mbembe', *New Frame* (5 September 2019), 16.
6   Andrew Geddes, *Governing Migration beyond the State: Europe, North America, South America, and Southeast Asia in a Global Context* (Oxford: Oxford University Press, 2021), 1.

and myths govern concrete evidence.[7] While facts no longer seem to matter,[8] they certainly exist.

International migrants currently comprise 3.6% of the global population.[9] It is indisputable that the estimated overall number of international migrants has increased in recent decades: up from 2.4% in 1960 to 2.8% in 2000 (Figure 1). However, the growth is only moderate. In actual numbers, the global migrant stock has almost quadrupled from 71.8 million in 1960 to 281 million in 2020. Nevertheless, these numbers must be understood in relation to the rapid overall growth of the human population (from 3.0 billion in 1960 to 7.8 billion in 2020). The figure of 281 million includes those who migrated from one country to live in another; many more, of course, moved within their countries of origin, migrating from villages and towns and from towns to cities.[10] Yet it is more astonishing when the same *international* migration statistics are flipped: the vast majority of people (96.4%) continue to live in the country in which they were born. The volume of human mobility tends to be exaggerated for certain, often political, purposes. Around the world, migration continues to be the exception rather than the rule.

7   See Jussi P. Laine, 'Safe European Home – Where Did You Go? On Immigration, B/Ordered Self and the Territorial Home', in Jussi P. Laine, I. Moyo and C. C. Nshimbi (eds), *Expanding Boundaries: Borders, Mobilities and the Future of Europe-Africa Relations* (London: Routledge, 2020), 216–36.

8   Mbembe, 'Thoughts on the Planetary', 15.

9   OM, *World Migration Report 2020* (Geneva: International Organization for Migration, 2020); UN DESA, *International Migrant Stock/International Migration Flows to and from Selected Countries*. United Nations Database, POP/DB/MIG/Flow/ (New York: UN Department of Economic and Social Affairs, Population Division, 2022).

10   Dario Tarchi, Francesco Sermi, Sona Kalantaryan, Simon Mcmahon, Pinelopi Kaslama, Marlene Alvarez Alvarez and Martina Belmonte, *Atlas of Migration – 2021*, D. Bongiardo, L. Carrozza, I. Crespi, A. Dara and V. Pisapia (eds) (Luxembourg: Publications Office of the European Union, 2021).

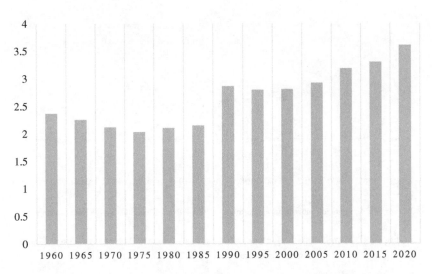

Figure 1. Global international migrant stock (% of population). Source: United Nations Population Division.

The share of migrants in the European Union (EU) (people living in a country other than that in which they were born) has climbed from 2.8% in 1960 to 12.2% in 2020. Yet, a large proportion of this can be explained by increased intraregional mobility, which for decades now has constituted one of the cornerstones of the European integration process. According to Eurostat and United Nations Department of Economic and Social Affairs (UN DESA) data, 5.1% (23 million people) of the 447.3 million people living in the EU were non-EU citizens in 2020, and almost 8.3% (37 million people) of all EU inhabitants were born outside the EU. There are considerable differences between the different member states, yet in all of them, the shares are remarkably lower than in most high-income countries. Ten years earlier, the share of third-country nationals (TCNs) in the EU was 4.6% (20.2 million people). The growth here can be considered quite modest – perhaps even too modest – as the immigration rate is no longer sufficient to balance out the negative natural population demographic inflicted by low birth rates and an ageing population (Figure 2). The natural change in the EU population remained positive – albeit decreasing – until 2011 but has been negative

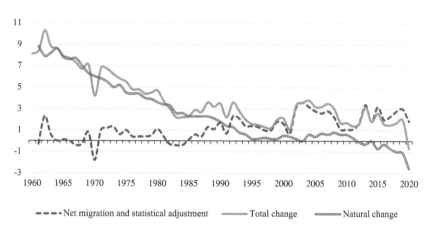

Figure 2. Population change by component (annual crude rates), EU, 1960–20.
Source: Eurostat (DEMO_GIND, 2021).

ever since (Figure 2). The total change remained positive due to net migration until 2020 when this number also became negative due to the reduced immigration resulting from the Covid-19 pandemic. In the EU, migration inflows declined in 2020 compared to 2019. Whereas in 2019, 2.9 million TCNs were granted permits to move to the EU, the number decreased to 2.2 million in 2020.[11]

Migration, as by now should go without saying, is a very complex phenomenon that comes in many shapes and forms. Following what came questionably to be heralded as a 'migration crisis' in 2015, the main focus was evidently shifted to the irregular forms of migration – to the extent that the terms 'migrant' and 'refugee' were occasionally used as synonyms. Free movement, migration and asylum were linked when large numbers of arrivals in Europe and secondary movement to other member states led to the reimposition of border controls between some EU member

11   Eurostat, 'Migration and Migrant Population Statistics – 2021', Online Data Codes: migr_imm1ctz and migr_pop1ctz; Tarchi et al., *Atlas of Migration – 2021.*

states.[12] Following Czaika and de Haas's earlier observation,[13] despite the extensive media and scholarly attention paid to irregular and other forms of 'unwanted' migration, the great majority of migrants still abide by the rules and regulations and move via regular channels. Geddes posits that the representation of asylum and third-country migration has been highlighted because it does not easily fit with a teleological representation of free movement and its relationship with the 'European project'.[14] Indeed, while free movement has been organized in this project as a core component of the EU's identity, migration and asylum have a much more ambiguous relationship with it, with a marked determination to organize the exclusion of those forms of migration defined by member states through their policies as unwanted, such as asylum seeking and irregular migration.[15]

Rather than migration per se, it is its chosen framing and representation that poses a problem. The widely shared images of desperate refugees trying to sneak into the EU over, under or through various fences have played into more enduring, often racialized, concerns about large-scale migration to the EU, reconfirming the perception that the situation is out of control and that order needs to be restored at 'our' borders.[16] The impact of framing is also evident in comparisons between the 2015–16 situation and the current Russian aggression against Ukraine. While in the former a little more than a million new arrivals were seen to challenge the resilience of the world's wealthiest continent, the around eight million who have fled from Ukraine (at the time of writing) have been met with appropriate yet unnoticed hospitality and unity. The apparent difference in the treatment of refugees in the EU demonstrates obvious limitations

---

12 Tanja Börzel and Thomas Risse, 'From the Euro to the Schengen Crisis: European Integration Theories, Politicisation, and Identity Politics', *Journal of European Public Policy* 25/1 (2018), 1–26.

13 Czaika and Haas, 'The Effect of Visas on Migration Processes', 893–926.

14 Geddes, *Governing Migration beyond the State*, 118.

15 Geddes, *Governing Migration beyond the State*, 119.

16 Jussi P. Laine, 'Ambiguous Bordering Practices at the EU's Edges', in Andrèanne Bissonnette and Élizabeth Vallet (eds), *Borders and Border Walls: In-Security, Symbolism, Vulnerabilities* (London: Routledge, 2020), 69–87.

to humanity,[17] highlighting the inability of European countries to meet their obligations, at least equally and unconditionally. It also proves that the alleged 'refugee crisis' in 2015–16 could have been avoided if there had been the political will to do so.

While there are certainly more people on the move today than in previous decades, as Mitchell, Jones and Fluri explicate,[18] the total number of irregular arrivals in Europe and the so-called Global North more generally has remained relatively modest, despite the political and media circus that has commonly presented the situation within a crisis frame.[19] The prevailing rhetoric depicting migration as a concern, problem or threat[20] continues to outperform the scientific evidence for immigration's positive economic and social impact.[21] Migration has been and will continue to be an important factor in EU population dynamics; many European countries will simply not be able to cope without migrants. As the statistics clearly indicate, migration – both regular and irregular – is a global rather than a European phenomenon. Although nearly half of international migrants are born in Asia, North America has recorded the largest gain in their absolute number.[22] More than a third of international migrants move between countries in the Global South, a greater share than those moving from the Global South to the Global North.

17   Addie Esposito, 'The Limitations of Humanity: Differential Refugee Treatment in the EU', *Harvard International Review* (14 September 2022).

18   Katharyne Mitchell, Reece Jones and Jennifer Fluri, 'Introduction' (co-authored with R. Jones and J. Fluri), in K. Mitchell, R. Jones and J. Fluri (eds), *Handbook on Critical Geographies of Migration* (London: Edward Elgar Press, 2019), 1–16.

19   Jussi P. Laine, 'Tabloid Media and the Dubious Terrain of Migration Reporting', *Ethical Space* 16/1 (2019), 34–40.

20   Laine, 'Exploring Links between Borders and Ethics'.

21   See Francine D. Blau and Christopher Mackie (eds), *The Economic and Fiscal Consequences of Immigration: A Report of the National Academies* (Washington DC: The National Academies Press, 2017); Martin Kahanec and Klaus F. Zimmermann (eds), *Labor Migration, EU Enlargement, and the Great Recession* (Berlin: Springer, 2016); Laine et al. (2021).

22   UN DESA, *International Migrant Stock/International Migration Flows to and from Selected Countries*.

Globally, by far the most striking increase has been witnessed in the number of those forcibly displaced by war, persecution and other violence. At the end of 1960, the total number of displaced people worldwide was 1.6 million; yet by the end of 2020, the figure had already risen to 82.4 million and has since continued to rise.[23] As such, between 1960 and 2020, the number of displaced people increased more than 50-fold. Of the 82.4 million, more than 26.4 million were refugees, which equates to 12% of all international migrants. The number of refugees worldwide decreased from 1990 (21.3 million) to a 26-year low in 2005 (13 million) before beginning to climb again. This moderate increase lasted until 2011, after which the rise has been more rapid. The share of refugees among migrants has also grown, indicating that forced displacements across national borders have continued to increase faster than voluntary migration. Yet by far the most significant increase is in the number of internally displaced persons (IDPs) – those who have not crossed a border at all. This figure hovered around five million throughout the 1990s and until 2005. The rise has since been increasingly rapid. By the end of 2020, the figure had reached 48 million according to the United Nations High Commissioner for Refugees (UNHCR), or even more than 55 million based on the estimates of the Internal Displacement Monitoring Centre (IDMC).[24] This significant group of the forcibly displaced often escapes media attention, populist threat narratives and migration statistics, for they do not travel internationally and therefore do not need to be hosted by another country. Apparently, in many fora, a person is perceived differently only when they have crossed the constructed political line.

The Covid-19 pandemic has had major implications for international migration flows. The foremost impact has been inflicted by travel restrictions, temporary border closures and reduced service provision capacities – for example, regarding the processes to apply for and obtain residence and work permits or to maintain integration programmes. The restrictive measures implemented both by EU member states, including the suspension of

---

23   UNHCR, 'Global Trends Forced Displacement – 2020', <https://www.unhcr. org/flagship-reports/globaltrends/>, accessed 11 November 2022.

24   IDMC, *Global Internal Displacement Database* (Geneva: Internal Displacement Monitoring Centre, 2020).

the registration of applications, and by third countries of migration transit and departure have substantially reduced the number of irregular arrivals, especially in the EU. Meanwhile, the Covid-19 pandemic has highlighted the vital contribution of migrants to keeping our societies and economies running.[25] Moreover, it has been acknowledged at the highest level that migrants play a key role in Europe's Covid-19 response capacity and recovery from the pandemic. According to a study by the European Commission's Joint Research Centre, 13% of key workers across the Union are immigrants, and in most countries, the share of extra-EU key workers is larger than the EU-mobile share.[26] In this sense, the crisis has been a significant moment of revelation as it accentuated the importance of migration and mobility for countries in Europe and around the world, often making distinctions between countries of origin and destination transit outmoded. As Commissioner for Home Affairs Ylva Johansson notes:

> We can't fight the virus without migrants. And our economies will not recover without migrants [...] If all migrants stopped working tomorrow, our economies would close down immediately. That shows migrants aren't 'them'. They're part of 'us'.[27]

Redefining migration

Human migration, as the widely accepted definition tells us, refers to the movement of people from one country to another across a political boundary. In practice, a person who moves several thousand kilometres from St Peterburg to Vladivostok within the Russian Federation or from

25 Claire Kumar and Elsa Oommen, 'Beyond Gratitude: Lessons Learned from Migrants' Contribution to the Covid-19 Response', ODI Working Paper 605, Overseas Development Institute (ODI), London, 2021; Tarchi et al., *Atlas of Migration – 2021*.

26 Francesco Fasani and Jacopo Mazza, *Immigrant Key Workers: Their Contribution to Europe's COVID-19 Response* (Ispra, Italy: European Commission – Joint Research Centre, 2020).

27 <https://storymaps.arcgis.com/stories/0bc1c0dcd2354263a00f7ed84f49155a>.

Nome in Alaska to Miami in Florida within the US is not considered a migrant, while a person who relocates a fraction of that distance – a matter of metres on some occasions – across a political boundary from, say, Strasbourg in France to Kehl in Germany is considered a migrant. This simplistic example here is not intended to level out the complexities of migration as a phenomenon but to highlight the role of borders as well as the political identifications that delineate them. As Gorodzeisky and Leykin note, the widely and uncritically used, seemingly politically neutral, statistical category of an 'international migrant/foreign-born' population ignores historical processes of both state formation and migration, thus privileging the current ethnonational definition of the state and legitimizing exclusionary policies.[28] Although where people happen to be born is arbitrary, 'the law of birth' continues largely to determine a person's legal recognition, political identification and thus mobility.[29] Citizenship understood in geographical terms as related to distinct exclusive territorial states remains people's most basic political identity.[30] Constructed in opposition to citizens, a nation's 'natives', migrants are constitutive of some of today's most denigrated and often dehumanized others – even while being represented as hardworking, desirable and prosperous.[31]

Despite the apparent trend by which borders have become increasingly understood as relations instead of fixed material things, the territorial fixity norm continues to underpin much of the modern geopolitical order and the entire international system in which we live and operate. This system of states is sovereignty, the overarching principle that orders

28   Anastasia Gorodzeisky and Inna Leykin, 'When Borders Migrate: Reconstructing the Category of "International Migrant"', *Sociology* 54/1 (2020), 142–58. See also Nicholas de Genova, 'Spectacles of Migrant "Illegality": The Scene of Exclusion, the Obscene of Inclusion', *Ethnic and Racial Studies* 36/7 (2013), 1180–98.

29   Laine, 'Exploring Links between Borders and Ethics'.

30   Simon Dalby, 'On "Not Being Persecuted": Territory, Security, Climate', in Andrew Baldwin and Giovanni Bettini (eds), *Life Adrift: Climate Change, Migration, Critique* (London: Rowman & Littlefield, 2017), 41–57.

31   Andrew Baldwin and Giovanni Bettini, 'Introduction', in Baldwin and Bettini (eds), *Life Adrift*, 1–21.

humanity's affairs; everything else supposedly follows from this mode of governance.[32] The fundamental argument behind the territorial state cartography that states represent nations stubbornly persists: ethnicity, in the form of a common identity, supposedly resides in places that can at least be approximately mapped as bounded territories.[33] Being unevenly transparent for different groups, depending on their origin, citizenship, material condition, and socio-professional belonging, borders are inevitably associated with discrimination, inequality and social injustice.[34] Despite the increasing complexity and processual and relational nature of the border concept, 'politics on the line' endures[35] and has, if anything, become only more strident: global politics is adamantly premised on territory and citizenship, and not on humanity.[36] Despite the frequent invocation of a universal humanity and cosmopolitan ethos to justify interventions under the responsibility to protect people in motion,[37] the underlying ontological premise for modern international relations continues to be tied to the unquestioned existence of and routinized relations between states. The criteria for people's access to a particular territory still depend on the paperwork related to their citizenship, often stubbornly derivative of their place of birth, not on the basis of their belonging to the species,[38] recognizing our broader planetary entanglement[39] and considering alternative forms of belongingness in transitioning to a less-bounded inclusivity.[40]

Coming up with convincing alternatives to state-centric teleology is undoubtedly challenging, and even if nationalism were understood more

32   Dalby, 'On "Not Being Persecuted"', 42.

33   Dalby, 'On "Not Being Persecuted"', 42.

34   Vladimir Kolossov and James W. Scott, 'Selected Conceptual Issues in Border Studies', *Belgeo: Revue belge de géographie* 1 (2013), 1–19.

35   R. Walker, *After the Globe, Before the World* (London: Routledge, 2010), 184.

36   Dalby, 'On "Not Being Persecuted"', 55.

37   Audra Mitchell, *International Intervention in a Secular Age: Re-enchanting Humanity?* (Abingdon: Routledge, 2014).

38   Dalby, 'On "Not Being Persecuted"', 55.

39   Mbembe, 'Thoughts on the Planetary'.

40   Jussi P. Laine, 'Beyond Borders: Towards the Ethics of Unbounded Inclusiveness', *Journal for Borderlands Studies* 36/5 (2021), 745–63.

reflexively,[41] it might well prove unsustainable. However, an important step in the right direction would be to consider a global model for mobility that allowed changing migration patterns to be managed in a way that ended discrimination based on mere place of birth. The very concept of 'native' is itself misleading, especially if the definition applied is borrowed from biology, as it often tends to be. A native species is found in a certain ecosystem due to natural processes such as natural distribution and develops in its surrounding habitat. Whereas transplanting or moving a plant or animal from its original habitat may cause it to atrophy or even die, this seldom happens to people. Rather, many seem to do much better in another environment than the one in which they happen to originate.

Hamid makes a persuasive appeal in this direction by urging us to challenge the juxtaposition between the migrant and the native.[42] He argues that humans as a migratory species have always moved across both time and geography. As none of us can be considered native to this moment, none of us is a native of the place we call home either. To be human, he maintains, is to migrate forward not only through time but also through space. To migrate is to grow as a person, as no punitive action will deter people from pursuing a better life:

> We move when it is intolerable to stay where we are. We move because of environmental stresses and physical dangers and the small-mindedness of our neighbors – and to be who we wish to be, to seek what we wish to seek.[43]

Amid the increasingly deterrent border and migration policies of the current era, these ideas may seem idealistic. However, they point towards the need to reconsider the key dualism not only on which much of modernity has been built, but also from which many of its key challenges are

---

41 Neil Walker, 'Teleological and Reflexive Nationalism in the New Europe', Euborders Working Paper 02, 2017 (Institut Barcelona d'Estudis Internacionals (IBEI), the Leuven Centre for Global Governance Studies (University of Leuven) and the Centre on Constitutional Change (CCC, Edinburgh)), <https://www.ibei.org/working-paper-02-euborders_145102.pdf>, accessed 26 April 2023.

42 M. Hamid, 'In the 21st Century, We Are All Migrants', *National Geographic* (August 2019).

43 Hamid, 'In the 21st Century, We Are All Migrants'.

derived. To follow Feldman, considering all of us as migrants might allow a greater degree of compassion for ourselves and thus a greater degree of compassion for others.[44] Once we abandon artificial distinctions between citizens and migrants, he reasons, we can learn much from the migrant experience about the more general alienation and atomization many contemporary citizens experience.[45] To overcome the migrant-hood condition, people must be empowered to constitute their own sovereign spaces from their particular standpoints. Instead of basing these spaces on categorical types of people, they emerge only as particular people present themselves to each other while questioning how they should inhabit it.

Human migration has been a persistent feature of human history and will continue to be so for years to come. While recurrent crises have consolidated particular representations of what is 'normal' about migration and have evidently shaped our responses,[46] it is important to remember that migration, for most of history, has been considered normal and not something to be fought against. Only recently have people on the move been depicted as a major problem. It is time to reverse this perception and, as Shah writes,[47] turn migration from a perceived crisis into the solution for manifold socioecological changes. As Mbembe argues, human mobility is normal; its governance is the challenge.[48]

Integration: A pivotal concept?

Formal laws, regulations and policies have been put in place in various countries to facilitate the settlement of immigrants and their integration

44   Gregory Feldman, *We Are All Migrants: Political Action and the Ubiquitous Condition of Migrant-hood* (California: Stanford University Press, 2015).
45   Feldman, *We Are All Migrants*, 105.
46   Geddes, *Governing Migration beyond the State*, 113.
47   Sonia Shah, *The Next Great Migration: The Beauty and Terror of Life on the Move* (New York: Bloomsbury, 2020).
48   Mbembe, 'Thoughts on the Planetary'.

into the host society. Various indicators have been defined to measure the level of integration (e.g. OECD/European Union 2015), with the aid of which immigrants tend to be categorized in relation to their success in achieving the predefined integration benchmarks set against a normative framework and presumably agreed, often nationally defined, standards. A glance at the prevailing public and political rhetoric suggests, first, that integration – understood as a sort of ideal end state – is indeed a desirable if unfeasible goal and that success in this respect is still often considered to depend more on the immigrant's characteristics and actions than on those of the receiving society. 'Society' here usually refers to the 'country' into which immigrants are expected to integrate themselves socio-economically and adapt to its sociocultural norms, values and customs. Used as a yardstick, integration thus continues to be assessed predominantly with quantitative measures of migrants' socioeconomic performance, commonly in contrast with the 'non-migrant' 'native' population.[49] Less attention is paid to who and what constitute the host population and society to which a migrant is expected to aspire. Central to the idea of a host population as a 'norm' is that it consists of a homogeneous group into which immigrants should integrate:[50] namely, a *nation*-state. It is argued here that this expectation is extremely biased and only accentuates the unfeasibility of the goal of integration by distorting the reality.

Meanwhile, many of the dominant academic approaches continue to remind us that integration is a two-way process in which both parties actively participate. Acknowledging this duality has also become popular in the associated policy circles. However, while certainly valuable in terms of checks and balances, the mere realization itself does little to blur the social boundaries and binaries between 'us' and 'them', 'insiders'

---

49   Evelyn Ersanilli and Ruud Koopmans, 'Do Immigrant Integration Policies Matter? A Three-Country Comparison among Turkish Immigrants', *West European Politics* 34/2 (2011), 208–34; Richard Alba and Nancy Foner, 'Integration's Challenges and Opportunities in the Wealthy West', *Journal of Ethnic and Migration Studies* 42/1 (2016), 3–22.

50   Sawitri Saharso, 'Who Needs Integration? Debating a Central, yet Increasingly Contested Concept in Migration Studies', *Comparative Migration Studies* 7/16 (2019), <https://doi.org/10.1186/s40878-019-0123-9>.

and 'outsiders', those who belong and those who are perceived as not belonging. As Klarenbeek argues, the concept of two-way integration remains underdefined, and its mere endorsement is insufficient to avoid or resolve the problems of a single-direction approach.[51] As she demonstrates convincingly, despite their good intentions, many dominant theoretical approaches to the two-way nature of integration have led to internal contradictions, only adding to and reinforcing, even if implicitly and unintentionally, a one-way integration discourse.[52] In other words, they have reconfirmed the existential separation between those who are considered to constitute 'society' by default and those who do not, and who therefore need to 'integrate' further.[53]

Even if it is bidirectional, the change both parties experience often remains completely unbalanced. This implies uneven power relations, normatively different responsibilities and thus different degrees of control of the process.[54] In moving up the social ladder, being 'well integrated' becomes the highest possible achievement for an outsider.[55] Yet by this logic even 'well-integrated' immigrants can never truly become insiders, for if they could do so, they would not be 'well integrated': integration would not even be an issue.[56] As long as the unquestioned image of an 'insider' continues to function as the benchmark against which the achievements of 'outsiders' are compared, the reproduction of social boundaries, inequality and the perceived difference they imply will continue to downplay any rhetorical commitments to the contrary. Such a reconfirmation of differences tends

51   Lea M. Klarenbeek, 'Reconceptualising "Integration as a Two-Way Process"', *Migration Studies* 9/3 (2019), 902–21.
52   Klarenbeek, 'Reconceptualising "Integration as a Two-Way Process"'.
53   Willem Schinkel, 'Against "Immigrant Integration": For an End to Neocolonial Knowledge Production', *Comparative Migration Studies* 6/31 (2018), 1–17.
54   David Miller, *Stranger in Our Midst: The Political Philosophy of Immigration* (Cambridge, MA: Harvard University Press, 2016); Klarenbeek, 'Reconceptualising "Integration as a Two-Way Process"'.
55   Willem Schinkel 'The Imagination of "Society" in Measurements of Immigrant Integration', *Ethnic and Racial Studies*, 36/7 (2013), 1142–61.
56   Kristine Horner and Jean-Jacques Weber, 'Not Playing the Game: Shifting Patterns in the Discourse of Integration', *Journal of Language and Politics* 10/2 (2011), 139–59.

to divert attention from the deeply rooted structural factors that maintain inequality to individual ones perceived as beyond *our* control.

The broadly established and increasingly elaborate systems for monitoring, categorizing and bordering reproduce otherness, maximizing its visibility in seeking to preserve and reconfirm a continuous positive version of the self, and the durability of the invisible social glue that is used to hold 'us' together. A 'drawing self' is constantly present behind the portraits of others.[57] The more negative the qualities attributed to 'them', the more positive 'we' seem in comparison,[58] and these representations seldom seek accuracy. Indeed, following Ahmed,[59] strangers are not those whom we do not recognize, but those whom we recognize as strangers. Instead of fixating on integration, it is these subtle forms of sociocultural bordering to which attention must be paid to advance our societies' resilience, well-being and fairness. Certainly, the immigrant's integration is not only shaped by explicit integration policies;[60] informal institutions among immigrants – such as religion and culture – can also determine its success, and immigrant groups may become either an accepted part of society at the same level as comparable 'native' groups, or they may isolate themselves and remain unrecognized and excluded.[61] However, more integration does not necessarily equate to more harmony, as changing power relations cause social friction.[62] An integrated society is not automatically 'better' or more socially just.

---

57 Dmitry Chernobrov, 'Ontological Security and Public (Mis)recognition of International Crises: Uncertainty, Political Imagining, and the Self', *Political Psychology* 37/5 (2016), 596.

58 Laine, 'Safe European Home – Where Did You Go?', 75.

59 Sara Ahmed, *Strange Encounters: Embodied Others in Post-Coloniality* (London: Routledge, 2000), 19.

60 Liza Mügge and Marleen van der Haar, 'Who Is an Immigrant and Who Requires Integration? Categorizing in European Policies', in B. Garcés- Mascareñas and R. Penninx (eds), *Integration Processes and Policies in Europe* (Cham: Springer, 2016), 77–90.

61 Garcés-Mascareñas and Penninx, *Integration Processes and Policies in Europe*.

62 Klarenbeek, 'Reconceptualising "Integration as a Two-Way Process"', 13.

Instead of continuing to fine-tune the analytical approach or fashioning yet another conceptualization of integration, this thesis claims that the entire premise of the key postulation guiding our thinking needs to be re-evaluated. Like the nocturnal drunkard looking for his lost keys under a streetlight because that is where they are easiest to see, we have continued to seek solutions to the challenges we face in the areas illuminated by our past state-oriented practices. Correspondingly, the key problems that European societies are addressing with their immigrant integration logics cannot be resolved through redefinitions or re-appropriations of the term itself.[63] A more fundamental readjustment is needed, and a key element of this endeavour is to advance the notions that people are not from a particular territorially bounded place and that the politics of belonging cannot be reduced to mere citizenship. Social, political and territorial demarcations persist largely because of the collective reproduction of their underlying essentialist conception and logic; yet belongingness and the conception of home are increasingly formed in relation to movement. In an increasingly mobile world, it is necessary to acknowledge the multi-layered aspects of belonging, which often straddle the boundaries of nation and state.

The inclusion and emplacement of migrants therefore needs to be understood as both a multi-level and multi-dimensional process, in which the different layers – if intertwined – may also have their own dynamics. While belongingness must often still be enacted within the frame of the respective nation-state, and belonging to a certain nation continues to have an undeniable appeal,[64] the assumed deeply rooted ideal linkage between these concepts needs to be rethought – just as it is necessary to re-think the relationship between citizenship and the state. As Yuval-Davis argues, people can simultaneously 'belong' in many different ways and to many different objects of attachment.[65] Belonging, she reasons, is not only

63   Fran Meissner and Tilmann Heil, 'Deromanticising Integration: On the Importance of Convivial Disintegration', *Migration Studies* 9/3 (2020), 740–59.

64   Jussi P. Laine, 'The Multiscalar Production of Borders', *Geopolitics* 21/3 (2016), 471.

65   Nira Yuval-Davis, 'Belonging and the Politics of Belonging', *Patterns of Prejudice*, 40/3 (2006), 199; Nira Yuval-Davis, Georgie Wemyss and Kathryn Cassidy, *Bordering* (Cambridge: Polity Press, 2019).

about social locations and constructions of individual and collective identities and attachments; it is also about how they are valued and judged.[66] Belongings are seldom clear-cut; rather, they are fragmented and coincidentally rearticulated as constellations in which national identification plays only a part.[67] This argument is made here in full acknowledgement of the incontrovertible fact that the idea of people being able to carry 'bundles of rights' with them across nation-state borders is one of the first lines of attack by nation-states when a perceived 'crisis' emerges.[68]

Conclusion: Towards belonging in a globalized world

To confront the simplistic relapse into state-centric thinking in times of 'crisis',[69] it is necessary to highlight shifting power relations at the global, regional and local levels.[70] Here, the increasing significance of the global level at the expense of regional integration and bilateral agreement has reawakened interest in interstate co-operation.[71] The rapid changes associated with globalization have decentred the state in some respects;[72] yet the legal power to determine who is and who is not admitted to the territory of a particular country and recognized as a citizen is an enduring

66   Yuval-Davis, 'Belonging and the Politics of Belonging', 204.
67   Laine, Moyo and Nshimbi, 'Borders as Sites of Encounter and Contestation'.
68   Jock Collins, 'Migration to Australia in Times of Crisis', in Cecilia Menjívar, Marie Ruiz and Immanuel Ness (eds), *The Handbook of Migration Crises* (Oxford: Oxford University Press, 2019), 817–31.
69   Laine, 'Ambiguous Bordering Practices at the EU's Edges'.
70   Paula García Andrade, 'EU External Competences in the Field of Migration: How to Act Externally When Thinking Internally', *Common Market Law Review* 55/1 (2018), 157–200.
71   Marion Panizzon and Micheline van Riemsdijk, Introduction to Special issue: 'Migration Governance in an Era of Large Movements: A Multi-Level Approach', *Journal of Ethnic and Migration Studies* 45/8 (2019), 1225–41.
72   Laine, 'The Multiscalar Production of Borders'.

arena of state control.[73] EU member states have insisted on maintaining absolute control of 'security matters' – a category into which migration is too often considered to fall. Despite the intra-EU levelling process intended to recommit member states to the duty of solidarity, an *extra-EU* co-operation strategy for third countries has gained ground as the member states have sought to renegotiate their obligations to the Union to maximize the policy space around migration and asylum – that is, to reaffirm migration as 'foreign policy'.[74]

While numerous scholars have urged that both the moral and economic imperatives of migration be recognized in line with what Juss[75] calls the 'global public interest', pleas for unbounded inclusiveness[76] have fallen prey to renationalized populist politics and methodological nationalism. Within contexts of socioeconomic stress and geopolitical instability – of which a prime example is the current crisis inflicted by the persistent pandemic – a strong state tends to be offered and broadly accepted as a solution to the perceived chaos, and simplistic politics as a cure for the complexities it has cultivated. These increasingly emotional reactions have not only largely overshadowed the scientific evidence pointing to the benefits of immigration, they have also turned a blind eye to the increasingly evident notion – for example, advocated by Jones and Wonders[77] – that the policies of nation-states often *produce* migration, harm and even violence.

---

73   Leanne Weber and Claudia Tazreiter, 'Introduction: Migration and Global Justice', in L. Weber and C. Tazreiter (eds), *Handbook of Migration and Global Justice* (Cheltenham: Edward Elgar, 2021), 1–15.

74   Panizzon and van Riemsdijk, Introduction to Special Issue: 'Migration Governance in an Era of Large Movements', 1228.

75   Satvinder Singh Juss, *International Migration and Global Justice* (Aldershot: Ashgate, 2016).

76   Laine, 'Beyond Borders', 745–63.

77   Lynn C. Jones and Nancy A. Wonders, 'Migration as a Social Movement', <https://www.law.ox.ac.uk/research-subject-groups/centre-criminology/centreborder-criminologies/blog/2019/05/migration-social>, accessed 17 November 2021. See also, N. A. Wonders and L. C. Jones, 'Challenging the Borders of Difference and Inequality: Power in Migration as a Social Movement for Global Justice', in Weber and Tazreiter, *Handbook of Migration and Global Justice*, 296–313.

While inclusive legal frameworks and efforts for effective global change are needed – the *Global Compact* being the first intergovernmentally negotiated agreement aiming for holistic and comprehensive change – the local level has been gaining importance as a setting for inter-ethnic coexistence and participatory action. In contrasting the rise of crisis frames and a politics of exclusion, human agency deserves to be restored to the centre to redefine the meaning of belonging in a globalized world.[78] In this endeavour, the place-bound social relations of individuals offer great potential. Ultimately, despite globalization processes, place continues to be an object of strong attachment[79] and an inescapable aspect of people's everyday lives and experiences.[80] However, once again, countering migrant exclusion requires more than universal appeals to inclusive egalitarian principles: abstract principles and norms need to be translated into concrete action, which is often more easily said than done. Achieving inclusivity requires concrete knowledge and practical guidance that encourage local administrations and other stakeholders to see this as part of their responsibility and fulfil their role in this respect.

Place-making by migrant populations has long been seen as an essential strategic response to the alienation, isolation and discrimination experienced by newcomers because it helps cement new identities as well as sustain and empower marginalized communities.[81] However, these new places may be accompanied by the negative implications of heightened ethnic differences through place-making.[82] A new understanding of being

78 Wonders and Jones, 'Challenging the Borders of Difference and Inequality'.

79 Per Gustafson, 'Place Attachment in Age of Mobility', in L. C. Manzo and P. Devine-Wright (eds), *Place Attachment: Advances in Theory, Methods and Application* (London: Routledge, 2014), 37–49.

80 Alisha Butler and Kristin A. Sinclair, 'Place Matters: A Critical Review of Place Inquiry and Spatial Methods in Education Research', *Review of Research in Education* 44/1 (2020), 64.

81 Deborah Phillips and David Robinson, 'Re•ections on Migration, Community, and Place', *Population, Space and Place* 21/5 (2015), 409–20.

82 Nick Gill, 'Pathologies of Migrant Place-Making: The Case of Polish Migrants to the UK', *Environment and Planning A* 42/5 (2010), 1157–73.

local – of belonging – should be sought through processes of inclusion and mutual recognition. These require continuous negotiation, but they fuel a social innovation in which the focus can be shifted from integration and assimilation to the co-creation of new transcultural spaces, economies and communities. This approach promotes social inclusion as a non-linear and reciprocal interaction through which new population groups negotiate new cultural meanings and tangible rights of citizenship with the existing populations within systems of socio-economic, legal and cultural relations whose basic characteristics need to be considered if a sustainable, equitable and resilient society is to be created for all. The resulting communities will not only be different; they will be better adapted to thrive in the context of the current era's seemingly endless uncertainty.

Bibliography

Ahmed, S., *Strange Encounters: Embodied Others in Post-Coloniality* (London: Routledge, 2000).

Alba, R. and Foner, N., 'Integration's Challenges and Opportunities in the Wealthy West', *Journal of Ethnic and Migration Studies* 42/1 (2016), 3–22.

Baldwin, A. and Bettini, G., 'Introduction: Life Adrift', in A. Baldwin and G. Bettini (eds), *Life Adrift: Climate Change, Migration, Critique*, 1–21 (London: Rowman & Littlefield, 2017).

Blau, F. D. and Mackie, C. (eds), *The Economic and Fiscal Consequences of Immigration*. A Report of the National Academies (Washington, DC: The National Academies Press, 2017).

Brambilla, C. and Jones, R., 'Rethinking Borders, Violence, and Conflict: From Sovereign Power to Borderscapes as Sites of Struggles', *Environment and Planning D: Society and Space* 38/2 (2020), 287–305.

Brambilla, C., Laine, J., Scott, J. W. and Bocchi, G., 'Introduction: Thinking, Mapping, Acting and Living Borders under Contemporary Globalisation', in C. Brambilla, J. Laine, J. W. Scott and G. Bocchi (eds), *Borderscaping: Imaginations and Practices of Border Making* (London: Ashgate, 2015), 1–9.

Butler, A. and Sinclair, K. A., 'Place Matters: A Critical Review of Place Inquiry and Spatial Methods in Education Research', *Review of Research in Education* 44/1 (2020), 64–96, <https://doi.org/10.3102/0091732X20903303>.

Chernobrov, D., 'Ontological Security and Public (Mis)recognition of International Crises: Uncertainty, Political Imagining, and the Self', *Political Psychology* 37/5 (2016), 581–96, <https://doi.org/10.1111/pops.12334>.

Collins, J., 'Migration to Australia in Times of Crisis', in C. Menjivar, M. Ruiz and I. Ness (eds), *The Handbook of Migration Crises* (Oxford: Oxford University Press, 2019), 817–31.

Czaika, M. and de Haas, H., 'The Effect of Visas on Migration Processes', *International Migration Review* 51/4 (2017), 893–926.

Dalby, S., 'On "Not Being Persecuted": Territory, Security, Climate', in A. Baldwin and G. Bettini (eds), *Life Adrift: Climate Change, Migration, Critique* (London: Rowman & Littlefield, 2017), 41–57.

Ersanilli, E. and Koopmans, R., 'Do Immigrant Integration Policies Matter? A Three-Country Comparison among Turkish Immigrants', *West European Politics* 34/2 (2011), 208–34.

Esposito, A., 'The Limitations of Humanity: Differential Refugee Treatment in the EU', *Harvard International Review* (14 September 2022).

Eurostat, 'Migration and Migrant Population Statistic – 2021', Online Data Codes: migr_imm1ctz and migr_pop1ctz, <https://ec.europa.eu/eurostat/statistics-explained/index.php?title=Migration_and_migrant_population_statistics>, accessed 27 April 2023.

Fasani, F. and Mazza, J., *Immigrant Key Workers: Their Contribution to Europe's COVID-19 Response* (Ispra, Italy: European Commission – Joint Research Centre, 2020).

Feldman, G., *We Are All Migrants: Political Action and the Ubiquitous Condition of Migrant-Hood* (Stanford, CA: Stanford University Press, 2015).

Garcés-Mascareñas, B. and Penninx, R., *Integration Processes and Policies in Europe – Contexts, Levels and Actors* (Dordrecht: Springer, 2016).

García Andrade, P., 'EU External Competences in the Field of Migration: How to Act Externally When Thinking Internally', *Common Market Law Review* 55/1 (2018), 157–200.

Geddes, A., *Governing Migration beyond the State: Europe, North America, South America, and Southeast Asia in a Global Context* (Oxford: Oxford University Press, 2021).

Genova, N. de, 'Spectacles of Migrant "Illegality": The Scene of Exclusion, the Obscene of Inclusion', *Ethnic and Racial Studies* 36/7 (2013), 1180–98.

Gill, N., 'Pathologies of Migrant Place-Making: The Case of Polish Migrants to the UK', *Environment and Planning A* 42/5 (2010), 1157–73.

Gorodzeisky, A. and Leykin, I., 'When Borders Migrate: Reconstructing the Category of "International Migrant"', *Sociology* 54/1 (2020), 142–58.

Gustafson, P., 'Place Attachment in Age of Mobility', in L. C. Manzo and P. Devine-Wright (eds), *Place Attachment: Advances in Theory, Methods and Application* (London: Routledge, 2014), 37–49.

Hamid, M., 'In the 21st Century, We Are All Migrants', *National Geographic* (August 2019).

Horner, K. and Weber, J.-J., 'Not Playing the Game: Shifting Patterns in the Discourse of Integration', *Journal of Language and Politics* 10/2 (2011), 139–59.

IDMC, *Global Internal Displacement Database* (Geneva: Internal Displacement Monitoring Centre, 2020).

IOM, *World Migration Report 2020* (Geneva: International Organization for Migration, 2020).

Jones, L. C. and Wonders, N. A., 'Migration as a Social Movement' (2019), <https://www.law.ox.ac.uk/research-subject-groups/centre-criminology/centreborder-criminologies/blog/2019/05/migration-social>, accessed 17 November 2021.

Juss, S. S., *International Migration and Global Justice* (Aldershot: Ashgate, 2006).

Kahanec, M. and Zimmermann, K. F. (eds), *Labor Migration, EU Enlargement, and the Great Recession* (Berlin: Springer, 2016).

Klarenbeek, L. M., 'Reconceptualising "Integration as a Two-Way Process"', *Migration Studies*, mnz033 (2019), <https://doi.org/10.1093/migration/mnz033>.

Kolossov, V. and Scott, J. W., 'Selected Conceptual Issues in Border Studies', *Belgeo: Revue belge de géographie* 1 (2013), 1–19.

Kumar, C. and Oommen, E., 'Beyond Gratitude: Lessons Learned from Migrants' Contribution to the Covid-19 Response', ODI Working Paper 605, Overseas Development Institute (ODI), London, 2021.

Laine, J., 'The Multiscalar Production of Borders', *Geopolitics* 21/3 (2016), 465–82.<https://doi.org/10.1080/14650045.2016.1195132>.

——, 'Tabloid Media and the Dubious Terrain of Migration Reporting', *Ethical Space* 16/1 (2016), 34–40.

——, 'Safe European Home – Where Did You Go? On Immigration, B/Ordered Self and the Territorial Home', in J. Laine, I. Moyo and C. C. Nshimbi (eds), *Expanding Boundaries: Borders, Mobilities and the Future of Europe-Africa Relations* (London: Routledge, 2020), 216–36.

——, 'Ambiguous Bordering Practices at the EU's Edges', in A. Bissonnette and É. Vallet (eds), *Borders and Border Walls: In-Security, Symbolism, Vulnerabilities* (London: Routledge, 2020), 69–87.

——, 'Exploring Links between Borders and Ethics', in J. W. Scott (ed), *A Research Agenda for Border Studies* (Camberley: Edward Elgar, 2020), 163–80.

——, 'Beyond Borders: Towards the Ethics of Unbounded Inclusiveness', *Journal for Borderlands Studies* 36/5 (2021), 745–63.

—— (ed.), 'Comparative Report and Social Innovation Practices', MATILDE – Migration Impact Assessment to Enhance Integration and Local Development in European Rural and Mountain Areas (870831), 2021.<https://doi.org/10.5281/zenodo.5017793>.

Laine, J., Moyo, I. and Nshimbi, C. C., 'Borders as Sites of Encounter and Contestation', in C. C. Nshimbi, I. Moyo and J. Laine (eds), *Borders, Sociocultural Encounters and Contestations: Southern African Experiences in Global View* (London: Routledge, 2020), 7–14.

Mbembe, A., 'Thoughts on the Planetary: An Interview with Achille Mbembe', *New Frame* (5 September 2019), 16.

Meissner, F. and Heil, T., 'Deromanticising Integration: On the Importance of Convivial Disintegration', *Migration Studies* mnz056 (2020), <https://doi.org/10.1093/migration/mnz056>.

Miller, D., *Stranger in Our Midst. The Political Philosophy of Immigration* (Cambridge, MA: Harvard University Press, 2016).

Mitchell, A., *International Intervention in a Secular Age: Re-enchanting Humanity?* (Abingdon: Routledge, 2014).

Mitchell, K., Jones, R. and Fluri, J., 'Introduction', in K. Mitchell, R. Jones and J. Fluri (eds), *Handbook on Critical Geographies of Migration* (London: Edward Elgar Press, 2019), 1–16.

Mügge, L. and van der Haar, M., 'Who Is an Immigrant and Who Requires Integration? Categorizing in European Policies', in B. Garcés- Mascareñas and R. Penninx (eds), *Integration Processes and Policies in Europe* (Cham: Springer, 2016), 77–90.

OECD/European Union, *Indicators of Immigrant integration 2015: Settling in* (Paris: OECD Publishing, 2015), <https://doi.org/10.1787/9789264234024-en>.

Panizzon, M. and van Riemsdijk, M., Introduction to Special Issue: 'Migration Governance in an Era of Large Movements: A Multi-level Approach', *Journal of Ethnic and Migration Studies* 45/8 (2019), 1225–41.

Phillips, D. and Robinson, D., 'Re•ections on Migration, Community, and Place', *Population, Space and Place* 21/5 (2015), 409–20.

Saharso, S., 'Who Needs Integration? Debating a Central, yet Increasingly Contested Concept in Migration Studies', *Comparative Migration Studies* 7/16 (2019), 7–16.

Schinkel, W., 'The Imagination of "Society" in Measurements of Immigrant Integration', *Ethnic and Racial Studies* 36/7 (2013), 1142–61.

——, 'Against "Immigrant Integration": For an End to Neocolonial Knowledge Production', *Comparative Migration Studies* 6/31 (2018), 1–17.

Shah, S., *The Next Great Migration: The Beauty and Terror of Life on the Move* (New York: Bloomsbury, 2020).

Tarchi, D., Sermi, F., Kalantaryan, S., Mcmahon, S., Kaslama, P., Alvarez Alvarez, M. and Belmonte, M., *'Atlas of Migration – 2021' EUR 30936 EN* (Luxembourg: Publications Office of the European Union, 2021), <https://doi.org/10.2760/979899, JRC127608>.

UN DESA, 'International Migrant Stock/International Migration Flows to and from Selected Countries', United Nations database, POP/DB/MIG/Flow/ (New York: UN Department of Economic and Social Affairs, Population Division, 2022).

UNHCR, 'Global Trends Forced Displacement' (2020), <https://www.unhcr.org/flagship-reports/globaltrends/>, accessed 11 November 2022.

Walker, N., 'Teleological and Reflexive Nationalism in the New Europe', Euborders Working Paper 02, September 2017 (Institut Barcelona d'Estudis Internacionals (IBEI), the Leuven Centre for Global Governance Studies (University of Leuven) and the Centre on Constitutional Change (CCC, Edinburgh)), <https://www.ibei.org/working-paper-02-euborders_145102.pdf>, accessed 26 April 2023.

Walker, R., *After the Globe, before the World* (London: Routledge, 2010).

Weber, L. and Tazreiter, C., 'Introduction: Migration and Global Justice', in L. Weber and C. Tazreiter (eds), *Handbook of Migration and Global Justice* (Cheltenham: Edward Elgar, 2021), 1–15.

Wonders, N. A. and Jones, L. C., 'Challenging the Borders of Difference and Inequality: Power in Migration as a Social Movement for Global Justice', in L. Weber and C. Tazreiter (eds), *Handbook of Migration and Global Justice* (Cheltenham: Edward Elgar, 2021), 296–313.

Yuval-Davis, N., 'Belonging and the Politics of Belonging', *Patterns of Prejudice* 40/3 (2006), 197–214.

Yuval-Davis, N., Wemyss, G. and Cassidy, K., *Bordering* (Cambridge: Polity Press, 2019).

ROBERTA MEDDA-WINDISCHER AND KARL KÖSSLER

Integration of Third-Country Nationals in Subnational Entities: Is Regional Citizenship a Viable Instrument?[1]

Introduction

The gradual decline of the Westphalian nation-state has undermined the monolithic concept of citizenship as being monopolized by one government level – the nation-state – and as being limited to one clear-cut group – citizens – clearing the way to new concepts such as 'regional citizenship'. In several respects, it is very much as summarized by the historian Hans Mommsen, recalled in the introduction of this volume: 'Die Nation ist tot, es lebe die Region.' (The Nation is dead, long live the Region.). In other words, the perception of the nation as the only marker of collective belonging in Europe has become increasingly outdated and in fact given way to other territorial identities, in particular a regional one. Unsurprisingly, this development has been accompanied by the decentralization of competences to sub-national authorities in such areas as social welfare, labour market, housing and language use. Also, this made it conceivable to think of such notions as regional, residence-based citizenship

---

1   This chapter draws on previous publications by the authors, in particular, Roberta Medda-Windischer and Karl Kössler, 'Introduction, Special Issue on Regional Citizenship', *European Yearbook of Minority Issues* 13 (2014), 61–78, and Roberta Medda-Windischer and Andrea Carlà (eds), *Migration and Autonomous Territories. The Case of South Tyrol and Catalonia* (Leiden: Brill, 2015).

for third-country nationals (TCNs). Particularly relevant in this regard is the extent to which rights – following the classical Marshallian conception civil, social and political rights – have been decentralized and how participation and belonging have been rescaled at the sub-national level. In this regard, as mentioned by the editors of this volume, the process of regionalization appears as a tool to go beyond a 'nation-cum-state paradigm', based on the slogan 'one nation, one culture, one state', recognizing simultaneously sub-state entities and state borders.

The main research questions in this context are as follows:

1. What alternatives exist to the traditionally exclusivist definitions of identity and belonging as exemplified by the monolithic concept of citizenship as a homogeneous and formal legal status bestowed by states and separating individuals in a binary manner?
2. To what extent does the concept of 'multi-level citizenship' (substate, state, transnational and supranational), encompassing in a three-dimensional way of rights, participation and sense of belonging, strengthen the integration processes of individuals and groups with migration background?
3. Under what conditions and to what extent can such alternative concepts of citizenship, in particular regional citizenship, be developed and reinforced?

Within this broad debate on alternative concepts of citizenship, this chapter concentrates on whether non-citizen membership, or 'denizenship', is a temporary deviation from membership as citizens, as opposed to a new model of membership in its own right that entails the decline of traditional citizenship and the concomitant rise of the concept of 'regional citizenship' based on residence. From the analysis of binary dimensions – sub-state and state levels – and by combining perspectives from regionalism and minority rights studies, this chapter aims to explore whether the concept of regional, residence-based citizenship can be considered as a means to strengthen the inclusion processes of TCNs. This is in line with the constructivist tradition highlighted by the introduction to this volume, which asserts that any groupings of people are communities based on fictitious constructions and narratives along the line of Anderson's definition of nations as 'imagined communities'.

This chapter is organized into four sections. The first and second parts provide a deeper overview of the above-mentioned trend towards differentiation that took citizenship beyond the nation-state level and the binary distinction between insiders (citizens) and outsiders (non-citizens). The third part briefly illustrates some emblematic examples of alternative forms of residence-based citizenship from Europe and beyond. The chapter concludes with some final remarks on how the citizenship approaches of sub-national territories impact individuals and groups with migration backgrounds.

The relevance of differentiated citizenship

Until quite recently, citizenship was taken for granted and uncontested because it appeared well-defined and not worthy of further exploration.[2] The 1990s, however, arguably saw the return of citizenship 'with a vengeance'[3] – a situation that is epitomized by the reform of citizenship legislation in a number of countries and the proliferation of multi-disciplinary research initiatives. Even though the notion of citizenship has undergone numerous shifts in its long history, citizenship, at its essence, concerns the relationship between an individual and a political community that has been historically linked to the Greek tradition of collective self-government and the Roman idea of the individual having a formal legal status.[4] While these historic precursors lay out the most basic and thus wholly general statement one can make about citizenship, the latter is today understood in manifold ways, though two main views have come to dominate.

2   See Stephen Castles and Alastair Davidson, *Citizens and Migration: Globalisation and the Politics of Belonging* (London: Macmillan, 2000), 1.

3   Catherine Dauvergne, 'Citizenship with a Vengeance', *Theoretical Inquiries in Law* 8/2 (2007), 489–507.

4   See J. G. A. Pocock, 'The Idea of Citizenship Since Classical Times', in Ronald Beiner (ed.), *Theorizing Citizenship* (Albany: SUNY Press, 1995), 29–52.

Many legal scholars, primarily those specialized in public law or international law, tend to subscribe to the traditional static view of citizenship as a formal legal status, which reflects – most visibly through a passport – full membership in a state and, as such, entails a set of particular rights and obligations. From this perspective, citizens and foreigners are 'correlative, mutually exclusive, exhaustive categories'.[5] It is this traditional understanding that is at the heart of a number of important ongoing debates. Among these are the debates about the increasing or decreasing value of citizenship,[6] the rise of dual citizenship,[7] the increasing convergence of citizenship regulation[8] through the 'migration of constitutional ideas'[9] and, not least, the insufficiency of *ius soli* and *ius sanguinis* as the sole sources of citizenship.[10] By contrast, mainly in social science and partly among experts in

5   Rogers Brubaker, *Citizenship and Nationhood in France and Germany* (Cambridge, MA: Harvard University Press, 1992), 46.

6   See on this debate in particular Ayelet Schachar, *The Birthright Lottery: Citizenship and Global Inequality* (Cambridge, MA: Harvard University Press, 2009); Christian Joppke, 'The Inevitable Lightening of Citizenship', *European Journal of Sociology* 51/1 (2010), 9–32.

7   See Peter J. Spiro, 'Dual Citizenship as Human Right', *International Journal of Constitutional Law* 8/1 (2010), 111–30.

8   See Randall Hansen and Patrick Weil, 'Introduction: Citizenship, Immigration and Nationality: Towards a Convergence in Europe?', in Randall Hansen and Patrick Weil (eds), *Towards a European Nationality: Citizenship, Immigration and Nationality Law in the EU* (Basingstoke: Palgrave Macmillan, 2001), 1–23.

9   Sujit Choudhry, *The Migration of Constitutional Ideas* (Cambridge: Cambridge University Press, 2006).

10   It is true that access to citizenship is increasingly determined by a combination of both principles, as classical *ius soli* countries have introduced *ius sanguinis* elements and vice versa (see Ayelet Schachar, 'Citizenship', in Michael Rosenfeld and András Sajó (eds), *The Oxford Handbook of Comparative Constitutional Law* [Oxford: Oxford University Press, 2012], 1002–19, 1006–10). But even as they are more often combined, these two principles have so far remained the exclusive sources of citizenship (see *United States v. Wong Kim Ark*, 169 U.S. 649 [1898]). Interestingly, in contrast to this traditional dualism, Schachar proposes the addition of *ius nexi* as a third title to citizenship. This could cover migrants who have often spent their whole lives in a country but sometimes still face the risk of expulsion (see Ayelet Shachar, 'Earned Citizenship: Property Lessons for Immigration Reform', *Yale Journal of Law and the Humanities* 23 [2011], 110–58).

European law, citizenship has recently come to be understood, especially fuelled by debates about EU citizenship, in a much broader sense as a three-dimensional concept that encompasses the following components: rights, participation and a sense of belonging.[11] Through the recognition of rights as one of these dimensions, commonly by invoking the classic rights-based citizenship notion of the sociologist T. H. Marshall,[12] this social science view also possesses a salient legal element. Yet, it then extends beyond the realm of law by adding participation as well as a sense of belonging to the political community as further building blocks of citizenship. Participation is hereby understood quite broadly as not only taking part in political life but more generally in civil society. A sense of belonging is considered crucial because it forms the basis for solidarity and trust, features that distinguish a community of interacting fellow citizens from a mere sum of individuals.

The development and diffusion of this three-dimensional understanding of citizenship must be seen in the context of increasing differentiation of a concept that was long perceived as monolithic. More precisely, the traditional citizenship notion focused on *one dimension* (the legal status), *one government level* as conferring this status (the nation-state level) and *one clear-cut group* holding this status (the citizens). From an extended perspective, this monolithic citizenship is closely tied to the paradigm of the Westphalian nation-state and thus historically contingent. It has been noted that the phenomenon of 'unitary citizenship is the historical exception' and a quite 'recent aberration'.[13] Just as the multifarious forces

11   See, for instance, Richard Bellamy, Dario Castiglione and Emilio Santoro, *Lineages of European Citizenship: Rights, Belonging and Participation in Eleven Nation-states* (Basingstoke: Palgrave Macmillan, 2004); Jo Shaw, *The Transformation of Citizenship in the European Union: Electoral Rights and the Restructuring of Political Space* (Cambridge: Cambridge University Press, 2007).

12   See T. H. Marshall, *Citizenship and Social Class* (Cambridge: Cambridge University Press, 1992 [1950]). Marshall proposed an evolutionary and rights-based concept of citizenship that starting with the conferral of civil rights, then political rights and at last social rights. That the Marshallian citizenship notion maintains its enduring influence is illustrated by the fact that many authors subscribing to this particular viewpoint explicitly refer to it.

13   Willem Maas, 'Varieties of Multilevel Citizenship', in Willem Maas (ed.), *Multilevel Citizenship* (Philadelphia: University of Pennsylvania Press, 2013), 1–21, 2.

of globalization, international migration and legal integration have set in motion the gradual decline of the Westphalian nation-state,[14] monolithic citizenship has also come under pressure. In Europe, it was not least the introduction of EU citizenship with the 1992 Treaty of Maastricht that provided a fillip for a conceptual differentiation of citizenship. This institutional development sparked a lively academic debate that has taken up the notion of three-dimensional citizenship. The trend towards differentiation also formed the basis for making the case for such notions as 'regional citizenship' and residence-based 'civic citizenship' of TCNs, terms that from the preceding monolithic perspective would have been summarily dismissed as blatant oxymorons. These notions suggest, respectively, that the concept of citizenship is no longer seen as being monopolized by *one government level*, that is, the nation-state,[15] nor as being limited to *one clear-cut group*, that is, citizens.[16]

14   See Richard Falk, 'Revisiting Westphalia, Discovering Post-Westphalia', *Journal of Ethics* 6/4 (2002), 311–52.

15   This phenomenon has been variously termed 'multi-level citizenship' (Joe Painter, 'Multi-Level Citizenship, Identity and Regions in Contemporary Europe', in James Anderson [ed.], *Transnational Democracy* [London: Routledge, 2002], 93–110; Maas, 'Varieties of Multilevel Citizenship'); 'nested scales of citizenship' (Joe Painter, 'European citizenship and the regions' *European Urban and Regional Studies* 15/1 [2008], 5–19); or 'citizenship constellations' (Rainer Bauböck, 'Studying Citizenship Constellations', *JEMS* 36/5 [2010], 847–59).

16   See Tomas Hammar, *Democracy and the Nation State: Aliens, Denizens and Citizens in a World of International Migration* (Aldershot: Avebury, 1994); Costica Dumbrava, 'Super-Foreigners and Sub-Citizens: Mapping Ethnonational Hierarchies of Foreignness and Citizenship in Europe', *Ethnopolitics* 14 (2015), 1–15.

Citizenship above and below the nation-state level

European citizenship

European citizenship is a matter that many commentators consider to be more symbolically than legally relevant.[17] In their view, the Maastricht Treaty has achieved little more than codifying the *acquis communautaire* on the position of the member states' citizens. It only added some particular elements such as active and passive voting rights in the elections for the European Parliament and municipal elections in the member state of residence (even if these are different from the state of which one is a citizen) and the right of petition to the European Parliament and the right of application to the Ombudsman.

Another position of these commentators is that European citizenship is just an additional dual citizenship, which encompasses both national and European citizenships without jeopardizing the principle that sovereignty remains strongly rooted in the member states. Given that the institution of Union citizenship has added little that is substantially new to the existing legal status of those who acquire it, sceptics dismiss European citizenship as being either a 'mercantile form of citizenship born out of the demands of economic integration, and/or empty rhetoric designed to enhance the Commission's legitimacy'.[18]

In spite of the modest character of the rights (and the complete absence of duties) attached to European citizenship, EU member states' heads of government who decided to insert the chapter on Union citizenship into the EU Treaty were probably attracted by the integrative potential that

---

17   Among the first critics, see Leon Brittan, 'Institutional Development of the European Community', in *Public Law* 92/4 (1992), 567–79, 574. More recently, see Christian Fernández, 'Patriots in the Making? Migrants, Citizens, and Demos Building in the European Union', *Journal of International Migration and Integration* 13/2 (2012), 147–63.

18   Theodora Kostakopoulou, 'European Citizenship and Immigration after Amsterdam: Openings, Silences, Paradoxes', *JEMS* 24/4 (1998), Adrian Favell (guest ed.), Special Issue 'The European Union: Immigration, Asylum and Citizenship'.

citizenship had manifested in the framework of the European nation-
states in the past 150 years. Thus, they sought, perhaps only rhetorically,
to exploit this potential and use it as a lever to secure their goal: to create
an 'ever closer Union of the peoples of Europe'.[19]

According to some scholars, Union citizenship entails the prospect of
a 'post-national' political arrangement, which may facilitate multiple mem-
berships by individuals in various overlapping and interlocking communities formed at various levels of governance.[20] Union citizenship occasions
the 'promise' of a heterogeneous, de-nationalized democratic community
in Europe.[21]

In this respect, the novelty of European citizenship may lie in its capacity to change our understanding of citizenship and prompt a rethinking
of membership with a view to opening up new forms of political community.[22] Stated another way, Union citizenship holds out the promise of

---

19   Preamble to the Treaty on European Union (TEU) (Maastricht, 7 February 1992).
      See also, the Preambles to the Consolidated Versions of the Treaty on European
      Union and the Treaty on the Functioning of the European Union, as amended by
      the Treaty of Lisbon, OJ C115, 9 May 2008, and the Preamble to the Charter of
      Fundamental Rights of the European Union, as amended by the Treaty of Lisbon.
      Likewise, article 1(2) TEU (Lisbon consolidated version, 2008) declares: 'This
      Treaty marks a new stage in the process of creating an ever closer union among
      the peoples of Europe, in which decisions are taken as openly as possible and as
      closely as possible to the citizens.' Among the recent studies on EU citizenship, see
      Elspeth Guild, Cristina J. Gortázar Rotaeche and Dora Kostakopoulou (eds), *The
      Reconceptualization of European Union Citizenship* (Leiden: Brill-Nijhoff, 2014).
20   Elizabeth Meehan, *Citizenship and the European Community* (London: Sage,
      1993); Elizabeth Meehan, 'Political Pluralism and European Citizenship', in Perry
      B. Lehning and Albert Weale (eds), *Citizenship, Demography and Justice in the New
      Europe* (London: Routledge, 1997), 69–85; Lorenzo Piccoli, 'Structuring Regional
      Citizenship: Historical Continuity and Contemporary Salience', in Roberta
      Medda-Windischer and Karl Kössler (eds), *Regional Citizenship as Loophole or Tool
      for Inclusion? A Comparative Appraisal on Autonomous Territories,* Special Issue,
      European Yearbook of Minority Issues, 13 (2014), 130–50.
21   Theodora Kostakopoulou, 'Towards a Theory of Constructive Citizenship in
      Europe', *Journal of Political Philosophy* 4/4 (1996), 337–58.
22   Theodora Kostakopoulou, 'European Citizenship: Writing the Future', *European
      Law Journal,* Special issue on EU Citizenship 13/5 (2007), 623–46.

what Kostakopoulou calls a 'constructive' approach to citizenship that is more respectful of diversity and more inclusive than nation-based models of citizenship.[23]

European citizenship would then consist of 'shared values, a shared understanding of rights and societal duties and shared rational intellectual culture which transcend organic-national differences.'[24] Obviating the need to favour one country's cultural heritage over that of another, the 'shared values' on which a specifically European identity might be constructed range from the respect for democracy, fundamental rights, including the rights of persons belonging to minorities, to equality, tolerance and the rule of law. These values find affirmation in the preamble and article 2 of the Treaty on European Union (Lisbon consolidated version, 2008), and in the Preamble to the EU Charter of Fundamental Rights. The latter refers to a 'peaceful future based on common values' and stipulates that the function of the Union and therefore of the European Court of Justice is to 'contribute to the development of these common values'.[25]

Clearly, the construction of a European identity along these lines, valuing ethno-cultural diversity, can be a powerful tool of integration for all those who have a legitimate stake in the EU's future, be they nationals of the member states or long-term residents who happen to be TCNs. However, that EU citizenship depends upon possession of the citizenship of a member state[26] has brought with it forms of exclusion and even

---

23   Kostakopoulou, 'European Citizenship'.
24   Joseph H. H. Weiler, 'The Reformation of European Constitutionalism', *Journal of Common Market Studies* 35/1 (1997), 118. For an analysis of the concept of 'citizenship of rights' developed by the Court of Justice of the European Union, see Alessandra Aparecida Souza Silveira, 'Citizenship of Rights and the Principle of the Highest Standard of Fundamental Rights' Protection', in Guild et al., *The Reconceptualization of European Union Citizenship*.
25   See Treaty on European Union (Lisbon consolidated version, OJ C115, 9 May 2008); EU Charter as amended by the Treaty of Lisbon (OJ C303, 14 December 2007).
26   See, article 9 TEU as amended by the Treaty of Lisbon (2008): 'Every national of a Member State shall be a citizen of the Union. Citizenship of the Union shall be additional to national citizenship and shall not replace it.' Many authors consider this aspect to be one of the great weaknesses of the European citizenship and, along these lines, the European Parliament has maintained that citizenship of the Union

discrimination against TCNs, some of whom have always lived on EU territory and have made the EU the centre of their socio-economic lives.[27]

Regional citizenship

While one dimension of multi-level citizenship concerns the European level, a second one pertains to the regional level.[28] If one focuses exclusively on the above-mentioned traditional understanding of citizenship as a formal legal status,[29] the regional dimension remains rather limited. As has been rightly pointed out, granting citizenship is, even in the face of globalization, one of the remaining exclusive domains of the state because it cannot be bestowed by either transnational economic actors[30] or by international or supranational institutions.[31] Even though a similar formal status entailing certain rights and obligations was commonly granted by cities until the nineteenth century, the reconfiguration of citizenship during that time made the nation-state the purportedly exclusive territorial frame of reference. Notwithstanding the gradual

---

should be defined as an autonomous concept. See also article 20 of the TFEU, as amended by the Treaty of Lisbon (2008).

27   Since the decisive qualifying factor for acquiring EU citizenship is through citizenship of a member state, this results in the exclusion from the European citizenship of approximately 20 million residents on the EU territory who are citizens of third countries.

28   See Medda-Windischer and Kössler, *Regional Citizenship as Loophole or Tool for Inclusion?*.

29   See the first section of this chapter.

30   Nonetheless, these actors often have considerable influence on states in citizenship matters. Arguably, this influence also contributes to an increasing focus on the accumulation of economically productive human capital in both immigration and citizenship policies. See Ayelet Shachar, 'Picking Winners: Olympic Citizenship and the Global Race for Talent', *Yale Law Journal* 120/8 (2011), 2088–139. This trend has been aptly termed 'citizenship by economic contribution'. Kim Barry, 'Home and Away: The Construction of Citizenship in an Emigration Context', *NYU Law Review* 81/11 (2006), 11–59, 36.

31   Even EU citizenship has a merely derivative character as it depends on possessing the citizenship of a member state.

decline of the Westphalian nation-state in recent decades, regions still play no more than a marginal role regarding formal citizenship. Most constitutions define this subject matter as an exclusive jurisdiction of the national government with regard to both its legislative and executive dimensions, with implementation usually being delegated to local branches of the national administration. Moreover, national governments have recently reinforced their leading role in a number of countries, including Germany in 1999 and Australia in 2007, by adopting a citizenship legislation in which they introduced citizenship tests and determined criteria for passing.

A notable exception to this centralization trend is Switzerland, where the cantons are empowered by virtue of article 37(1) of the Swiss Constitution[32] to establish their own criteria for naturalization. The fact that Swiss cantons make effective use of this opportunity in practice results in substantial variation. For instance, the requirement of residence in the respective canton ranges from only two years in Geneva to 12 years in Nidwalden.[33] Other sub-national entities like the German *Länder* are not authorized to (co-)regulate access to citizenship, but they still have a significant bearing on it through their discretion in applying national regulations concerning naturalization.[34] Further, in other countries, sub-national entities can exert only a degree of influence in the area of citizenship which is, in the absence of a significant legislative and executive role, dependent on their ability to set the agenda and lobby the national government. This has arguably been the case with the restrictive turn of Belgium's 2012 citizenship reform, which brought legislation adopted by the National Parliament more in line with Flemish preferences.

---

32 Article 37 (1) reads as follows: 'Any person who is a citizen of a commune and of the Canton to which that commune belongs is a Swiss citizen.' Due to this conception of a 'multi-level citizen', a naturalization candidate has to meet the requirements stipulated at the municipal, cantonal, and national levels (article 38 (2)).

33 See Gianni D'Amato, 'Switzerland', in Christian Joppke and F. Leslie Seidle (eds), *Immigrant Integration in Federal Countries* (Montreal: McGill-Queen's University Press, 2012), 162–90, 179–80.

34 See Ines Michalowski, 'Required to Assimilate? The Context of Citizenship Tests in Five Countries', *Citizenship Studies* 15 (2001), 749–68.

Taking this three-dimensional understanding of citizenship as a point of departure,[35] multi-level constellations are quite different and much more susceptible to a substantial role of sub-national entities. From a comparative perspective, regions with a significant share of 'old minorities' are particularly active in this regard. For these regions, creating a cohesive community through some sort of regional citizenship based on rights, participation and a sense of belonging is usually an important element of a broader minority nation-building project, which is aimed at competing with the rivalling project of the majority.[36] Even if regions typically cannot rely in this regard on the (national) power to grant formal citizenship, real-life socialization patterns of newcomers actually often occur on a regional scale. In other words, 'immigrants are naturalised as citizens of Belgium, Germany, Italy […] but they are socialised as Walloons or Flemish, Bavarians or Hamburgers, Venetians or Sicilians.'[37]

In this context, the creation of a distinct sub-national political community based on rights, participation and belonging can be a means to a different end. In some cases, the construction of regional citizenship is rather inclusive towards immigrants.[38] This may result, for example, from the perception that a sense of belonging of newcomers, which is at least as

35   See the first section of the chapter.

36   See André Lecours and Geneviève Nootens, 'Understanding Majority Nationalism', in Alain-G. Gagnon, André Lecours and Geneviève Nootens (eds), *Contemporary Majority Nationalism* (Montreal: McGill-Queen's University Press, 2011), 3–18.

37   Dietrich Thränhardt, 'Immigration and Integration in European Federal Countries. A Comparative Evaluation', in Dietrich Thränhardt (ed.), *Immigration and Federalism in Europe. Federal, State and Local Regulatory Competencies in Austria, Belgium, Germany, Italy, Russia, Spain and Switzerland* (Osnabrück: Institut für Migrationsforschung und Interkulturelle Studien, 2013), 7–20, 7.

38   See the contributions by Eve Hepburn, 'Is There a Scottish Approach to Citizenship? Rights, Participation and Belonging in Scotland', Dirk Gebhardt, 'The Difference That Being a Minority Territory Makes: Exploring Immigrant Citizenship in Catalonia vs. Andalusia and Madrid', Eduardo J. Ruiz-Vieytez, 'Regional Citizenship and the Evolution of Basque Immigration and Integration Policies', and Heidi Öst, 'The Concept and Impact of Regional Citizenship of the Åland Islands on the Inclusion of Migrants', in Medda-Windischer and Kössler, *Regional Citizenship as Loophole or Tool for Inclusion?* .

strong regarding the region as the national level,[39] is crucial for winning them over as political allies against the national government, for realizing the social capital[40] or for unlocking the endogenous economic potential[41] of the region. In other cases, it is quite exclusive and characterized by a rationale of fending off newcomers. In these sub-national entities, the 'cultural turn in citizenship discourse and practice'[42] that is most clearly illustrated by the trend towards citizenship tests with culture-related contents may be even more pronounced than at the national level. A prime example is the 2003 Flemish decree on *inburgering* (citizenization),[43] which reflects a strong emphasis on language, culture and values of the receiving society, that is, the society of the region, and thus starkly contrasted with, until then, quite liberal national policies.[44]

While granting formal citizenship remains a stronghold of the national government, creating regional citizenship in the broader three-dimensional sense may be an alternative project, which most sub-national governments are able to realize on the basis of their existing legislative powers. In this regard, most relevant are their competences in such areas as social welfare,

39 See Luis Moreno, 'Local and Global: Mesogovernments and Territorial Identities', *NEP* 5/3–4 (1999), 61–75.

40 See Robert D. Putnam (with Robert Leonardi and Raffaella Y. Nanetti), *Making Democracy Work: Civic Traditions in Modern Italy* (Princeton, NJ: Princeton University Press, 1993).

41 See Michael Keating, 'The Political Economy of Regionalism', in Michael Keating and John Loughlin (eds), *The Political Economy of Regionalism* (London: Routledge, 1997), 17–40.

42 Schachar, 'Citizenship', 1013.

43 Marco Martiniello, 'Belgium', in Joppke and Seidle, *Immigrant Integration in Federal Countries*, 58–77, 71 and 77. Martiniello uses the term 'citizenization' but, at the same time, underlines that a literal translation of *inburgering* is impossible.

44 See Marie-Claire Foblets and Zeynep Yanasmayan, 'Language and Integration Requirements in Belgium: Discordance between the Flemish Policy of "Inburgering" and the Federal Legislator's View(s) on the Integration of Newcomers and Migrants', in Ricky Van Oers, Eva Ersbøll and Dora Kostapoulou (eds), *A Re-Definition of Belonging? Language and Integration Tests in Europe* (Leiden: Brill-Nijhoff, 2010), 271–306.

labour market, housing and language use.[45] The Flemish government made extensive use of these competences in order to define the boundaries of regional (social) citizenship. For instance, in a decree from 1999, the government made access to care insurance dependent on a designated period of residence in the Flemish region, while residence in *any* part of Belgium is sufficient in the rest of the country. Another example is the reform of housing legislation in 2006 that made the willingness to learn Dutch a condition for access to social housing for all residents of the region.[46] Beyond the powers of ordinary legislation, some sub-national governments may rely on the additional tool of guaranteeing particular rights in quasi-constitutional documents, which are due to strict amendment procedures quite firmly entrenched, in their efforts to create regional citizenships. In many cases, fundamental rights catalogues of national constitutions are 'a floor rather than a ceiling' – regions are in principle empowered to expand this minimum standard.[47] The 2006 Statute of Catalonia is, in this regard, particularly far-reaching as it includes an entirely new Title I with as many as 40 provisions.[48] The comprehensiveness of this fundamental rights catalogue and its central position at the beginning of the statute clearly demonstrates the ambition to make it a visible symbol of regional citizenship.[49]

45   See Karl Kössler, 'Immigration and Integration in Multilevel Systems: A Challenge between Regional Autonomy and Intergovernmental Cooperation', in Medda-Windischer and Carlà), *Migration and Autonomous Territories*, 27–61, 36–8.

46   Whereas the Belgian Constitutional Court ruled that this requirement could not apply to French-speaking people in the municipalities enjoying the constitutionally guaranteed 'language facilities', this requirement was upheld with regard to all other individuals (Belgian Constitutional Court, Judgement No. 101/2008 of 10 July 2008).

47   See G. Alan Tarr, 'Subnational Constitutions and Minority Rights: A Perspective on Canadian Provincial Constitutionalism', *Rutgers Law Journal* 40/4 (2009), 767–92, 791.

48   These are grouped into civil and social rights (articles 15–28), political and administrative rights (articles 29–31), linguistic rights and obligations (articles 32–6) as well as governing principles, which shall guide public policy (articles 37–54).

49   See Michael Keating and Alex Wilson, 'Renegotiating the State of Autonomies: Statute Reform and Multi-Level Politics in Spain', *WEP* 32/3 (2009), 536–58, 550.

Under scrutiny, certain limits for any citizenship construction by sub-national governments emerge from both the national and the European levels. As to the national level, this is demonstrated, for instance, by judgements of the Spanish Constitutional Court. This body recognized only some of the entitlements enshrined in the regional statutes, such as participatory rights, as fully fledged individual rights and 'downgraded' others, such as the many social rights, to guiding principles (*principios rectores*) that are not directly enforceable.[50] With regard to the supranational level, the prohibition of discrimination on the basis of nationality (article 18 of the Treaty on the Functioning of the European Union; TFEU) is most relevant.[51] As famously declared by the ECJ in *Bickel and Franz*, this provision not only protects EU citizens with residence in the respective region but equally applies to those without it.[52] The only EU citizens not covered by article 18 of the TFEU are therefore citizens of the same member state, who are *not* at the same time residents of the respective region.[53] These intricacies remind us that any construction of regional citizenship does not take place in a vacuum, but rather is situated in a multi-level context and thus inextricably interrelated with rules stemming from national and supranational legal orders. As a result of this legal pluralism, the situation concerning the statuses that different groups of people hold within this multi-level context is also highly complex.

Citizens, EU-citizens and immigrants as denizens

In liberal democracies, citizenship gives individuals the right to vote, run for office and participate freely in public activities, while also requiring the obligation of paying taxes and possibly serving in the military. This has, in turn, led many to proclaim the increasing irrelevance of citizenship

---

50 Spanish Constitutional Court, Sentencia del Tribunal Constitucional 247/2007 and 31/2010.

51 For an in-depth analysis, see Dimitry Kochenov, 'Regional Citizenships and EU Law: The Case of the Åland Islands and New Caledonia', *ELR* 35 (2010), 307–24.

52 European Court of Justice, Case C-274/96 Bickel and Franz [1998] ECR I-7637, 24.

53 Government of the French Community (C-212/06) (2008) ECR. I-1683, 63.

in the nation-state. According to this argument, since many social rights can now be achieved without political rights and since an increasing number of political rights are now available at the sub-national and supra-national level, national citizenship no longer matters in this new post-national era.[54]

Despite these arguments, it is undoubtedly far too early to dismiss the relevance of the nation-state and citizenship for several reasons. First, the right to vote and run for office in national elections are still extremely consequential. Non-citizens, even if they are permanent residents and long-time workers, have limited opportunities to participate in the democratic process at the national level. Since citizenship, immigration and asylum policies are generally implemented at the national level, despite the efforts at the EU level to adopt common guidelines and cases in which non-citizens are allowed to participate in local elections, non-citizens are generally still excluded from decisions that may directly affect their own lives.

Second, even though many social rights are generally guaranteed to everyone regardless of their citizenship, there are several countries where non-citizens are still excluded or hampered in accessing significant social benefits. In other words, while the modern welfare state undeniably provides greater benefits to immigrants than at earlier points in history, non-citizens continue to receive significantly fewer social benefits than people with national citizenship.

Third, although citizenship is generally not relevant for most private sector employment, it is nonetheless important in the allocation of many public sector jobs. Within the EU itself, while EU citizens can automatically live and work in another EU country, TCNs have the right to reside and work in an EU country other than the country into which they have

---

54 See David Jacobson, *Rights across Borders: Immigration and the Decline of Citizenship* (Baltimore, MD: Johns Hopkins University Press, 1996), 8; Saskia Sassen, *Losing Control? Sovereignty in an Age of Globalisation* (New York: Columbia University Press, 1996), 95; Saskia Sassen, 'The De Facto Transnationalizing of Immigration Policy', in Christian Joppke (ed.), *Challenge to the Nation-State* (Oxford: Oxford University Press, 1998), 49–85; Yasemin N. Soysal, *Limits of Citizenship: Migrants and Postnational Membership in Europe* (Chicago: University of Chicago Press, 1994).

immigrated only after five years of continued residence and fulfilment of certain integration requirements.[55] Moreover, EU preference for employment is a principle commonly accepted and even included in the Framework Employment Directive.[56]

In short, despite the argument that the concept of citizenship has undergone a process of transformation into what Christian Joppke calls 'citizenship light',[57] national citizenship endures as an essential and lasting feature of modern life.

TCNs in Europe today, however, settle for something less than full citizenship and in this sense, they are currently 'denizens'.[58] They have permanently settled on the territory of the member states and become de facto citizens in so far as they gained social and civil rights. However, their political and electoral rights remain by and large circumscribed, along with eligibility for welfare benefits and public sector jobs.[59] As noted by Elspeth Guild, 'it is difficult to avoid the conclusion that the member states consider third-country nationals, even after five years of stable and lawful residence in the Union, an intrinsically *suspect* category.'[60]

---

55 See Council Directive 2003/109/EC of 25 November 2003 concerning the status of third-country nationals who are long-term residents, OJ L 016, 23 January 2004.

56 Article 3(2) of the Council Directive 2000/78/EC of 27 November 2000 establishing a general framework for equal treatment in employment and occupation reads thus: 'This Directive does not cover differences of treatment based on nationality.'

57 Among others, see Christian Joppke, *Citizenship and Immigration* (Cambridge: Polity Press, 2010).

58 Hammar, *Democracy and the Nation-State*; Kees Groenendijk, 'The Legal Integration of Potential Citizens', in Rainer Bauböck et al. (eds), *Acquisition and Loss of Nationality*. Vol. I (Amsterdam: Amsterdam University Press, 2006), 385–410.

59 Elspeth Guild, Kees Groenendijk and Sergio Carrera (eds), *Illiberal Liberal States. Immigration, Citizenship and Integration in the EU* (Farnham: Ashgate, 2009); Jo Shaw, *The Transformation of Citizenship in the European Union* (Cambridge University Press, Cambridge, 2007).

60 Elspeth Guild, *The Legal Elements of European Identity – EU Citizenship and Migration Law* (The Hague: Kluwer Law International, 2004), 252; emphasis added.

This 'suspicion' vis-à-vis TCNs is difficult to justify given that many of these individuals have often lived their entire lives within the territory of the member states and have made this territory the centre of their socioeconomic life. The question is, thus, whether non-citizen membership or 'denizenship' is a temporary deviation from membership as citizens, or rather, is it a new model of membership in its own right that entails the decline of traditional citizenship and the concomitant rise of the concept of 'regional citizenship' based on residence.

To find a remedy to the civic and social inclusiveness deficit of TCNs in Europe and identify an appropriate criterion to confer rights and duties to TCNs, many suggest the concept of abode or domicile, possibly even conditional upon permanent residence or residence for a certain number of years.[61] In this perspective, the *Nottebohm* concept of a *genuine and effective link*[62] can be moulded and developed into a broader concept in the area of integration of TCNs.

State practice suggests that an effective link to a state might include habitual and lawful residence in the state – in addition to factors such as birth on a state's territory, descent from citizens or marriage to a citizen.

---

61 A *'jus domicilium'* has been proposed by a number of scholars since the Treaty of Maastricht. Among them, see Marie José Garot, 'A New Basis for Citizenship: Residence', in Massimo La Torre (ed.), *European Citizenship: An Institutional Challenge* (The Hague: Kluwer Law International, 1998); Kees Groenendjik, 'Citizens and Third Country Nationals: Differential Treatment or Discrimination?', in Jean-Yves Carlier and Elspeth Guild (eds), *The Future of Free Movement of Persons in the EU* (Brussels: Bruylant, 2006), 94–5; Jean-Yves Carlier, 'Incola est. About European Citizenship', in Anita Böcker et al. (eds), *Migration Law and Sociology of Law* (Nijmegen: Wolf Legal Publications, 2008), 161–8; Fernández, 'Patriots in the Making?.

62 The *Nottebohm* concept derives from the International Court of Justice's case *Liechtenstein v. Guatemala* (*Nottebohm case* – ICJ [International Court of Justice Reports, 1955), in which the ICJ described citizenship as being 'a legal bond having as its basis a social fact of attachment, a genuine connection of existence, interest and sentiments, together with the reciprocal rights and duties. It may be said to constitute the juridical expression of the fact that the individual upon whom it is conferred [...] is in fact more closely connected with the population of the State conferring nationality than with that of any other State' (4).

Long-term residence is, for instance, a well-established and globally practised principle upon which citizenship is legitimately granted through naturalization. The 1997 Convention on Nationality firmly establishes lawful and habitual residence as a legitimate means of granting citizenship generally and, therefore, of looking beyond *jus soli* and *jus sanguinis* in determining the link an individual has with a state.[63] In other words, in addition to the links one is born with, 'genuine and effective' links with a state can also be acquired over time.

Bruno Nascimbene argued, back in 1996, that citizenship will gradually lose its significance in favour of the concept of abode or habitual and lawful residence, which will become the most appropriate standard to establish the link or tie between an individual and a civil or social community.[64]

Currently, long-term residence is the basis for acquiring the status of long-term resident, implying the right not to be expelled and a conditioned freedom of movement in the EU. The Directive 2003/109 concerning the Legal Status of TCNs who are Long-Term Residents (LTRD) sets out a status that is acquired by TCNs after five years of lawful residence in one member state.[65] The status provides rights of continued residence and economic activity as well as protection against expulsion and, once acquired, the status also allows the individual to take up residence and economic activities in other member states. The LTRD does, however, leave to member states a wide margin of discretion in the implementation of its provisions. For instance, for those who are admitted into one member state, the conditions that must be fulfilled before they will be able to acquire the status of long-term resident include a requirement on integration, generally linked

63 Article 6(3) of the 1997 European Convention on Nationality states thus: 'Each State Party shall provide in its internal law for the possibility of naturalization of persons lawfully and habitually resident on its territory. In establishing the conditions for naturalization, it shall not provide for a period of residence exceeding ten years before the lodging of an application.'

64 Bruno Nascimbene (ed.), *Nationality Laws in the European Union* (Milano: Giuffré, 1996), 10.

65 Council Directive 2003/109/EC.

to knowledge of the language(s), culture, and history of the country of new residence, to be imposed at the discretion of each member state.[66]

In short, a legal abode or habitual and lawful residence represents a sound legal criterion for allocating rights and duties to TCNs and enhancing their inclusion in the receiving community. The concept of abode appears to be a more objective basis for selection than the subjective national concepts of citizenship and corresponds with the principle of equal treatment. The relevance of this mechanism for the inclusion of TCNs will, however, depend not only on how it will be implemented by member states but also on their political willingness to effectively integrate TCNs.

Alternative forms of citizenship: Some emblematic examples

Residence-based/regional citizenship

The first example of residential citizenship is the civic citizenship introduced by the European Commission back in 1999 with the Tampere European Council where residence was introduced as the main criterion to recognize equal rights and duties to TCNs. This concept was then applied in the LTRD: TCNs acquire a long-term residence status after five years of residence in an EU member state. It provides the right not to be expelled as well as the right to take up residence and start economic activities in another EU member state. However, discretionary requirements on integration, such as tests on language, history or culture of the country of residence, can be imposed on TCNs.

The second example is Catalonia. Here, the concept of residential citizenship for foreign citizens residing in Catalonia has been widely developed and applied through institutional policies and legal documents. The main idea is that what makes a Catalan is not a matter of blood, descent or ethnic

---

66 See articles 5(2) and 15 of the Council Directive 2003/109/EC. For an overview of the integration criteria introduced by many European states, see R. van Oers et al., *A Re-Definition of Belonging? Language and Integration Tests in Europe* (Leiden: Martinus Nijhoff, 2010).

origin but the decision to accept a 'shared civic identity' or 'a common public culture': this means accepting a set of values, such as human rights and democratic values, gender equality and freedom of religious beliefs, but also that Catalan language and culture must be shared by everyone as the basis for communication and participation (as in Quebec).

Third, Italy and particularly a recent judgement of the Constitutional Court on the exclusion of foreign citizens from admission to the national civil service (no. 119/2015; Giuliano Amato/*giudice redattore*). According to the Italian Constitutional Court, this exclusion was not legitimate and reasonable because, among the other arguments, it was unfair to exclude foreign citizens and lawfully resident citizens in Italy from participating in a community that must be considered broader and more inclusive than a community based on a narrow and strict sense of citizenship. The Constitutional Court has accepted the concept of residential citizenship for all those, including foreign citizens, who belong on a stable and regular basis to the community of residence. This is because the civil service is considered an important tool for inclusion and social cohesion, through which it is possible to nurture the common good (*bene comune*).

Municipal forms of citizenship

In Italy, other forms of residential citizenship on a local basis are found in Torino and Florence, where this symbolic citizenship of foreign citizens is recognized when they acquire the LTRD status or long-term permits (*permesso di soggiorno per soggiornanti di lungo periodo*). In both cities, the municipal authorities have also signed agreements (*Patto di condivisione/ Torino* e *Patto di cittadinanza/Florence*) with the Muslim communities whereby their members accept to share a set of common values in addition to commit themselves to follow certain rules and actively engage in projects. The idea is to enhance the sense of belonging and participation in the community of residence.

The last example is in New York. Here the idea by the then mayor de Blasio has been to issue a municipal identification card based on residence for all New Yorkers, including the undocumented immigrants living in the city (one out of ten New Yorkers have participated, approx. 850 thousand persons). With this card, undocumented migrants can, for instance, pick up their children at school or attend school meetings without having the fear of being stopped; they could even open a back account. In order to attract documented persons to avail of the opportunity, the municipal identification card provides some benefits, such as discounts on prescription drugs or free membership to important museums. Surveys have shown that this card has been successful especially among immigrants (approximately three-fourths) in increasing their sense of belonging to the city of residence.

Conclusion

The concept of regional citizenship is nurtured by a common moral and emotional identification with a specific area, sharing key constituent principles and a collective concept of the self. In mainstream communities, this concept of identification could be stretched to include individuals and groups originating from migration. In a nation organized as a social community, whose members consider themselves a nation (Renan's 'daily plebiscite'),[67] there is no need for a shared ethnicity or religion. It is the sentiment of the members of a nation that define it as such, and this sentiment can only spring from one or all of these traits, or from something totally different, such as a common territory. The consciousness of belonging to a shared territory and a common political organization, having a collective destiny with the rest of the society, is at the core of the concept of regional citizenship based on a common territorial identity.

This alternative form of citizenship, although largely symbolic, could unite all those who live in a given territory, regardless of their language, religion and/or ethnic background. This is in line with the approach of this volume, according to which identities, like borders, are social constructions which are continually framed and reframed. The concept of

---

67   E. Renan, 'Qu'est-ce qu'une nation ?' (1882) *Bulletin hebdomadaire*, Association scientifique de France.

regional citizenship represents a form of post-ethnic sovereignty, in which the nation is viewed as the result of progressive creation by the groups, through forms of free and spontaneous union, which entail voluntary acceptance of common principles, a shared sense of belonging, loyalty to one's adopted community and concomitant feelings of mutual trust among the individuals who belong to this political organization and live in the same territory.

The concept of regional citizenship would be an additional identity, alongside one's identity/ies, which may be based on language or religion, similar to European citizenship and its relation to the citizenship of the various EU member states.[68] It would therefore be a common and overarching identity, overlapping with the single and multiple identities, without blotting them out but rather respecting and protecting them.[69]

The creation of a common shared identity around the concept of regional citizenship would be based on both common values – such as human rights, democracy, tolerance, equality and respect for the environment – and on a commitment to future challenges, not limited to a specific group. Thus, all individuals and groups living in a given territory would fundamentally share the same vision of a future – a concept capable of uniting people in a broader community, regardless of the emotional bonds among the members of this community that are often fragile and distant.[70]

68 See Treaty on European Union (TEU), signed in Maastricht on 7 February 1992, in force since 1 November 1993; see also, Treaty of Lisbon amending the Treaty on European Union and the Treaty Establishing the European Community, signed in Lisbon, 13 December 2007.

69 On multiple identities, see, among others, A. K. Appiah, 'Race, Culture, Identity: Misunderstood Connections', in A. K. Appiah and A. Gutman (eds), *Color Consciousness: The Political Morality of Race* (Princeton, NJ: Princeton University Press, 1996), 30–105; R. Bauböck, 'Farewell to Multiculturalism? Sharing Values and Identities in Societies of Immigration', *Journal of International Migration and Integration* 3/1 (2002), 1–16; A. Zolberg, 'Modes of Incorporation: Toward a Comparative Framework', in V. Bader (ed.), *Citizenship and Exclusion* (London: Macmillan, 1997), 139–54.

70 Along the same lines, the Preamble of the Charter of Fundamental Rights of the EU states, 'The European people, in creating an ever closer union among them, are resolved *to share a peaceful future based on common values*' (Emphasis added

However, this change of perspective on the meaning of citizenship is not easy to achieve and has its own problems: some groups may not be open and experimental while others may jealously guard their inherited identities. In the end, sincere willingness for continuous interaction, mutual adjustment and accommodation on all sides lies at the heart of any successful pluralist and cohesive society.

---

by the authors). See Charter of Fundamental Rights of the EU, 2000/C 364/01, proclaimed on 7 December 2000, amended by the Lisbon Treaty, 2007/C 303/01, 14 December 2007.

LEAH SIMMONS WOOD

'Taking back control': Brexit and UK Border Policies

In 2016, the Brexit Leave campaign was centred on the notion of taking back 'control'. Declaring that the UK had reached 'Breaking Point!', the conservative government promised a new-found control over British borders and laws.[1] The campaign responded to the 'European migration crisis' declared in 2014. It capitalized on the emergence of far-right movements, and their accompanying prejudice, across European Union (EU) member states – enabled by a framework where 'prejudicial language […] informs discourses, policies, strategies, and techniques'.[2] Taking this into account, I consider what is meant and implied by 'regain control'. Further, I question whether, and if so when, the UK did not have control of both its external and internal borders.[3] In doing so, I maintain that despite the ruptures in social continuities caused by Brexit, particularly as it coincided with the Covid-19 pandemic which has disrupted cross-border mobility on a global scale, the UK has always had control over its borders. Implications of this 'control' lie with the enormity of its humanitarian consequences, the price

1   H. Stewart and R. Mason, 'Nigel Farage's Anti-Migrant Poster Reported to Police', *The Guardian* (16 June 2016), <https://www.theguardian.com/politics/2016/jun/16/nigel-farage-defends-ukip-breaking-point-poster-queue-of-migrants>.

2   V. Bello, 'The Spiralling of the Securitisation of Migration in the EU: From the Management of a "Crisis" to a Governance of Human Mobility?', *Journal of Ethnic and Migration Studies* 48/4 (2020), 8.

3   Through the term 'internal borders', I refer to the structural and racist complications that migrants encounter once they reach their 'final' destination. These align with notions of migrant 'non-belonging' and as 'undeserving' that underpin policies such as the 'culture of disbelief' and the 'hostile environment' in the UK. See N. El-Enany, *(B)Ordering Britain* (Manchester: Manchester University Press: 2020).

of which is migrant lives seeking refuge in the UK and the EU. My argument lends credence to Castles' theory that 'the real key to effective migration management', a central political agenda point since the early 2000s, is 'reducing North-South inequality'.[4] By maintaining a global racial order as established under colonialism,[5] 'government policy creates the crisis which it claims to solve'.[6]

To critique the political myth that Brexit would provide a means to 'regain control', we must consider the UK's membership in the EU between 1 January 1973 and 1 January 2021. The political narrative of 'taking back control' refers to the colonial context that dominated the world prior to the UK's accession to the European Economic Community (EEC), later forming the EU. Informed by El-Enany's argument on the centrality of empire in understanding Britain's borders and colonial rule, I understand 'regained' as a nostalgia for imperial power. The misconception in the campaign's narrative lies in its disregard of the UK-EU 'flexible membership' with regard to the four freedoms – movement, goods, capital and services – of EU border control, allowing it to opt in and opt out of different policies. Together with the non-binding nature of the Geneva Convention (1949) and of international law regimes generally, this guaranteed the UK's retention of its border control after the decline of its empire.

Investigating Britain's external border policy contributes to understanding how the UK has sought to manage diversity within the country and exert its influence within the Union to support its own domestic policy. Attention is thus paid to the Dublin Regulation and resettlement/asylum procedures and programmes, as examples of policies that Britain has been in and not in favour of, respectively. This brief history of UK-EU relations illustrates how the UK used its membership in the EU to its advantage, specifically with regard to border control. Despite the focus on asylum policies and procedures, awareness of the dangerous nature of dichotomies

---

4   S. Castles, 'Why Migration Policies Fail', *Ethnic and Racial Studies* 27/2 (2004), 205.

5   N. El-Enany, 'Introduction: Britain as the Spoils of Empire', in *(B)Ordering Britain*, 3.

6   L. Mayblin, 'The Death of Asylum and the Search for Alternatives', *Discover Society: New Series* 1/1 (2021), <https://doi.org/10.51428/dsoc.2021.01.0003>.

between migrants is made. For example, the concept of 'mixed migration', prominent in policy circles, is often ignored with discriminative realities.[7] Notwithstanding the dominant political and media narrative that the UK lost control of its borders when it joined the EU, locating this notion within the colonial roots of the modern British nation-state and of the institution of the EU will illustrate that 'European integration has [actually] served to accommodate and reinforce its border control regime'.[8] Rather than strengthening control of the UK external border, Brexit forms part of a continuum of legacies of the empire seeking to define British identity, contingent, in part, on racial exclusion.

From here, a discussion of the 'hostile environment' – a means for internal, as well as external, bordering – ensues. This policy finds legal expression in the Immigration Acts of 2014 and 2016, advancing the UK's 'culture of disbelief' and its ties to the 'push-pull theory', which seeks to simplify the complexity of irregular migration and asylum seeking. Colin Yeo, an influential immigration barrister in the UK, explains that 'pull factors' refer to qualities that attract a migrant to a certain destination over another.[9] The 'hostile environment' was established in response to

---

7   The term 'mixed migration' refers to both the overlapping and numerous reasons that motivate someone to migrate and the multiple migration flows that take place. Van Hear explains that the reason this is often ignored in policy is that policy regimes tend to conceptualize migrants as moving for a sole reason, categorizing them under labels such as refugee, family migrant, labour migrant, student and so on. See N. Van Hear, *Mixed Migration: Policy Challenges, The Migration Observatory* (Oxford: University of Oxford, 2011), <https://migrationobservatory.ox.ac.uk/resources/primers/mixed-migration-policy-challenges/>. International agencies developed the term of 'mixed migration' in response to the collapse in faith in the asylum seeking processes at the turn of the century. Arguably, this is happening again in current times. See Alison Mountz, 'The Death of Asylum: Hidden Geographies of the Enforcement Archipelago', *New Books Network* (9 April 2021), <https://newbooksnetwork.com/the-death-of-asylum?fbclid=IwAR3GhqFqfRzosQTTR8p3rBYs5UODvGobd5pxTn4nPhL1po4wNNNdQ3lZiUc>.

8   El-Enany, *(B)Ordering Britain*, 174.

9   C. Yeo, 'Introduction', in *Welcome to Britain: Fixing Our Broken Immigration System* (London: Biteback Publishing, 2020), 11.

this 'policy imaginary',[10] aiming to deter migrants from seeking refuge in the UK, despite the lack of supporting evidence.[11] This background allows for a better understanding of the UK's new post-Brexit asylum policy, as part of what is increasingly being recognized in scholarship as the 'death of asylum' – 'the erosion of people's rights to seek asylum'.[12] It is important to acknowledge that the idea that Brexit will make Britain hostile obscures the fact that racism has long informed and, in turn, produced hostile policies.[13]

Last, it can be argued that the Covid-19 pandemic has exposed the political myth of Brexit as a vehicle for 'taking back control' of the UK's borders. The pandemic has imposed a global liminal state, and yet it has been politicized to further government objectives. This is addressed with reference to travel bans and the UK Coronavirus Red List.

In 2004, the Labour Prime Minister Tony Blair referred to Britain as having 'the best of both worlds' with regard to European co-operation and migration policy. He stated:

> We are not obliged to have any of the European rules here, but where we decide in a particular area, for example to halt the trafficking in people, for example to make sure that there are proper restrictions on some of the European borders that end up affecting our country, it allows us to opt in and take part in these measures.[14]

10   L. Mayblin, 'Imagining Asylum, Governing Asylum Seekers: Complexity Reduction and Policy Making in the UK Home Office', *Migration Studies* 7/1 (2019), 1.

11   Y. Maccanico et al., 'The Shrinking Space for Solidarity with Migrants and Refugees: How the EU and Member States Target and Criminalize Defenders of the Rights of People on the Move', *Transnational Institution* (2018), <https://www.tni.org/en/publication/the-shrinking-space-for-solidarity-with-migrants-and-refugees> accessed 7 August 2022=3.

12   A. Mountz, *The Death of Asylum: Hidden Geographies of the Enforcement Archipelago* (Minneapolis: University of Minnesota Press: 2020). See also N. Nyabola, 'The End of Asylum', in *Travelling While Black: Essays Inspired by a Life on the Move* (Oxford: Hurst, 2020), 53–9.

13   M. Goodfellow, 'Racism and the UK's Immigration System', *Migration Mobilities Bristol* (11 May 2021).

14   Tony Blair, 25 October 2004, House of Parliament. See A. Geddes, 'Getting the Best of Both Worlds? Britain, the EU and Migration Policy', *International Affairs* 81/4 (2005), 723, <https://www.standard.co.uk/hp/front/blair-defends-asylum-move-7225795.html>.

Indeed, despite the freedom of movement of workers from member states[15] as a fundamental principle of the EU internal market programme since its inception, Lawyers For Britain explained the three-fold motivations behind the UK's ability to control its borders, regardless of its EU membership. First, the majority of migrants who come to the UK are non-EU, and thus unaffected by internal EU regulations. Second, although EU citizens had the right to seek work in the UK, they never had the right to permanent abode. Third, and in conjunction with the previous point, the UK retained its right to border control in the 1997 Amsterdam Treaty by opting out of the Schengen agreement – which abolished border controls between member states.[16]

Conversely, the British government played an active role in the development of the Eurodac Convention (2000) to support an effective application of the Dublin Regulation. Through this database, migrants' fingerprints are collected and computerized, to address unregulated and 'illegal' migration from the 'point-of-entry'.[17] This strategic and selective 'use of the EU as an alternative, co-operative venue for migration policy management [...] reinforced rather than overturned established patterns.'[18] By allocating responsibility for processing asylum claims to other member states, the UK sought to externalize its domestic political concerns.

The expansion of the 'hostile environment' – the political strategy seeking to deter migrants by creating hard borders – across Europe draws on the dual policies of externalization and securitization. These policies allowed the UK to maintain control over its borders through its membership in the EU. Indeed, the EU system of managing asylum rests on a person

15 As stated in article 3(2) of the EU: this includes the rights of movement and residence of workers, and the entry of their family members, as well as the right to work in another member state.

16 Lawyers For Britain, 'Can the UK Control Its Borders If It Remains in the EU?', *The UK and the EU: Benefits, Misconceptions and Alternatives*, <http://lawyers-inforbritain.uk/b-m-a/can-the-uk-control-its-borders-if-it-remains-in-the-eu/>.

17 <https://eur-lex.europa.eu/legal-content/EN/TXT/HTML/?uri=URISERV:l33081>.

18 Geddes, 'Getting the best of Both Worlds?', 723.

arriving in EU territory and subsequently presenting their application. Notwithstanding the disastrous consequences for asylum seekers, including the creation of huge confinement and detainment centres in Southern Europe, the Dublin III Regulation (2013) seeks to allocate responsibility for asylum applications in the EU by 'the issue of a transit visa, the legal presence of a close family member, or in the absence of these, the first physical contact with territory'.[19] The UK's geographic positioning meant the state was a major proponent of 'burden sharing', allowing for deportations back to the first 'point of entry' or safe country encountered – usually in Southern Europe. Through 'externalization and securitization' the UK's integration into the EU has allowed it to use its membership 'as a potential solution to domestic issues'.[20] This has led to much controversy between member states. In August 2020, for instance, Pierre-Henri Dumont, the Calais representative in the French national assembly, accused the UK 'of lacking even an ounce of humanity for making it so difficult for people to claim asylum in the UK'.[21] Whether or not Dublin III 'remains the main problem in achieving solidarity among Member States',[22] the EU context is, despite its limitations, 'still the single most favourable context for co-operation'.[23] In this sense, the UK's flexible relationship with the EU had previously allowed for adaptable participation and solidarity with regard to 'burden-sharing'. The UK retained the right of relocation during the Brexit transition period until 1 January 2021, with a rise in the number of deportations in December 2020.[24] Now, as a third-party state to the EU, it is debatable that leaving the EU has weakened the UK's ability to control its

19   El-Enany, *(B)Ordering Britain*, 204.

20   El- Enany, *(B)Ordering Britain*, 209.

21   'More or Less: Covid Testing Capacity, Refugee Numbers and Mascara', *BBC Sounds* (16 September 2020).

22   S. Angeloni and F. M. Spano, 'Asylum Seekers in Europe: Problems and Solutions', *International Migration and Integration* 19 (2018), 484.

23   A. Niemann and N. Zaun, 'EU Refugee Policies and Politics in the Times of Crisis: Theoretical and Empirical Perspectives', *Journal of Common Market Studies* 56/1 (2017), 15.

24   M. Townsend, 'UK Races to Deport Asylum Seekers Ahead of Brexit', *The Guardian* (6 December 2020).

borders having lost access to Dublin III, with implications for the freedom of movement of UK nationals. More recently, the Home Office announced its plans to send people seeking asylum in the UK to Rwanda for the applications to be processed – continuing to push the border further away. This constitutes a persistent attempt to externalize the UK's immigration 'issues'. The plan has been met with both national and international uproar and legal condemnations, foreseeing future challenges in 'protecting' the UK border.[25] In this regard, the EU actually served to support the UK's externalization objectives.

Furthermore, the UK participates in the United Nations (UN) Refugee Resettlement programme, leading Conservative MP Tim Loughton to declare that the UK has 'resettled more "genuine" refugees genuinely escaping war zones than any other EU Member State since 2016'.[26] The idea of 'genuine refugees' alludes to the UK's 'culture of disbelief', where they are considered to be economic migrants cheating the system.[27] Moreover, the statement is misleading and fuels an already 'highly charged and not always well informed' public debate.[28] Following a rise in asylum claims in the 1990s, the UK Home Office developed the 'culture of disbelief', which led to a decline in successful asylum claims from 87% in the 1980s to 4% the following decade.[29] In reality, the UN programme constitutes only 6% of the total number of asylum claims made to the EU. The Migration Observatory at the University of Oxford emphasizes that 'the key word here appears to be resettled'[30]: the Home Office was referring to a specific asylum process organized by the UN – in which the international organization identifies refugees across the globe and transfers them to a safe country. This does not include the 94% of refugees who claim asylum by arriving at a safe destination first. Although a third of people in the UK arrive through resettlement programmes, claiming asylum through an

25   M. Townsend, Priti Patel's Rwanda Plan for UK Asylum Seekers Faces Its First Legal Challenge', *The Guardian* (7 May 2022).
26   'More or Less', *BBC Sounds*.
27   Mayblin, 'The Death of Asylum and the Search for Alternatives'.
28   Geddes, 'Getting the best of Both Worlds?', 725.
29   Yeo, 'Introduction', 14.
30   'More or Less', *BBC Sounds*.

alternative route is both difficult and dangerous. In fact, out of the 80 million people displaced globally at the end of 2019, 22,800 were resettled and only 3,560 to the UK.[31] The country ranks sixth in terms of accepting asylum applications within the EU, following Germany, France, Sweden, Austria and Italy.[32] This illustrates how the UK retained control of its borders during its membership to the EU, relying on a misconception by the general public of the word 'resettled' to further its objectives.

Immigration is not just about an 'Other', or 'them', but is also about 'us.'[33] In a first-hand account of living as a migrant in Britain, it has been noted how the country is undergoing 'a period of rejection […] as the aggressive rhetoric of adhering to "British values" has catapulted itself into social policy.'[34] Indeed, 'race' is central to defining 'Britishness' and nationality, drawing attention to the internal border: functional, organizational and conceptual. In the organizational aspect, the 'effect of the hostile environment for policy was to deny long-settled former colonial subjects and their descendants access to […] vital services and to detain and expel them', forcing them to live below the poverty line.[35] In terms of conceptual borders, de Noronha – an academic and author of *Against Borders: The Case for Abolition* (2022) – states that 'ideas about race are sedimented and reflect colonial histories' and that we 'need to pay attention to the ways in which race shifts and gets reconfigured through immigration control'. He centres issues of 'class and race' in the 'expansion and intensification of the border in the wake of Brexit'.[36] The complexity of shifting immigration laws and the legacy of the twentieth-century fear of the 'Other' has meant that Britain's racialized subjects have been continuously excluded by the state's attempt to regain control. The notion of multiculturalism – cultural

31   Mayblin, 'The Death of Asylum and the Search for Alternatives'.
32   'More or Less', *BBC Sounds*.
33   B. Anderson, Introduction, *Us and Them?: The Dangerous Politics of Immigration Control* (Oxford: Oxford Scholarship Online, 2013), 9.
34   K. Yates, 'On Going Home', in N. Shukla, *The Good Immigrant* (London: Unbound, 2017), 109.
35   El-Enany, *(B)Ordering Britain*, 8.
36   L. De Noronha, 'Race, Class and Brexit: Rethinking from Detention', *Verso Blogs* (9 March 2018).

plurality – is undermined by an understanding of 'Britishness' as intrinsically white. Racism and nationalism are fundamentally linked in the UK, furthering the argument that the UK has always retained control of its borders through its understanding of who belongs. The 'culture of disbelief' and the 'hostile environment' seek to deter migrants from trying to reach the UK and the EU, aligning with notions of belonging and 'deserving'. The 'culture of disbelief' appears as 'a colonial-style set of assumptions about applicants' dishonesty and behaviour, particularly marked in the handling of family reunion and asylum claims',[37] further alluding to the current and ongoing 'death of asylum' as a category of protection.[38] Moreover, understanding internal borders allows for a better comprehension of 'migrant journeys', during which asylum seekers continue to encounter borders regardless of their physical location.

Internal borders are perpetuated by the hostile environment 'explicitly and implicitly' through the 'push-pull theory' with the objective of reinforcing the external border to migrants.[39] Where life-saving is considered a 'pull factor', policymakers seek to justify the human rights violations that occur at sea and on external territories.[40] While this maintains a strong external border, it also enhances the argument that the price of these policies is found in the number of migrant deaths. Although 'categorisations facilitate administrative processes', they fuel the 'policy imaginary' of pull factors,[41] regardless of the theory's 'inability to explain real-world patterns and processes of migration' and its limited supporting evidence.[42] El-Enany's historical approach to understanding the UK's immigration law underlines this exclusive categorization of migrants through the 'culture of disbelief' and locates the UK's 'low recognition rate of claims originating from its

---

37 F. Webber, *Borderline Justice: The Fight for Refugee and Migrant Rights* (London: Pluto Press, 2012), 2.

38 Mountz, 'The Death of Asylum'.

39 H. De Haas, 'A Theory of Migration: The Aspirations-Capabilities Framework', *Comparative Migration Studies* 9/8 (2021), 1.

40 Maccanico et al., 'The Shrinking Space for Solidarity', 9.

41 Mayblin, 'Imagining Asylum, Governing Asylum Seekers', 4.

42 Mayblin, 'Imagining Asylum, Governing Asylum Seekers', 8.

former colonies'.[43] She describes Brexit 'as a nostalgia for Empire' based on unaddressed colonial legacies, including racism.[44] The 2016 referendum ignores the fact that the EU had supported Britain's border control from its inception, with its membership application in 1973 contingent on the exclusion of its Commonwealth and racialized subjects.[45]

The prior UK Home Secretary Patel's new post-Brexit Asylum and Immigration policy, publicly declared on 24 March 2021, will extend the exclusive point-based system established in 2008.[46] The three main objectives of the new immigration plan include: 'increasing the fairness and efficacy of [the] system to provide protection for those in genuine need of asylum; to deter illegal entry to the UK; to remove more easily from the UK those with no right to be here'.[47] The policy sees an expansion of the category of 'irregularized' migrants.[48] The United Nations High Commissioner for Refugees (UNHCR) has expressed concern at the plan's 'discriminatory two-tiered approach to asylum, differentiating between those who arrive through legal pathways [...] and those who arrive irregularly', and states that 'attempts to relieve pressure on the UK asylum system by narrowing access to it [...] are neither effective nor sustainable ways to address the system's current weakness'.[49] The success of these increasingly harsh asylum

---

43   El-Enany, (B)Ordering Britain, 204.

44   El-Enany, (B)Ordering Britain, 212–13.

45   El-Enany, (B)Ordering Britain, 177.

46   The point-based system subdivided migrants and their applications to come to the UK into five separate categories: highly skilled workers, skilled people with a job offer, low-skilled, students and temporary workers. The system was modelled on an Australian immigration system and created additional barriers to people seeking to settle in the UK.

47   <https://www.gov.uk/government/consultations/new-plan-for-immigration/new-plan-for-immigration-policy-statement-accessible>.

48   D. Casciani, 'Priti Patel Pledges Overhaul of Asylum Seeker Rules', BBC World News (24 March 2020).

49   'UNHCR Observations on the New Plan for Immigration Policy Statement of the Government of the United Kingdom', UNHCR (4 May 2021), <https://www.unhcr.org/uk/60950ed64/unhcr-observations-on-the-new-plan-for-immigration-uk?fbclid=IwAR2woQbO6hxKooEo6TnP8a9Am6-Zvb7ryaRjJ5WRo7vQXdvyixYIg6cSk9g>.

policies is unfounded, and undermines the system on a global scale with huge moral and ethical implications and loss of life.[50] Within El-Enany's framework of UK immigration law as an 'ongoing project of colonialism, sustained via the structure of law'[51] and Gilroy's concept of 'post-colonial melancholia',[52] this calls for a sceptical approach to reviewing the previous prime minister Boris Johnson's comment about 'building a more global Britain'.[53]

The Covid-19 pandemic has altered the context and conditions in which Brexit was expected to occur at the time of the referendum, including influences on the labour market with high levels of unemployment, and has added additional barriers to cross-border mobility on a global scale. While Sumption, from the Migration Observatory at the University of Oxford, has declared 'uncertainty as the theme of the future' in this area, continuities of racial exclusion in both internal and external bordering have been evident over the last year.[54] Once again, this reveals that although measures have been implemented to strengthen the UK's external border, bordering methods and their consequences are consistent with previous processes. The anti-Brexit political campaign group, Led By Donkeys, exposed, through a video published on social media outlets, the 'real danger at our borders', calling attention to the hypocrisy of the notion of taking back control. While the 2016 referendum campaign promised that regaining border control would increase the security and protection of British nationals, Hassan Akkad questions the government's response to the pandemic and what this tells us about border security.[55] Despite the use of the virus as a justification

50   A. Connelley, 'What's Behind the UK's Harsh Post-Brexit Asylum Overhaul?', *New Humanitarian* (11 May 2021).

51   El-Enany, *(B)Ordering Britain*, 2.

52   P. Gilory, 'Race Is Ordinary: Britain's Post-Colonial Melancholia', *Philosophia Africana* 6/1 (2003), 32.

53   D. Boffey, 'European Parliament Votes through Brexit Deal with Big Majority', *The Guardian* (28 April 2021).

54   M. Sumption, Resolution Foundation, 'A New Era: What do Brexit and Covid Mean for Migration and the UK Labour Market?' (17 December 2020), <https://www.resolutionfoundation.org/events/a-new-era/>.

55   Hassan Akkad, 'Exposed: The Real Scandal at Our Borders', *Led By Donkeys*, Twitter (26 April 2021).

for border controls, the video questions who the enemy is and on whom
the doors are being closed. Stierl argued that Europe is united by 'migrant
deterrence' and has 'used coronavirus to extend the hostile environment to
the Mediterranean'.[56] This raises the question of whether the UK, through
bilateral agreements, will continue to be united in EU deterrence policies
despite its status as a third-party state. The overwhelming majority in the
European Parliament backing the Brexit trade and security deal suggests
that this is a possibility, demonstrating the UK's ongoing relations with
with the Union.[57]

Concerning internal borders, the pandemic has revealed racist narratives with respect to both immigration and the UK's reliance on migrant
workers in essential work and frontline jobs. Migrants were twice as likely to
contract the virus than citizens, while also bearing the dual vulnerability of
status and low salary. Fear of detection, denouncement and deportation has
reduced the already limited access to basic services, including health care.[58]
The effects of the hostile environment in constructing migrants as scapegoats have been exposed by the virus – highlighting the argument of the
legacies of Britain's 'colonial past' and its 'imperial present'.[59] Furthermore,
travel bans and the UK Coronavirus Red List also reveal some of the political incoherencies across Global North countries with regard to policy
during the pandemic. Travel bans were imposed on countries of the Global
South far earlier than on developed nations. Kenyan human rights lawyer
Nyabola states that 'it didn't matter that the dreaded virus had come to
Africa, rather than from it', reminding us that 'racism is humanity's original sin – as crude violence [...] but also as bureaucratic exclusion'.[60] The

56   M. Stierl, 'Migration: How Europe Is Using Coronavirus to Reinforce the Hostile
      Environment in the Mediterranean?', *The Conversation* (20 May 2020), <https://
      theconversation.com/migration-how-europe-is-using-coronavirus-to-reinforce-
      its-hostile-environment-in-the-mediterranean-137840>.
57   Boffey, 'European Parliament Votes'.
58   M. Panizzon, 'Covid-19 Was a Big Test for the UN Migration Initiatives. Did They
      Succeed?', *Open Democracy* (2 February 2021).
59   M. Goodfellow, *Hostile Environment: How Immigrants Became Scapegoats*
      (London: Verso, 2019).
60   Nyabola, *Travelling While Black*, xii, xviii.

Red List contained many overlaps with countries that require a visa to enter the UK, which, in turn, is 'conceived of as the frontline defence in expressing countries' fears of conquest and invasion, in many cases from the same territories that these powers spent the previous century conquering and invading'.[61] Mobility restrictions provide a powerful tool for discrimination, where 'bordering practices' both 'reflect' and 'make racial hierarchies'.[62] This shows how the pandemic has been politicized in the attempt to strengthen the UK's borders – internal and external. While the virus in some ways stresses the uncertainty imposed initially by Brexit, the politics surrounding the pandemic have revealed continuities in race relations and exclusions prevalent since the days of empire.

The UK's Brexit campaign was centred on the narrative of 'regaining control'. This statement is misleading, responding to the immediate political 'crisis' of immigration across the EU. Supporting evidence was found through an investigation of Britain's colonial history and its 'flexible relationship' with the EU, underlining the imperial nature of the UK's present state and of the Brexit campaign. Despite common political and media perceptions, the UK was able to strategically use the EU to externalize asylum and immigration policies with the objective of furthering its domestic agenda. In this way, the strengthening of the UK external border is reinforced by internal bordering. In addition, while the Covid-19 pandemic imposed a threshold of waiting, travel bans and the Red List expose how it has been politicized: border controls have been established for migrants as opposed to the common threat of the virus. Within the UK, the virus revealed and heightened national and international inequalities – ultimately the key motive for continued international migration. Policies that aim to strengthen the border in light of this come at the price of migrant lives. Uncertainty marks the context in which Brexit and its new asylum policy are taking place; however, continuities in the treatment and condition of migrants and racialized people in policy and practice remain

---

61 Nyabola, *Travelling While Black*, 139.
62 L. De Noronha, 'Deporting Black Britons: Mobility and Race-Making in the Life Stories of Criminalized "Deportees"', in *Race, Nation and Migration*, Migration Mobilities Bristol blog (23 March 2021).

prevalent. The Brexit campaign was highly politicized and relied on a generally poorly informed public opinion. This chapter has sought to place the campaign within its historical context in order to understand its roots and implications with the hope of creating a more inclusive future for migrants in the UK.

Bibliography

Policy reports and papers

<https://migrationobservatory.ox.ac.uk/press/migration-observatory-reviews-potential-post-brexit-immigration-policies/>.
<https://migrationobservatory.ox.ac.uk/resources/primers/mixed-migration-policy-challenges/>.
<https://www.ole.bris.ac.uk/bbcswebdav/pid-5272143-dt-content-rid-19987366_2/courses/SPOLM0042_2020_TB-2/More-detention-fewer-safeguards-How-the-new-EU-Pact-on-Migration-and-Asylum-creates-new-loopholes-to-ignore-human-rights-obligations.pdf>.
UNHCR Observations on the New Plan for Immigration Policy Statement of the Government of the United Kingdom (4 May 2021), <https://www.unhcr.org/uk/60950ed64/unhcr-observations-on-the-new-plan-for-immigration-uk?fbclid=IwAR2woQbO6hxKooEo6TnP8a9Am6-Zvb7ryaRjJ5WRo7vQXdvyixYIg6cSk9g>.

Newspaper articles and blog posts

Aitkin, A., 'Migrant Crossings: What Happens to Migrants Who Reach the UK?', *BBC* (24 March 2021), <https://www.bbc.co.uk/news/explainers-53734793>.
Boffey, D., 'European Parliament Votes Through Brexit Deal with Big Majority', *The Guardian* (28 April 2021), <https://www.theguardian.com/politics/2021/apr/28/european-parliament-votes-through-brexit-deal-with-big-majority?utm_term=2fa5f1e6079443f1013d5bb00dacc9c0&utm_campaign=ThisIsEurope&utm_source=esp&utm_medium=Email&CMP=thisiseurope_email>.

Casciani, D., 'Priti Patel Pledges Overhaul of Asylum Seeker Rules', *BBC* (24 March 2021).

Chigudu, S., ' "Colonialism Never Really Ended": My Life in the Shadows of Cecil Rhodes', *The Guardian* (14 January 2021), <https://eulawanalysis.blogspot. com/2020/09/first-analysis-of-eus-new-asylum.html>.

Connelley, A., 'What's Behind the UK's Harsh Post-Brexit Asylum Overhaul?', *The New Humanitarian* (11 May 2021), <https://www.thenewhumanitarian.org/ analysis/2021/5/11/whats-behind-uk-harsh-post-brexit-asylum-overhaul?utm _source=The+New+Humanitarian&utm_campaign=1d99d0eee0-EMAIL_ CAMPAIGN_5_11_2021_DAILY&utm_medium=email&utm_term=0_ d842d98289-1d99d0eee0-75666022>.

Goodfellow, M., 'Racism and the UK's Immigration System', *Migration Mobilities Bristol* (11 May 2021), <https://migration.bristol.ac.uk/2021/05/11/racism-and-the-uks-immigration-system/>.

Grierson, J. et al., 'Teenager Found Dead Trying to Cross Channel in Dinghy with Shovels for Oars', *The Guardian* (19 August 2020), <https://www.theguardian. com/world/2020/aug/19/sudanese-teenager-found-dead-on-beach-near-cal ais-sangatte>.

Hassan Akkad, 'Exposed: The Real Scandal at Our Borders', *Led By Donkeys*, Twitter (26 April 2021).

The Independent, <https://www.independent.co.uk/news/uk/politics/theresa-may-conference-speech-article-50-brexit-eu-a7341926.html>.

Kibasi, T., 'Biden's Tariffs Threat Shows How Far Brexit Britain Is from Controlling Its Own Destiny', *The Guardian* (30 March 2021), <https://www.theguardian. com/commentisfree/2021/mar/30/biden-tariffs-brexit-britain-eu-big-tech>.

Panizzon, M., 'Covid-19 Was a Big Test for the UN Migration Initiatives. Did They Succeed?', *Open Democracy* (2 February 2021).

Rankin, J., 'EU Rejects British Plan for Post-Brexit Return of Asylum Seekers', *The Guardian* (20 August 2020), <https://www.theguardian.com/politics/ 2020/aug/20/eu-rejects-british-plan-for-post-brexit-return-of-asylum-seek ers?fbclid=IwAR0097u3lyLoCJbyUnefsu83P4ecjRsyJ-483kFShJ46B85CzJg-0Dm4Z8A>.

Stierl, M., 'Migration: How Europe Is Using Coronavirus to Reinforce Its Hostile Environment in the Mediterranean', *The Conversation* (13 May 2020), <https:// theconversation.com/migration-how-europe-is-using-coronavirus-to-reinfo rce-its-hostile-environment-in-the-mediterranean-137840>.

Townsend, M., 'UK Races to Deport Asylum Seekers Ahead of Brexit', *The Guardian* (6 December 2020), <https://www.theguardian.com/uk-news/ 2020/dec/06/uk-races-to-deport-asylum-seekers-ahead-of-brexit?fbclid= IwAR3_ClKdLGvVlBnIh92UeLtRYOC8809YrcvGY98tVVPvPmQZPmx8 bD9r7Ms>.

——, 'Priti Patel's Rwanda Plan for UK Asylum Seekers Faces Its First legal Challenge', *The Guardian* (7 May 2022), <https://www.theguardian.com/world/2022/may/07/priti-patels-rwanda-plan-for-uk-asylum-seekers-faces-its-first-legal-challenge>.

Podcasts

Mountz, Alison, 'The Death of Asylum: Hidden Geographies of the Enforcement Archipelago', *New Books Network* (9 April 2021), <https://newbooksnetwork. com/the-death-of-asylum?fbclid=IwAR3GhqFqfRzosQTTR8p3rBYs5UOD vGobd5pxTn4nPhL1po4wNNNdQ3lZiUc>.

'More or Less: Covid Testing Capacity, Refugee Numbers and Mascara', *BBC Sounds* (16 September 2020), <https://www.bbc.co.uk/sounds/play/mooomksw>.

Webinars

Sumption, Madeleine, Resolution Foundation, 'A New Era: What Do Brexit and Covid Mean for Migration and the UK Labour Market?' (17 December 2020), <https://www.resolutionfoundation.org/events/a-new-era/>.

Scholarship

Anderson, B., *Us and Them: The Dangerous Politics of Immigration Control* (Oxford: OUP's Oxford Scholarship Online, 2013).

Bertram, C., *Do States Have the Right to Exclude Immigrants?* (Cambridge: Polity Press, 2018).

Bhambra, G., 'Brexit, Empire and Decolonisation,' History Workshop Blog (19 December 2018), <https://www.historyworkshop.org.uk/empire-decolonisation/brexit-empire-and-decolonization/>.

Castles, S., 'Why Migration Policies Fail', *Ethical and Racial Studies* 27/2 (2004), 205–27.

De Haas, H., 'A Theory of Migration: The Aspirations-Capabilities Framework', *Comparative Migration Studies* 9/8 (2021), 1–35.

De Haas, H., Castle, S. and Miller, M., *The Age of Migration: International Population Movements in the Modern Age* (Basingstoke: Palgrave Macmillan, 2013).

De Noronha, L., 'Deporting Black Britons: Mobility and Race-Making in the Life Stories of Criminalised "Deportees"', *Race, Nation and Migration*, Migration Mobilities Bristol blog, <https://migration.bristol.ac.uk/2021/03/23/deporting-black-britons-mobility-and-race-making-in-the-life-stories-of-criminalised-deportees/> (23 March 2021).

——, 'Race, Class and Brexit: Thinking from Detention', *Verso Blogs* (9 March 2018), <https://www.versobooks.com/blogs/3675-race-class-and-brexit-thinking-from-detention?fbclid=IwAR0097u3lyLoCJbyUnefsu83P4ecjRsyJ-483kFS hJ46B85CzJg-0Dm4Z8A>.

El-Enany, N., *(B)Ordering Britain: Law, Race and Empire* (Manchester: Manchester University Press, 2020).

Geddes A., 'Getting the Best of Both Worlds? Britain, the EU and Migration Policy', *International Affairs* 81/4 (2005), 723–40.

Gilory, P., 'Race Is Ordinary: Britain's Post-Colonial Melancholia', *Philosophia Africana* 6/1 (2003), 32.

Goodfellow, M., *Hostile Environment: How Migrants Became Scapegoats* (London: Verso, 2019).

Mayblin, L., 'Imagining Asylum, Governing Asylum Seekers: Complexity Reduction and Policy Making in the UK Home Office', *Migration Studies* 7/1 (2019), 1–20.

——, 'The Death of Asylum and the Search for Alternatives', *Discover Societies: New Series* 1/1 (2021), <https://doi.org/10.51428/dsoc.2021.01.0003>.

Niemann, A. and Zaun, N., 'EU Refugee Policies and Politics in Times of Crisis: Theoretical and Empirical Perspectives', *Journal of Common Market Studies* 56/1 (2017), 3–22.

Nyabola, N., *Travelling While Black: Essays Inspired by a Life on the Move* (London: Hurst, 2020).

Peers, S., *EU Justice and Home Affairs Law* (Oxford: Oxford University Press, 2001).

——, 'EU Law Analysis: First Analysis of the EU's New Asylum Proposals', *EU Law Analysis* (25 September 2020), <https://eulawanalysis.blogspot.com/2020/09/first-analysis-of-eus-new-asylum.html>.

Stierl, M., 'Reimagining Europe through the Governance of Migration', *International Political Sociology* 14 (2020), 252–69.

Van Houtum, H., 'The Political Extreme as the New Normal: The Cases of Brexit, the French State of Emergency and Dutch Islamophobia', *Fennia – International Journal of Geography* 195/1 (2017), 85–101.

Webber, F. and Sedley, S., *Borderline Justice: The Fight for Refugee and Migrant Rights* (London: Pluto Press, 2012).

Yates, K., 'On Going Home', in N. Shukla (ed.), *The Good Immigrant* (London: Unbound, 2017).

Yeo, C., *Welcome to Britain: Fixing Our Broken Immigration System* (London: Biteback Publishing: 2020).

ANDREA CARLÀ

Navigating the Implications of Consociational Power-Sharing Regimes: Power-Sharing and (De)securitization in Northern Ireland and South Tyrol[1]

Changing boundaries and drawing new boundaries have long been contested issues in both Northern Ireland and South Tyrol. The partition of Ireland left unresolved the tensions between the Catholic and Protestant segments of the population and between the Republican and Unionist nationalist claims, which ended in the so-called Troubles that bloodied Northern Ireland societies for decades. Similarly, the demise of the Hapsburg Empire and the annexation of South Tyrol with its German- and Ladin-speaking population by the Italian state turned into a low-intensity conflict in the 1950s and 1960s. In both Northern Ireland and South Tyrol, consociational power-sharing institutions (liberal and corporate type, respectively) were seen as the solution to resolve the tension between the potentially conflictual segments of the population and between the peripheral region and the central state, though with different degrees of success so far.

In Northern Ireland, the 1998 Good Friday Agreement foresaw a liberal form of consociational power-sharing system that contributed towards

1   This chapter is partially based on: Andrea Carlà, 'Fear of Others? Processes of Securitization in South Tyrol', *Research and Science Today* 2/18 (2019), 9–25 and Andrea Carlà, 'Fear of Others: Processes of (De)Securitisation in Northern Ireland', *Journal on Ethnopolitics and Minority Issues in Europe* 20/1 (2021), 45–77. While working on this publication, the author has greatly benefited from the intellectual exchange through the SECUREU (Securitization of Migrants and Ethnic Minorities and the Rise of Xenophobia in the EU) Jean Monnet Network (<https://www.europenowjournal.org/secureu-2022/>).

putting an end to the violence, but many political and social issues among the Northern Irish communities are still unresolved. The region continues, thereby, to mirror the problems of divided societies. Brexit and the re-establishment of borders between the UK/Northern Ireland and the EU/Ireland have brought further challenges. On the contrary, South Tyrol and its 1972 second Statute of Autonomy is often considered by practitioners and in public opinion as a successful example of conflict resolution and minority protection through regional corporate consociation in contexts ranging from Bosnia-Herzegovina to Tibet and more recently Ukraine. At the same time, in the past decades, both polities have become more complex due to the arrival, from foreign countries, of migrants whose presence challenges established boundaries and identities.

In light of these institutional frameworks and their outcomes, this chapter adopts a 'from-above' perspective that analyses the consequences of institutional constellations on social processes in both Northern Ireland and South Tyrol. In particular, it aims to explore the implications of con-sociational power-sharing regimes on the relationship between potentially conflictual segments of the population and their identities. The chapter asks how consociational power-sharing institutions interplay with the way the different political communities in Northern Ireland and in South Tyrol see and perceive each other. To what extent do they challenge and affect how these communities perceive themselves and their boundaries vis-à-vis the 'others'? Do the liberal and corporate forms of consociationalism have a different impact in this regard?

To investigate these questions, I combine the fields of ethnic politics and research on consociationalism with security studies. In particular, I explore and compare the interaction between power-sharing insti-tutional arrangements in Northern Ireland and South Tyrol and pro-cesses of (de)securitization, which refers to the process through which an issue is considered (or not any longer) as an existential threat and through an us-versus-them lens. In the past decades, (de)securitization has become a popular and recurrent term used by researchers and prac-titioners in a variety of political, economic and social contexts. Many scholars have used the concept of (de)securitization to analyse varied perceived security problems related to minority politics. Building on this scholarship, I analyse to what extent, how and on what terms (de) securitization dynamics have unfolded vis-à-vis the presence of diverse communities and the power-sharing context in the two case studies. Comparing Northern Ireland and South Tyrol, I explore whether consociationalism (whether in the liberal or corporate form) can help overcome friend-enemy distinctions and us-versus-them frameworks. Understanding securitization as a speech act, I trace (de)securitizing moves and their historical evolution as they have developed in political discourses at the elite level. Methodologically, I rely on discourse analysis of the electoral manifestos of the main political parties in Northern Ireland and South Tyrol since the implementation of power-sharing institutions as well as selected speeches of main political leaders.

In this way, I provide new insights into debates surrounding consociationalism and institutional solutions for divided societies and their impact. Though often presented as the best solution, consociationalism is also criticized for entrenching ethnic identities and division. I argue that rather than designing and thinking about alternative institutions to overcome ethnic diversity, it is necessary to focus on how consociational solutions address negative connotations and perceptions of 'the other' and normalize ethnic cleavage and minority/majority relations; namely the extent to which they address (de)securitization processes.

The chapter is structured in four parts. First, I present my theoretical framework, discussing how the concept of securitization might be applied to the theory of consociationalism. Thereafter, I present the specific consociational mechanisms foreseen by the Good Friday Agreement in Northern Ireland and the second Statute of Autonomy in South Tyrol and provide background information, stressing similarities and differences in the two case studies. Third, I present the analysis of processes of (de)securitization in political discourses in Northern Ireland and South Tyrol and of how the different political communities perceive each other, whether in positive or negative terms. In the conclusion, I draw inferences on the interplay between consociational institutions and processes of (de)securitization and discuss how cross-fertilization among research fields and the application of the concept of securitization enriches our understanding of institutional solutions for divided societies.

Theoretical framework: When consociationalism meets securitization

Since its first theorization by A. Lijphart, many scholars and practitioners have embraced the concept of consociationalism as the best institutional framework to address conflicts in plural and divided societies. Consociationalism is an 'elite-oriented' top-down theory[2] that considers the different (ethnic) segments of the population in a plural society as its 'constructive elements'.[3] It thus aims at recognizing and protecting them by guaranteeing access to power through four main mechanisms: executive power-sharing, proportionality, mutual veto and segmental autonomy. Under specific conditions, such system is seen as successful at bringing peace and ending violence while providing political stability. Indeed, according to the theory, over time, intergroup co-operation in consociational arrangements has the potential to foster trust among the political elite – trust that will later trickle down to society at large. In this way, consociationalism can lessen inter-group divisions and weaken identity politics.[4] However, it should be clarified that consociationalism does not aim at transcending ethnic diversity.[5]

There are different types of consociations. Scholars distinguish between the so-called corporate consociationalism and liberal consociationalism. The former, which, as shown below, is used in South Tyrol, accommodates groups by identifying them in advance based on ascriptive criteria, thereby assuming group identities as fixed. Instead,

---

2   Henry Jarrett, *Peace and Ethnic Identity in Northern Ireland* (London: Routledge, 2018), 49.

3   Arend Lijphart, *Democracy in Plural Societies: A Comparative Exploration* (New Haven, CT: Yale University Press, 1977), 42.

4   John McGarry and Brendan O'Leary, 'Consociational Theory, Northern Ireland's Conflict, and Its Agreement 2. What Critics of Consociation Can Learn from Northern Ireland', *Government and Opposition* 41/2 (2006), 249–77.

5   John McGarry, 'Conclusion: What Explains the Performance of Power-Sharing Settlements', in Allison McCulloch and John McGarry (eds), *Power-Sharing Empirical and Normative Challenges* (London: Routledge, 2017).

liberal consociationalism, which resembles what is used in Northern Ireland, rewards groups that have emerged spontaneously in democratic elections, thus assuming ethnic identity as fluid and flexible.[6] Though most scholars prefer the liberal version, corporate consociationalism is much more common in practice.[7]

Institutional mechanisms for divided societies such as consociational systems are generally evaluated and analysed along four main dimensions: the extent to which they (1) bring peace and end violence; (2) manage to provide political stability and functional governments; (3) are fair and bring justice; (4) transform society, overcoming ethnic divisions and cleavages and fostering cross-ethnic behaviour. In this regard, among the criticisms of consociational theory is the fact that consociational mechanisms empower ethnic elites, thus decreasing incentives for moderation and entrenching divisive identities.[8] Along these lines, some scholars prefer alternative conflict management tools designed to dilute ethnic identities and discourage ethnic appeals.

This criticism and perspective reflect a common normative bias that seems to imply that dis-homogeneous societies and high degree of diversity is *the* problem; hence, the need to transcend and weaken ethnic diversity and identities in order to have peace, democracy and stability arises. In reality, diversity by itself is not necessarily a problem: there are hundreds

---

6   Arend Lijphart, 'Constructivism and Consociational Theory', *apsa-cp* 12/1 (2001), 11–13.

7   Allison McCulloch, 'Consociational Settlements in Deeply Divided Societies: The Liberal-Corporate Distinction', *Democratization* 21/3 (2012), 501–18.

8   Furthermore, consociationalism is criticized for various other reasons: that it is difficult to be adopted, inapt to mitigate conflict in severely divided societies, and undemocratic and ineffective; it causes government gridlocks and political instability; it endangers individual rights; it does not deal with the problems of minority within minority and those segments of the population that are not included in the consociational pact. For an overview of criticisms and replies, see Brendan O'Leary, 'Debating Consociational Politics', in Sid Noel (ed.), *From Power Sharing to Democracy* (Montreal: McGill-Queen's University Press, 2005).

of national minorities and communal groups in the world, and many of them do not quarrel but more often live and co-operate peacefully.[9] What is then the actual challenge faced by plural societies?

To answer this question, I refer to the concept of (de)securitization, developed within the field of Security Studies. Securitization is the process through which an issue is considered as an 'existential threat, requiring emergency measures and justifying actions outside the normal bounds of political procedure'.[10] As developed by the so-called Copenhagen School, which first theorized the concept, this process is not based on objective facts; securitization happens not because a real existential threat exists, but because an issue is presented as a threat. Critically, securitization has an identity component and exclusionary effects, acting as a principle of categorizing and othering. Indeed, it is based on a friend-enemy distinction and us-versus-them framework, delimiting the group to be secured, which group poses a threat and which does not, as well as who is an insider and who is an outsider.[11] As the antithesis of securitization, de-securitization refers to the unmaking of the institutionalized representation of an issue as threatening and the transformation of the friend-enemy logic.[12]

9   Jams Fearon and David Laitin, 'Explaining Interethnic Cooperation', *American Political Science Review* 90/4 (1996); Jason Sorens, *Secessionism: Identity, Interest, and Strategy* (Montreal: McGill-Queen's University Press, 2012).

10   Barry Buzan, Ole Wæver and Jaap de Wilde, *Security. A New Framework for Analysis* (Boulder, CO: Lynne Rienner Publishers, 1998), 23–4.

11   See Josefina Echavarría Alvarez, 'Re-thinking (In)security Discourses from a Critical Perspective', *asteriskos* 1–2 (2006), 61–82; Pinar Bilgin, 'Identity/Security', in Peter Burgess (ed.), *The Handbook of New Security Studies* (London: Routledge, 2010), 81–9; Xavier Guillaume and Jef Huysmans, 'Citizenship and Securitizing', in Xavier Guillaume and Jef Huysmans (eds), *Citizenship and Security* (London: Routledge, 2013), 20; Andrea Carlà, 'From Security Considerations to De-securitising the Discourse on "Old" and "New" Minorities', in Roberta Medda-Windischer, Caitlin Boulter and Tove H. Malloy (eds), *Extending Protection to Migrant Populations in Europe* (London: Routledge, 2020).

12   It should be pointed out that de-securitization can be understood in several ways. See for example, Lene Hansen, 'Reconstructing Desecuritization: The Normative-Political in the Copenhagen School and Directions for How to Apply It', *Review of International Studies* 38/3 (2012), 526–46.

The concept of (de)securitization has been used in a variety of contexts, including in studies on ethnic conflict and politics of ethno-nationalism. Research demonstrates how specific minorities, such as the Palestinian citizens of Israel and the Russian minorities in Baltic states, have been securitized by states and national majorities being presented as antagonistic to the majority society or as a threat to the sovereignty and unity of the country.[13] Alternatively, scholars have shown how all parties involved in ethnic tensions and conflicts have acted as securitizing actors, as observed, for instance, in Aceh/Indonesia and in Bosnia-Herzegovina.[14]

Building on these works, I apply the concept of (de)securitization to scholarship on institutional design for plural and divided societies and consociationalism in order to argue that the issue at stake is not to transform societies, dilute ethnic identities and limit ethnic mobilization. Instead, the challenge is to address negative connotations and perceptions towards 'the other' and tackle 'the making and breaking of identity as an existential threat';[15] in other words, to deal with securitization processes and the use of us-versus-them logic and friend-enemy distinctions in regard to the relationship between majorities and minorities. Dealing with and designing institutions for divided societies imply addressing the securitization/desecuritization of diversity and minority issues in order to normalize cultural cleavages and minority-majority relations. Thus, following Calu's study, I reflect on the impact of consociational institutions put in place to accommodate minorities and ethnic tensions on (de)securitization processes and the portrayal of other communities as a threat to society.[16] The successful

---

13   Ronnie Olesker, 'National Identity and Securitization in Israel', *Ethnicities* 14/3 (2014), 371–91; Graeme P. Herd, and Joan Löfgren, ' "Societal Security", the Baltic States and EU Integration', *Cooperation and Conflict* 36/3 (2001), 273–96.

14   Yandry K. Kasim, 'Securitization and Desecuritization in Indonesia's Democratic Transition: A Case Study of Aceh Separatist movement', paper presented in the 8th Pan-European Conference on International Relations, 18–21 September 2013, Warsaw; Niels van Willigen, 'From Nation-Building to Desecuritization in Bosnia and Herzegovina', *Security and Human Rights* 21/2 (2010), 127–38.

15   Marius-Ionut Calu, 'Non-Dominant Groups in Kosovo: A Marginalised View on (De)Securitisation of Minorities after Conflict', *Journal on Ethnopolitics and Minority Issues in Europe* 20/1 (2021), 147.

16   Ionut Calu, 'Non-Dominant Groups in Kosovo', 152.

history of South Tyrol, with its corporate consociational institutions, and the struggle of Northern Ireland and its liberal type of consociational tools make the two an ideal comparison to analyse the ability and challenges of different forms of consociationalism in addressing divided societies and their interplay with (de)securitization processes.

In this contribution, I reframe the concept of (de)securitization, stressing its identity component in the definition of threats. I thus define securitization as the subjective process through which an issue is considered a threat wherein 'others' (cultural, political, religious, etc.) come to be perceived in prevalently exclusionary forms centred on a 'we versus them' dichotomy, implying homogeneous entities in opposition or competition. In this way, I explore the (de)securitization moves developed in Northern Ireland and South Tyrol after the establishment of consociational systems, revealing whether, who, what and in what terms is perceived as a threat, affecting relations between the different segments of the population.

To conduct the analysis, I adopt the Copenhagen School's understand securitization as a speech act. In this perspective, language has performative power and 'by saying the words, something is done'.[17] However, it should be clarified that this is not enough to define a threat; rather this discursive securitizing move is concluded only when the public accepts that the issue at stake is a threat. Furthermore, I understand securitization as a continuum and a multifaceted process, in the sense of the development of simultaneous processes of (de)securitization by a variety of actors and a 'sum of actions' without a clear beginning and ending.[18] Thus, I trace (de)securitization processes as they develop in the political discourses of all main political parties in Northern Ireland and South Tyrol. Specifically, in the former case I conducted a critical discourse analysis of the electoral programmes for the elections of the Northern Ireland Assembly from 1998 to 2017 of the parties constantly represented in the assembly since the Good Friday

---

17   Buzan et al., *Security. A New Framework for Analysis*, 26.

18   See Ali Bilgic, *Rethinking Security in the Age of Migration* (New York: Routledge, 2013); Faye Donnelly, 'The Queen's Speech: Desecuritizing the Past, Present and Future of Anglo-Irish Relations', *European Journal of International Relations* 21/4 (2015), 917.

Agreement. In addition, I looked at party programmes used before the agreement, that is, the manifestos for the 1997 Westminster parliamentary election. In South Tyrol, I analysed electoral programmes of the last 2018 election for the South Tyrolean Parliament together with selected political party's programmes and discourses of the political forces elected in the South Tyrolean Parliament since the turn of the century. In addition, I considered some previous political discourses of historical political forces. The analysis focuses on political parties and forces represented in the Northern Ireland Assembly or South Tyrolean Parliament because, as pointed out by Vuori, I use the electoral results and the strength of these parties in the assembly/parliament as a proxy of the public acceptance of their discourses.[19] In both Northern Ireland and South Tyrol, I analysed the discourse of more moderate and more extreme political forces within each segment of the population (respectively British unionists and Irish nationalists and Italian speakers and German speakers) as well as parties that crosscut the segmental cleavage. Table 1 presents the parties analysed in the two cases and their affiliation along the segmental cleavage.

19   Juha A. Vuori, 'Illocutionary Logic and Strands of Securitization: Applying the Theory of Securitization to the Study of Non-Democratic Political Orders', *European Journal of International Relations* 14/1 (2008), 65–99. Thus, this chapter takes for granted the level of public endorsement of (de)securitizing discourses and does not present a specific analysis in this regard.

Table 1. Analysed party and affiliation

Northern Ireland				South Tyrol	
British unionists	Irish nationalists	Others	German	Italian	Inter-ethnic
Ulster Unionist Party (UUP)	Social Democratic and Labour Party (SDLP)	Alliance Party of Northern Ireland (APNI)	Südtiroler Volkspartei (SVP)	Movimento Sociale Italiano (MSI)	Verdi-Grüne-Vërc
Democratic Unionist Party (DUP)	Sinn Féin		Süd-Tiroler Freiheit	Alleanza Nazionale (AN)	Team K
			die Freiheitlichen	Unitalia	
				Forza Italia/ Popolo della Libertà	
				L'Alto Adige nel cuore	
				Lega	
				Partito Democratico (PD)	

Consociationalism in Northern Ireland and South Tyrol

There are great differences in the history and dynamics of the tensions in Northern Ireland and South Tyrol, not least the degree of violence and death toll.[20] In particular, the Troubles of Northern Ireland constitute

20   The Troubles left over 3,600 dead (for the most part civilians) and more than 30,000 injured; clearly these numbers cannot be compared with the few tens of deaths and injured in South Tyrol, despite hundreds of terrorist attacks, most of which did not target people.

an overlap of religious, ethno-national and socio-political cleavages with the contraposition between Catholic-Irish-nationalist/republicans versus Protestant-British-unionist/loyalists, though this contraposition does not completely grasp the complexity and shifting dynamics of Northern Ireland population's identities.[21] Instead, the tensions in South Tyrol reflect a more clearly defined ethno-linguistic-national cleavage with the contraposition among German, Italian and Ladin speakers.[22]

However, at the same time, it is possible to mention some common traits. The end of the First World War was followed by a turning point event in both countries: the partition of the island and the annexation of South Tyrol by the Italian state as spoiled of war. Following partition, Northern Ireland society experienced decades of political and economic discrimination and domination of the Catholic population by the Protestant majority, which in the late 1960s led to the Troubles when a civil rights and anti-discrimination campaign turned into a low-intensity conflict over the constitutional status of Northern Ireland. Similarly, after annexation, South Tyrol witnessed fascist oppression and the attempt of the Italian State to Italianize the area also through the immigration of Italian speakers from the rest of the peninsula. Furthermore, both cases rely on an international

---

21   Duncan Morrow, 'Sectarianism in Northern Ireland: A Review', Ulster University Press, 2019, <https://www.ulster.ac.uk/__data/assets/pdf_file/0016/410227/ A-Review-Addressing-Sectarianism-in-Northern-Ireland_FINAL.pdf>, accessed 15 December 2022, 10, 13. According to the 2011 census, 41.5% of the population is Protestants and 41% Catholic. Furthermore, in a 2019 survey, 39% of the persons described themselves as British, 25% as Irish, 1% Ulster, 27% Northern Irish 29% and 8% as others. It should also be noted that in 2011, 4.3% of the population was born outside of UK and Ireland. See Northern Ireland Statistics and Research Agency, 'Northern Ireland Census 2011 Key Statistics Summary Report', (2014), 53, 84–85; NILT, '2019 Northern Ireland Life and Times Survey', *ARK* (2019), <https://www.ark.ac.uk/nilt/2019/Community_Relations/NINATID.html>, accessed 15 December 2022.

22   In the last 2011 census, 69.4% of the South Tyrolean population affiliated with the German-speaking group, 26.1% with the Italian-speaking group and 4.5% with the Ladin group. In addition to the official linguistic groups, foreign population represents today more than 9% of the inhabitants in the province.

agreement, the 1998 Good Friday Agreement and the De Gasperi-Gruber Agreement, signed in 1946 by Austria and Italy, which committed to provide some forms of protection and political autonomy to the German-speaking inhabitants of South Tyrol. However, the failed implementation of the agreement by the Italian state led to tensions and bomb attacks that affected the province in the 1950s and 1960s.[23]

Last, but particularly relevant for the scope of this chapter, in both Northern Ireland and South Tyrol consociational power-sharing arrangements have been introduced to bring an end to the tensions in the two contexts, though in the liberal and corporate type of consociation, respectively. Furthermore, in both cases, consociational mechanisms combine with extensive territorial autonomy, owing to which both regions have extensive powers in several matters, such as health and social services.

As consociational mechanisms, the Good Friday Agreement as well as the South Tyrolean second Statute of Autonomy foresee the use of the proportional system for the election of the Northern Ireland Assembly and the South Tyrolean Provincial Parliament, whose members in both cases should designate themselves as part of a specific segment of the population. While in Northern Ireland the category of 'others' is included in addition to 'unionists' and 'nationalists', in South Tyrol the choice is limited to the linguistic groups (Italian, German and Ladin).[24] In both systems, there is the possibility of cross-community voting procedures (for key decisions in Northern Ireland and for the approval of the South Tyrolean provincial budget) and a sort of veto power. This is the 'petition of concern', according to which 30 members of the Northern Ireland Assembly can ask to vote with cross-community support; similarly, in South Tyrol, the linguistic groups can request a separate vote by linguistic group and challenge a contested law before the Italian Constitutional Court for legislation that regards the vital interests of a group.

---

23   Only with the 1972 second Statute of Autonomy has the De Gasperi-Gruber agreement been fulfilled.

24   More precisely, people in South Tyrol can declare themselves as 'other', but have to then choose their affiliation to one of the official linguistic groups. The category of 'other' is not foreseen by the consociational mechanisms.

The liberal element of the Northern Ireland system relies mainly on the use of the d'Hondt procedure for the formation of the Northern Ireland Executive, whose composition is determined on the basis of parties' assembly seat share. Since 'the d'Hondt allocation is difference blind' and operates 'according to the strength of representation won by parties in the Assembly, not their national identity', the Northern Ireland consociation 'does not privilege particular identities'.[25] Instead, the corporate South Tyrol system identifies the linguistic groups (Italian, German and Ladin) as constituent parts of the provincial government, whose composition must reflect the numerical strength of the groups as represented in the Provincial Parliament. Furthermore, another corporate element of the South Tyrol system is the so-called ethnic quota system, according to which public employment and public resources are distributed among the linguistic groups in proportion to their numerical strength, which is calculated based on a declaration of linguistic belonging or aggregation (Italian, German or Ladin speaker). Thus, Northern Ireland's liberal system is more prone to deal with flexible identities and processes of transformation of the society, whereas South Tyrolean corporate institutions are designed based on pre-determined categories and with the goal of maintaining and protecting distinct cultures and identities.

The Northern Ireland and South Tyrolean governments differ further because the former has a joint head of the Executive composed of the first and deputy first minister chosen, respectively, by the main unionist and nationalist parties. Instead, in South Tyrol the head of the government is the president, who is de facto a German speaker, and there are two/three vice presidents (from each linguistic group).

Finally, both the Good Friday Agreement and the South Tyrolean second Statute of Autonomy contain provisions in matters of cultural autonomy and cultural rights, though the former is set out in a vaguer manner. Indeed, the Good Friday Agreement refers to the importance of respecting, understanding and tolerating linguistic diversity, in particular

---

25 John McGarry and Brendan O'Leary, 'Power Shared after the Death of Thousands', in Rupert Taylor (ed.), *Consociational Theory: McGarry and O'Leary and the Northern Ireland Conflict* (London: Routledge, 2009), 15–84, 71.

the Irish language, Ulster-Scots as well as the languages of the various ethnic communities of the island, although the enactment of specific measures is delegated to future government actions. Various other identity-related issues were touched upon by the agreement but not clearly resolved, leaving space for the rise in tensions in the following years. Instead, the Second Statute of Autonomy establishes several linguistic rights and cultural autonomy forms, including mandatory bilingualism/trilingualism of public signs and public officers and education in the mother tongue, implemented through three separate school systems.

Naturally, both documents contain specific elements and provisions that make the two systems unique. In particular, the Northern Ireland consociational system has an international and transnational dimension and is 'built within an overarching confederal and federal' framework that addresses the relations between Northern Ireland and the Republic of Ireland and between the latter and the UK.[26] This framework includes the cross-border North-South Ministerial Council, which fosters co-operation between the Northern Ireland Assembly and the Irish Parliament. The British-Irish Intergovernmental Conference and the British-Irish Council – composed of members of the British and Irish governments; the parliaments in Scotland, Wales and Northern Ireland; and representatives of the Isle of Man and the Channel Islands – cover the East-West relations between the UK and the Republic of Ireland. Instead, the second Statute of Autonomy of South Tyrol does not have this external dimension. However, this aspect is included in the De Gasperi-Gruber Agreement between Italy and Austria, which represents the international basis for South Tyrol's autonomy. Indeed, on the one hand, the agreement recognized Austria as the protector of its kin people and, on the other hand, it included measures to promote cross-border relations, such as mutual recognition of degrees and facilitating frontier traffic and exchange of goods. These cross-border activities have further developed, leading to the creation in 2011 of the

---

26 Brendan O'Leary, cited in Joanne McEvoy, *Power-Sharing Executives* (Philadelphia: University of Pennsylvania Press, 2015), 64.

European Grouping for Territorial Cooperation called 'European Region Tyrol-South Tyrol-Trentino' to develop and coordinate common policies.[27]

Furthermore, the Good Friday Agreement incorporates other specific provisions. These include constitutional changes in the Republic of Ireland (removing from its constitution the claim on the entire island), the principle of consent according to which Northern Ireland's constitutional status can change if a majority of the population in both the Republic and Northern Ireland wish it and measures to deal with the violent past like decommissioning of weapons by paramilitary forces and the release of paramilitary prisoners. Noteworthy in the South Tyrol system is the creation of joint commissions for the implementation of the Statute and its development and extensive financial provisions, including the fact that 90% of the taxes collected in South Tyrol are allocated to the Province, guaranteeing remarkable economic resources.

Following the Good Friday Agreement and the second Statute of Autonomy, Northern Ireland and South Tyrol have had quite a different experience, since the former faced several difficulties and setbacks, whereas South Tyrol witnessed a long period of peace, stability and prosperity. Indeed, though the Good Friday Agreement has brought relative peace and reduced violence, many contentious issues, such as weapon decommissioning and the reform of the police, remained and took some years to be resolved through further agreements.[28] In particular, various identity-related issues were not clearly settled by the Good Friday Agreement and continued to spark political tensions, and, consequently, minor paramilitary activities,

---

27 It should be noted that in both cases the development of the EU and the Schengen agreement, which emptied the state borders between Italy and Austria and between Ireland and the UK of their meaning, contributed to the functioning of the consociational power-sharing arrangements.

28 In 2001, the Northern Irish police force (the Royal Ulster Constabulary), which was considered supporting the unionist/protestant population, was transformed into the Police Service of Northern Ireland (PSNI) with a 50% recruitment policy from people with Catholic background. Regarding the issue of weapon decommissioning, considered by unionist political forces a prerequisite to enter in the government, only in 2005 did the Provisional Irish Republican Army announced its disarmament.

protests and riots resurfaced occasionally. Only with the 2014 Stormont House Agreement and the 2015 Fresh Start Agreement was there some progress on symbolic issues related to parades and flags and the legacy of the past.[29] Instead, the Irish language and related legislation continue to be an unresolved highly politicized topic. Furthermore, although shared cultural activities and specific policy measures have been taken, segregation, sectarianism and sectarian hate crimes persist and are part of everyday life in many areas.[30] Therefore, scholars speak of 'uneasy peace rather than deep reconciliation'.[31]

In this context, fulfilling a common criticism of consociationalism, governments in Northern Ireland have been characterized by political instability and modest results. Shortly after the Good Friday Agreement, the parties that led the peace negotiations (i.e. the Ulster Unionist Party [UUP] and the Social Democratic and Labour Party [SDLP]) were overtaken by less moderate parties, the Democratic Unionist Party (DUP) and Sinn Féin, which since 2003 are the main parties within respectively the unionist and nationalist political arena. The DUP and Sinn Féin have not managed to collaborate properly within the consociational framework, and the government was suspended several times, in 2000, between 2002 and 2007 and again between 2017 and 2020. So far, Northern Ireland has experienced only two full-term consecutive assemblies and executives in 2007–11 and 2011–16 led by Sinn Féin and the DUP, respectively. However, political achievements have been modest, and moments of tension and contention remained. In addition, in the past years, Brexit, opposed by the majority of Northern Ireland's population, which voted to 'Remain' in the 2016 referendum (56%), as well as the issue regarding the re-establishment of the border between the UK and the EU/the Republic of Ireland are

---

29   The agreements foresaw a Commission on Flags, Identity, Culture and Tradition, and institutions to address the legacy of the Troubles, including an Oral History Archive and a Historical Investigations Unit. Furthermore, the responsibility over parades has been devolved to the Northern Ireland Assembly.

30   Morrow, *Sectarianism*.

31   Brigid Laffan, cited in David Torrance, 'Devolution in Northern Ireland, 1998–2018', Briefing Paper, CBP 8439 (2018), 19.

undermining the political co-operation established by the Good Friday Agreement and the agreement itself.[32]

On the contrary, South Tyrol's second Statute of Autonomy notably contributed to resolving conflicts and helped foster peaceful cohabitation by providing a feeling of protection among the language groups, in particular the German-speaking population.[33] As foreseen by the consociational theory, the consociational mechanisms have encouraged elites' inter-ethnic collaboration and the development of mutual trust, which in a process of social learning have spilled over into the society at large.[34] South Tyrol has thereby witnessed a long period of political stability, characterized by the dominance of the Südtiroler Volkspartei (SVP), the party that has historically represented the German- and Ladin-speaking population, which has continued to govern the province, mostly in coalition with centre/centre-left Italian parties and since 2018 with the Lega, as mandated by the consociational mechanisms. Not surprisingly, most of South Tyrol's population defines cohabitation as good or satisfactory.[35] Peace and political stability came together with remarkable economic growth, both absolutely and in comparison with the rest of Italy, making South Tyrol an extremely wealthy and prosperous area. Consequently, thanks to the financial provisions of the autonomy, the provincial government can count on remarkable resources.[36]

However, at the same time, the linguistic divisions within the South Tyrolean population have been maintained in many aspects of social and political life. Indeed, each group has created its own organizations (such

---

32   Morrow, *Sectarianism*, 21.

33   Bertus de Villiers, 'Power-Sharing Options in Complex Societies – Possible Lessons from South Tyrol for Young Democracies on Ways to Protect Ethnic Minorities at a Regional Level', *JEMIE* 16/1 (2017), 9.

34   Joseph Marko, 'Is there a South Tyrolean "Model" of Conflict Resolution to be Exported?', in Jens Woelk, Francesco Palermo, Joseph Marko and the European Academy Bozen/Bolzano (eds), *Tolerance through Law. Self-Governance and Group Rights in South Tyrol* (Leiden: Martinus-Nijhoff, 2008).

35   ASTAT, *Südtiroler Sprachbarometer/Barometro linguistico dell'Alto Adige 2014* (Bolzano: Provincia Autonoma di Bolzano-Alto Adige, 2015).

36   In 2018, the provincial budget was about € 6 billion.

as trade unions, youth and sports associations, and mass media), though in past years there have been improvements in terms of increasing interaction and inter-ethnic civil society initiatives.[37] In particular, South Tyrolean political life remains characterized by an ethnic cleavage with many people still voting along linguistic lines, despite the presence of inter-ethnic parties. In this context, since the 1980s, within the German-speaking political arena, right-wing nationalist pro-independence political forces (today the Süd-Tiroler Freiheit and die Freiheitlichen) have challenged the power of the SVP, growing remarkably after the turn of the century, but experiencing a significant setback in the last 2018 elections.[38] Other aspects reveal the persistence of underlying and unresolved tensions within South Tyrolean society. Indeed, whereas South Tyrol is a bilingual territory, part of its population, especially Italian speakers, still struggle with the second language and are not bilingual. Furthermore, the South Tyrolean population maintains a distinct sense of identity along the linguistic division, and one-third (and the majority of Italian speakers) think that their language group is disadvantaged in various sectors of public life.[39] This discomfort of the Italian-speaking group is referred to as the *disagio degli italiani* (uneasiness of Italians) and has been behind the strength of Italian nationalist right-wing parties in the province in the 1980s and 1990s; however, in the past decade (until the 2022 national election) these parties seemed to have lost appeal.[40] At times these underlying tensions among the linguistic groups come at the fore of public debate.

37   See Günther Pallaver, 'South Tyrol's Consociational Democracy: Between Political Claim and Social Reality', in Woelk et al., *Tolerance through Law*; Günther Pallaver, 'South Tyrol's Changing Political System: From Dissociative on the Road to Associative Conflict Resolution', *Nationalities Papers* 42/3 (2014), 376–98.

38   In the 2013 provincial elections, these nationalist parties together received more than 25% of the votes, and among them Die Freiheitlichen was the second most voted party in the province with 17.9% of the votes. In 2018, these percentages reduced to 13.5% and 6.2%, respectively.

39   Most of the German-speaking population (80.7%) identify with the term *Südtiroler* (South Tyrolean in German language), whereas the majority of the Italian language group (59%) identifies as *Italian*, and 18.7% chose *Altoatesino* (an Italian term for South Tyrolean). See ASTAT, *Südtiroler Sprachbarometer*, 170, 185–6, 189.

40   As in the rest of Italy, the last 2022 national election saw even in South Tyrol the growth of the nationalist right-wing party Fratelli d'Italia.

Analysis

As shown above, Northern Ireland and South Tyrol represent two different forms of consociationalism which have so far presented divergent outcomes in terms of peace and political stability. Instead, the following analysis of political party programmes shows that there are some similarities in the way the experience with such consociational mechanisms have related to processes of (de)securitization in the two regions.

In Northern Ireland, most analysed political forces, across the unionist-nationalist divide, have carried out a variety of de-securitizing discourses, which in some cases were manifested even before the Good Friday Agreement, but increased over time after the implementation of the agreement and its consociational mechanisms. Most political programmes present a view of Northern Ireland which embraces diversity and avoids using processes of othering between the different Northern Irish communities and traditions. This view ranges from UUP's commitment to a 'multicultural, multi-ethnic society in which everyone plays a part'[41] to Sinn Féin's call for a society where 'difference is celebrated and cultural diversity is encouraged',[42] being epitomized in Alliance Party of Northern Ireland's (APNI) vision of an 'integrated and shared societies'.[43] The only exception is represented by the DUP, which took more than a decade after the agreement to overcome a language of fear and a grammar of security that contraposes the Northern Irish communities.

Interestingly, except in the Sinn Féin case, this approach turns in a strong criticism against some of the consociational elements of the Good Friday Agreement, like the petition of concern for fostering divisions and thereby encouraging securitization processes. Such mechanisms are seen as 'entrenc[hing] divisions and divid[ing] the community',[44]

---

41   UUP, *Ulster Unionists Manifesto 2003*, Ulster Unionist Party (2003).

42   Sinn Féin, *Sinn Féin Assembly Election Manifesto 2007. Delivering for Ireland's Future. Saoirse, Ceart agus Síocháin* (2007), 41.

43   APNI, *Forward. Faster, Manifesto 2016*, Alliance Party of Northern Ireland (2016), 20.

44   DUP, *Moving Forward, Manifesto 2011*, Democratic Unionist Party (2011), 25.

'institutionalis[ing] sectarianism' and fostering 'politics of "them" versus "us" over control of territory and resources',[45] or endangering the proper functioning of the government.[46] At the same time, most parties have expressed concerns about direct rule, which is 'unaccountable' and 'remote',[47] and, more recently, they raised the fear of Brexit, considered as undermining the Good Friday Agreement and 'the biggest threat to the economic, social and political interests' of Northern Ireland.[48]

However, though they all present a de-securitizing perspective, these discourses diverge since most of the time they develop within a unionist or Irish/nationalist standpoint that stresses the specific needs of their own community and focuses on the constitutional status of Northern Ireland (i.e. the emphasis on being part of the UK or the goal of a united Ireland). Thus, with the exception of the APNI, binary codes and polarized schemes have not completely disappeared. Furthermore, all analysed Northern Ireland political parties continue to securitize other political forces throughout confrontational and contentious tones both across the unionist-nationalist divide and within the own community of reference, for example, DUP's fear of radical republican demands, APNI's concerns for the threat posed by DUP and Sinn Féin politicians' incapacity, and UUP's vision of Sinn Féin and DUP as polarizing the society.

Similar to Northern Ireland, in South Tyrol most of the past securitizing discourses regarding the presence in the province of different linguistic groups have disappeared. Long gone is the expression of a 'death march' for the German-speaking population, coined by the Canon M. Gamper in 1953 to represent the continuous immigration of Italian speakers in the province,[49] which, according to SVP leader S. Magnago, 'is strangling us in

45 APNI, *The Alternative. An Agenda for a United Community, Manifesto, Assembly Election, 7 March 2007*, Alliance Party of Northern Ireland (2007), 4.
46 See SDLP, *Build a Better Future, SDLP Manifesto 2016*, Social Democratic and Labour Party (2016).
47 UUP, *For All of Us, Ulster Unionist Party Assembly Election Manifesto 2007*, Ulster Unionist Party (2007), 32.
48 SDLP, *Make Change Happen, Manifesto 2017*, Social Democratic and Labour Party (2017), 3.
49 Cited in Georg Grote, *The South Tyrol Question, 1866–2010* (Bern: Peter Lang, 2012), 86.

our own Heimat'.[50] At the same time, mostly gone is the vision of Italian speakers as a minority suppressed by the German-speaking population, which first emerged in the late 1950s.[51] In the years following the second Statute of Autonomy, this type of discourse became popular, particularly in the 1980s and 1990s when it was successfully carried out by fascist/post-fascist political forces (i.e. Movimento Sociale Italiano [MSI] and Alleanza Nazionale [AN]), which aimed at protecting the interests and rights of the Italian-speaking population against the South Tyrolean autonomy and its measures that protect the German-speaking group. However, today, such political forces and discourses have mostly lost their political appeal.[52] Right-wing Italian parties that have inherited this nationalist tradition, like *L'Alto Adige nel cuore*, de-emphasize the conflictual aspects of the relationship between Italian and German speakers, avoiding in part the use of the ethnic card and no longer seeing the other linguistic groups, the autonomy and key measures of minority protection as a danger.

Furthermore, today most political programmes across the linguistic spectrum see multilingualism as an added value and an opportunity, and they have a positive understanding of the presence of different (German, Ladin, Italian) groups in the province. For example, it is considered by die Freiheitlichen as an opportunity 'to act as a bridge between the German and Italian cultural and economic areas, offering our homeland and its people prosperity, quality of life and great opportunities',[53] whereas the Green Party 'consider(s) precious the plurality of language' and 'see(s) in interaction among various cultures a great opportunity'.[54]

50 Cited in Maurizio Ferrandi, 'Silvius. L'oratore di Castelfirmiano', Alto Adige - Storia e storie (2013), <http://www.altoadigestory.it/index.php/la-galleria-degli-antenati/silvius>, accessed 1 September 2023. Translation from Italian by the author.

51 See Grote, *The South Tyrol*, 21.

52 The last party carrying on this type of discourses with slogans such as 'South Tyrol to Italy, Italy to Italians' was Unitalia, which has not longer been elected since 2013. See Unitalia, *Linee Guida* (n.d.). This and the following citations from South Tyrolean political forces were translated from Italian or German by the author.

53 die Freiheitlichen, *Das freiheitliche Wahlprogramm zur Landtagswahl 2018* (2018).

54 Verdi-Grüne-Vërc, *Grün bewegt/Spinta verde. Wahlprogramm Landtagswahl 2018/ Programma per le elezioni provinciali 2018* (n.d.), 6.

As in Northern Ireland, except for the German parties, in the discourses of all the other Italian or inter-ethnic political forces, this de-securitizing vision came together with criticism against some of the consociational elements of the second Statute of Autonomy, such as the ethnic proportion and the separate school system, which maintain the separation among the linguistic groups, speaking of 'ethnic cages'[55] and the 'last wall of Europe'.[56]

However, some securitizing aspects persist. Indeed, discourses of fear continue to be used by German nationalist parties against the Italian state, perceived as a threat since being part of Italy 'has made us politically and economically dependent',[57] and 'as long as South Tyrol is part of Italy, developments that endanger the survival of the German and Ladin minorities can never be ruled out'.[58] On the other side of the linguistic spectrum, Italian right-wing parties, such as L'Alto Adige nel cuore/Fratelli d'Italia Uniti, highlight the danger of German nationalist parties whose initiatives are considered a 'detriment to the cohabitation'.[59] Finally, although some parties – the Green, Team K and the Partito Democratico (PD) – refuse the use of binary codes and the view of South Tyrolean society as divided along linguistic lines and want to overcome the Italian-German polarization, German parties maintain a defensive attitude and a vision of South Tyrol as composed of linguistic groups that should remain distinct. In the past, such a position was summarized in the statement by the SVP politician Anton Zelger, at the time Provincial Councillor for German school and culture: 'the more we will separate, the more we will understand each other'.[60] Such a radical slogan has turned into a more moderate claim of the

55   Alexander Langer, 'Opzione 1981: le gabbie etniche', ondazione Alexander Langer Stiftung (1986), <https://www.alexanderlanger.org/it/144/283>, accessed 1 September 2023.

56   Michaela Biancofiore, cit. in AndreaCarlà, 'New and Old Minorities: Migration Politics in South Tyrol', Eurac Research (2013), 32–33, <https://bia.unibz.it/esploro/outputs/report/New-and-Old-Minorities-Migration-Politics/991005772551101241>, accessed 1 September 2023.

57   Süd-Tiroler Freiheit, *Programm der Süd-Tiroler Freiheit für die Landtagswahl 2018* (2018), 1.

58   die Freiheitlichen, *Das freiheitliche*.

59   Alto Adige nel cuore/Fratelli d'Italia Uniti, *Patto prima del voto* (19 October 2018).

60   Cit. in Maurizio Ferrandi, 'La profezia di Anton', *salto.bz* (9 March 2019). Translation from Italian by the author.

need that the linguistic groups reinforce their culture before interacting,[61] or the opposition to the development of an 'egalitarian uniformity porridge'.[62]

Differences between Northern Ireland and South Tyrol emerge when looking at how these discourses intersect with the presence of new communities stemming from recent migratory flows from foreign countries. Indeed, in Northern Ireland, the de-securitizing framework goes beyond the main Northern Ireland communities to include, sooner or later, other ethnic minorities as well as, with the exception of the DUP, new minorities resulting from migration. This is considered in some cases as 'a positive development, something to be welcomed, not feared' and as enriching Northern Ireland culturally and economically.[63] Instead, in South Tyrol there emerged a process of securitization of migration in which migrants are considered as a cultural and social threat. Such a process intersects with the discourses surrounding South Tyrolean linguistic groups and their mutual relationships. For example, in past discourses of German parties, migration was presented as undermining the effectiveness of some of the measures to protect the South Tyrol groups and altering the demographic equilibrium between the Italian- and German-speaking groups, since migrants were believed to integrate more into the Italian-speaking group and 'become tomorrow's Italians'.[64] However, at the same time, some South Tyrolean political manifestos present alternative non-securitizing and de-securitizing discourses that see migration in positive terms and address migrants as 'an opportunity for change, enrichment and renewal'.[65]

61 Südtiroler Volkspartei, *Das neue Programm der Südtiroler Volkspartei* (8 May 1993), 15.

62 die Freiheitlichen, *Das freiheitliche*.

63 Sinn Féin, *Sinn Féin Assembly*, 47.

64 Sven Knoll, *Meilenstein in der Einwanderungspolitik: Landtag genehmigt gezielte Anwerbung von EU-Arbeitskräften* (2011).

65 Verdi-Grüne-Vërc, *Grün bewegt/Spinta verde*, 47.

Conclusion

Governing divided or plural societies such as South Tyrol and Northern Ireland remains a difficult challenge. Indeed, despite decades of public debates on multiculturalism and cosmopolitanism, the myth of the nation-state – with its slogan, one nation, one state, one culture, one language – persists. In the past years, we have witnessed how populist and right-wing political forces pursued processes of re-nationalization of the political agenda. Thereby, equality in many countries continues to be seen mainly as sameness or at best toleration, and differences are accepted as an exception rather than a natural fact of the human society. Challenging this myth of the nation-state, consociational theory is one of the favourite options to deal with a diverse society and ethnic tensions, pursuing the sharing of the state between different segments of the population.

In this chapter, I enrich scholarship on consociationalism and advance our understanding of this type of institutional mechanism by applying the concepts of securitization and de-securitization, borrowed from the field of security studies. On the one hand, securitization helps explain why processes of discrimination and marginalization persist even in apparently democratic countries. Indeed, illiberal actions can be justified and accepted because diversity is articulated as a threat and as a matter of security.[66] On the other hand, the securitization lens highlights that the problem is not the existence of diversity and ethnic mobilization, thereby the debate on the need to overcome and dilute ethnic distinctions; rather, it is how others and diversity are perceived and the framing of relations among groups in terms of a friend-enemy logic. Thus, in addition to the degree of peace, stability and justice that they foster, consociational measures (as well as other types of institutional solutions) should be evaluated based on the extent to which they address processes of securitization and de-securitization.

From the analysis of Northern Ireland and South Tyrol emerges a correlation between the consociational power-sharing regime foreseen by the Good Friday Agreement as well as the second Statute of Autonomy

---

66   Olesker, 'National Identity'.

and processes of de-securitization, respectively. In both cases, the diversity and multiculturalism of the regions have been increasingly celebrated in political discourses and the different segments of the population do not see each other as a threat. However, these de-securitizing discourses present some limits since there are different de-securitizing perspectives which might not be compatible with each other, and some securitizing elements persist, whether in regard to other political forces or the constitutional status of the region.

Furthermore, it should be noted that there might be differences in the way that the liberal consociations in Northern Ireland and the South Tyrolean corporate mechanisms interact with processes of securitization. First, despite the violent past, de-securitizing discourses seem to have developed more quickly and prominently in Northern Ireland. Instead, in South Tyrol the second Statute of Autonomy sparked an adverse reaction by part of the Italian-speaking community, which still reverberates today, and it took two decades to be overcome. Second, though within a specific unionist or Irish/nationalist perspective, the various de-securitizing discourses developed in Northern Ireland tend to include the other segment of the population in the vision of a shared society. Instead, in line with the corporate logic of seeing identities as fixed, some South Tyrolean discourses present a stronger emphasis on the need to maintain and preserve the distinction among South Tyrolean groups rather than foster a shared society. In addition, such a perspective and the rigidity of the corporate system have negative repercussions for the inclusion of new communities stemming from recent migratory flows and their diversity.

To conclude, cross-fertilization among research fields provides new reading keys to analyse the institutional design and identify the best policy solutions. However, it should be stressed that securitization and de-securitization are ongoing processes, and Brexit as well as the Covid-19 pandemic may have had several effects on Northern Ireland and South Tyrol discourses, for which further research is necessary.

ALEXANDRA TOMASELLI

Divided across Borders: The Impacts of the Creation of States on Indigenous Peoples and Their Rights in Northern Europe[1]

Introduction

This chapter challenges belonging and borders from a decolonial perspective by focusing on the impact of the creation of states on the Indigenous Sámi people in the three Nordic States (Norway, Sweden and Finland) and the Russian Federation. In this frame, it aligns with the arguments of this volume's editors that not only borders and identities are socially constructed concepts but also human societies are much more complex than the idea, or the ideal, of a nation-state, being rather characterized by diversity and multiple identities. This, however, does not mean that borders, in the legal and political sense, have not affected or do not impact peoples' daily lives. This is particularly evident in the case of Indigenous Peoples, such as the Sámi, who live across national frontiers, and, as the volume editors argue, enter those power dynamics and processes of inclusion and exclusion that are present in all types of borders. Indeed, as discussed below, Sámi, as an Indigenous People, become excluded also *within* the majoritarian societies they live in. This reflects those internal

---

1   My arguments have evolved from my previous co-authored publication titled 'The Frustrations of the Right to Political Participation of Minorities: Practical Limitations in the Case of the Nordic Sámi and the Roma', *European Yearbook of Minority Issues* 8 (2009), 2011, pp. 149–185.

boundaries and physical and psychological demarcations that the volume editors also highlight, and that trigger responses, as in the case of the Sámi peoples.

Indigenous Peoples across the world, although in different ways and at different times, have been dispossessed of their lands. The Indigenous Sámi peoples of Northern Europe and the Russian Federation are no exception.

Two doctrines of international law have, inter alia, contributed to legitimizing such dispossessions. The *terra nullius* principle (literally 'nobody's land') was a Roman legal concept that originally referred to a land that was beyond the Roman Empire's borders and that did not belong, or no longer belongs, to anybody, or was not subject to any sovereignty.[2] This legal fiction legitimized the taking over and the colonization of, for example, the British settlers both in Australia and New England (US),[3] and, after the 1884–85 Berlin Conference, of the various European powers in Africa.[4]

Some Indigenous Peoples and various colonizers did sign several treaties or agreements, including in Northern Europe, but these were largely ignored, and territorial rights were considered valid only in accordance with a state-run order.[5] Since many Indigenous Peoples were nomads or did not crop the land, they were further considered unable to hold any ownership rights over their lands and were thus dispossessed of their territories – determined as *terra nullius*.[6] This doctrine has been ultimately rejected both at national and international levels.[7]

2   Charles Geisler, 'New *Terra Nullius* Narratives and the Gentrification of Africa's "Empty Lands"', *Journal of World Systems Research* 28/1 (2012), 15–29, 18.

3   Jérémie Gilbert, *Indigenous Peoples' Land Rights under International Law: From Victims to Actors* (Ardsley: Transnational Publishers, 2006), 29; Colin Samson, 'The Rule of *Terra Nullius* and the Impotence of International Human Rights for Indigenous Peoples', *Essex Human Rights Review* 5/1 (2008), 1–12, 4.

4   Gilbert, *Indigenous Peoples' Land Rights under International Law*, 27.

5   Gilbert, *Indigenous Peoples' Land Rights under International Law*, 26.

6   Samson, 'The Rule of *Terra Nullius*', 4–5; Geisler, 'New *Terra Nullius* Narratives', 18.

7   In 1975, the International Court of Justice in the *Western Sahara* case recognized the fictitious nature of this principle. In the early 1990s, the Australian *Mabo* finally contributed to the authoritative rejection of this principle. International Court of Justice, *Western Sahara*, Advisory Opinion, 16 October 1975, ICJ Reports 1975, 12, paras 82–3; High Court of Australia, *Mabo and Others v. Queensland (No. 2)*, 175

Another international law principle that contributed to depriving Indigenous Peoples of their rights to freely stay and proclaim their territorial rights was the *uti possidetis* doctrine. It was widely applied in the process of the creation of the Latin American states and promoted by the European descendants (Creoles) as well as in the decolonization process after the Second World War, especially in Africa.[8] The *uti possidetis* doctrine, which also derives from Roman law, originally applied to the litigations on the ownership of a real property (*uti possidetis, ita possideatis*, that is, 'as you possess, so you may possess').[9] In the processes of decolonization, it was used in the sense of leaving 'the place as one received it'.[10] Indigenous Peoples complained that they were denied possession and ownership of their traditional lands on the basis of this doctrine, which was later combined with the 'Blue or Salt Water Thesis'. Where the *uti possidetis* doctrine secured the national borders as they stood at the time of independence, the 'Blue or Salt Water Thesis' legitimized the independence of only those colonies that were separated from their colonizers by blue or saltwater.[11]

Therefore, the majority of the modern nation-states were eventually founded without taking into consideration the peoples that originally inhabited the same land which came to form the territories of these new

---

CLR 1 F.C. 92/014, 3 June 1992, <http://www.austlii.edu.au/au/cases/cth/HCA/ 1992/23.html>, accessed 13 January 2022. Nevertheless, some authors have argued that the principle is still used in the case, for example, of the current land grabbing in Africa. See Geisler, 'New *Terra Nullius* Narratives', 19–24, Samson, 'The Rule of *Terra Nullius*', 6–11, and Andrew Fitzmaurice, 'The Genealogy of Terra Nullius', *Australian Historical Studies* 38/129 (2007), 1–15.

8   Siegfried Wiessner, 'Indigenous Sovereignty: A Reassessment in Light of the UN Declaration on the Rights of Indigenous Peoples', *Vanderbilt Journal of Transnational Law* 41 (2008), 1141–76, 1154; Gilbert, *Indigenous Peoples' Land Rights under International Law*, 36–7.

9   Gilbert, *Indigenous Peoples' Land Rights under International Law*, 36.

10 Wiessner, 'Indigenous Sovereignty: A Reassessment', 1150.

11 Gilbert, *Indigenous Peoples' Land Rights under International Law*, 35–6. For example, France and its former African colonies were separated by saltwater. Thus, such colonies could become independent but in the way that they were shaped by colonizers, with no regard for Indigenous traditional lands and territories *within* such colonies.

states. Often, if not always, Indigenous Peoples have been excluded from the benefits of the creation of new states and have been subject to assimilation and annihilation. Still today, many Indigenous Peoples live across borders and are divided by superimposed international frontiers that represent the first fragmentation and dispersion of their peoples and cultures and continue to have repercussions nowadays. This is the same for the Indigenous Sámi peoples of Northern Europe and Russia.

Against this background, as mentioned, this chapter aims to challenge belonging and borders from a decolonial perspective. It provides some insights into the impacts of the creation of states on the Sámi peoples by reporting some examples from the dense history of Northern Europe and Russia and focusing on the current challenges that these peoples face in such areas. In the first section, it offers some facts and data as well as the main historical events that have shaped the relations between the Sámi and the four states they are now divided into, including the peculiar system of the Sámi Parliaments. Second, it looks at three main hurdles that the Sámi face today, namely the limited powers and impact of the Sámi Parliaments, the discrimination against the Sámi and the main issues regarding their cross-border co-operation today, which was further exacerbated by the pandemic. This second part of the chapter also points at whether these three above-mentioned factors may partially, if not totally, embody both an inheritance of the creation of the states and of the imposition of national frontiers on territories that were ancestrally and wholly inhabited by the Sámi peoples before. It also suggests that these factors illustrate the continuation of a colonial approach. Finally, the chapter provides the reader with some concluding remarks summarizing its arguments and highlighting the persistent colonial structure that continues to exist within the three Nordic countries and Russia. They also point at the recent establishment of the preparatory works to create Truth and Reconciliation Commissions (TRCs) as a way to rebalance such state supremacy.

This chapter offers only a brief overview of the most significant historical events, acts and legislative measures regarding the Sámi peoples in Norway, Sweden and Finland, and it is far from being exhaustive. In particular, it should be noted that the situation of the Sámi people that live in the Russian Federation differs significantly from those of the Sámi peoples residing in the three Nordic countries, mainly due to a systematic lack of implementation of Indigenous rights in Russia.[12] This is why this chapter focuses more on the Sámi peoples in the three Nordic countries, although it will briefly refer to the situation in Russia as well.

The Sámi people in Northern Europe: From one territory to four states

Main facts and major historical events

Between 50,000 and 100,000[13] Sámi live in the nor-thern regions of the Scandinavian and the Kola

12   Natalia Nikolaevna Averyanova, Aleksey Pavlovich Anisimov and Galina Nikolaevna Komkova, 'Debatable Issues on Land Rights Protection of Indigenous Small-Numbered Peoples of the North, Siberia and the Far East of the Russian Federation', *International Journal on Minority and Group Rights* 28/2 (2021), 331–50. Moreover, the geopolitical and economic consequences of the Russian attack to Ukraine from early 2022 on is likely to affect negatively Indigenous Peoples and their rights within Russia since they already stand at the fringes of the Russian society.

13   These figures differ in the various sources, and there is no instrument to assess the population of the Sámi people. Laila Susanne Vars, 'Sápmi', in IWGIA (ed.), *The Indigenous World – 2021* (IWGIA: Copenhagen, 2021), 506–18, 507; National Sámi Information Centre et al., *The Sámi. An Indigenous People in Sweden* (Västerås: Edita Västra Aros, 2007), 4; Resource Centre for the Rights of Indigenous Peoples, *The Sámi People. A Handbook. We are the Sámi – Fact Sheets: An Introduction to Indigenous Issues of Norway* (Karasjok: Resource Centre for the Rights of Indigenous Peoples, 2006), 1; Timo Koivurova, 'The Draft for a Nordic Saami Convention', in *European Yearbook of Minority Issues* 7 (2006/7), 103–36, 1; Malgosia Fitzmaurice, 'The Sámi People: Current Issues Facing an Indigenous People in the Nordic Region', *Finnish Yearbook of International Law* 8 (1997), 201–42, 214; Lars-Anders Baer, 'The Rights of Indigenous Peoples. A Brief Introduction in the Context of the Sámi', *International Journal on Minority and Group Rights* 8 (2001), 245–67, 247; Barbara Ann Hocking, 'Evaluating Self-Determination of Indigenous People through Political Process and Territorial

Peninsulas.[14] They occupy a territory that today belongs to four states –
Norway, Sweden, Finland and the Russian Federation.[15] The majority of
the Sámi people nowadays work in non-traditional activities while only
approximately 10% of Sámi people are employed in reindeer herding,
and others in agriculture, fishing and commercial activities.[16] There are
nine Sámi languages, all of which derive from the Finno-Ugric language
family.[17]

Historically, the Sámi were called 'The Lappons' but this terminology has long been rejected. Across the dense history of these countries,
the interaction between the Nordic countries' populations and the Sámi
passed through diverse phases. One of the most important historical records

---

Rights: The Status of the Nordic Saami from an Australian Perspective', *Finnish
Yearbook of International Law* 12 (2002), 289–323, 292; Lauri Hannikainen and
Anne Nuorgam, 'Cross-Border Cooperation of the Northern Indigenous Saami
People', *Europa Ethnica* 3/4 (2008), 82–9, 90; Eva Josefsen, 'The Saami and the
National Parliaments – Channels for Political Influence', *Gáldu Čála – Journal of
Indigenous Peoples Rights* 2 (2007), 8.

14   Approximately 50,000 to 65,000 Sámi live in Norway (i.e. between 1.06% and 1.38%
     of the total population), 20,000 in Sweden (i.e. around 22% of the total popula-
     tion), 8,000 in Finland (i.e. approx. 0.16% of the total population) and 2,000 in
     Russia (too little to compare to the total population). National Sámi Information
     Centre et al., *The Sámi. An Indigenous People in Sweden*, 4; Koivurova, 'The Draft
     for a Nordic Saami Convention', 1; Vars (2021), 'Sápmi', 507.

15   The current territory of Norway belonged to Denmark, became part of Sweden
     in 1812 and gained independence in 1905; Finland belonged to Sweden until 1808,
     when it became part of Russia, and was finally proclaimed independent in 1917.
     Hocking, 'Evaluating Self-Determination of Indigenous People through Political
     Process and Territorial Rights', 295.

16   Josefsen, 'The Saami and the National Parliaments – Channels for Political
     Influence', 8.

17   Reetta Toivanen, 'From Ignorance to Effective Inclusion: The Role of National
     Minorities within the Finnish Consensus Culture', in Peter A. Kraus and Peter
     Kivisto (eds), *The Challenge of Minority Integration: Politics and Policies in the Nordic
     Nations* (Warsaw: De Gruyter Open Ltd., 2015), 110–40, 122; Mariya Riekkinen
     and Markku Suksi, 'The Sámi Assembly in Finland', Online Compendium
     Autonomy Arrangements in the World (2019), <www.worldautonomies.info>, ac-
     cessed 11 January 2022.

regards the act of the Swedish Crown that gave the *Birkarls*, a people living in the surroundings of the modern Tampere, the right to trade and to levy taxes from the Sámi in 1328 and to the Sámi the right not to be prevented from (free) hunting.[18] Two centuries later, in 1543, King Gustav Vasa of Sweden stated that the Sámi may enjoy 'certain rights' on the side of the Lapland border. In 1584, a letter of the king recognized that the Sámi had an 'immemorial right' to move freely throughout the northern areas. However, in 1673 the so-called Lappmark Proclamation – which promoted the migration to the northern territories – accorded to non-Sámi farmers the possibility to freely settle into Sámi territories. At the same time, between 1670 and 1750, the Nordic states (which were Denmark, which included current Norway, and Sweden, which included current Finland) pursued conversion campaigns vis-à-vis the Sámi and made their religion illegal.[19] Conversely, in 1886, a Swedish Government Bill declared for the Sámi a right to vacant land.[20] The most important act, nevertheless, is the so-called Lapp Codicil of 1751 which was added to the Stromstad Treaty on the drawing of the border between Norway and Sweden. This act granted the Sámi people the right to cross the border for reindeer herding purposes, following the natural reindeer migration. This act has been considered the 'Magna Carta' of the Sámi.[21]

Nevertheless, during the twentieth century, the Sámi were subjected to assimilation policies. In mid-1800, Norway started a process of *fornorskning* (literally 'norwegianization') with a national budget named *Finnefindet* (i.e. 'the Lapp fund') aimed to 'promote the teaching of Norwegian in the transitional districts and to ensure the *enlightenment* of the Sámi people'.[22]

18   National Sámi Information Centre et al., *The Sámi. An Indigenous People in Sweden*, 10 and 32–3.
19   Riekkinen and Suksi, 'The Sámi Assembly in Finland'.
20   National Sámi Information Centre et al., *The Sámi. An Indigenous People in Sweden*, 10 and 32–3.
21   Hocking, 'Evaluating Self-Determination of Indigenous People through Political Process and Territorial Rights', 295–6; National Sámi Information Centre et al., *The Sámi. An Indigenous People in Sweden*, 10 and 34–5; Hannikainen and Nuorgam, 'Cross-Border Cooperation of the Northern Indigenous Saami People', 90–1.
22   Emphasis added. Henry Minde, 'Assimilation of the Sámi – Implementation and Consequences', *Gáldu Čála – Journal of Indigenous Peoples Rights* 3 (2005), 6–33, 12;

In Sweden, Sámi reindeer herders were victims of the segregation policy, and reindeer grazing activities were restricted, thereby affecting Sámi's traditional lifestyle. Many Sámi families were forced to migrate south between the 1920s and 1930s.[23] In 1922, the Swedish 'National Racial Biology Institute', fully funded and supported by the Swedish Parliament, focused on the risks and the 'threat for the society' caused by mixed marriages with Sámi individuals, a conviction that was also widely shared by society at the time.[24] The Swedish government officially apologized for pursuing these assimilation policies in 1998.[25]

In Finland, assimilation policies aimed at promoting the migration and the settlement of non-Sámi population in the northern areas caused a heavy loss of Sámi language and culture.[26] In particular, the 1809 Treaty of Fredrikshamn between Sweden and Russia (which gave and ruled the current territory of Finland until 1917) kept the previous treaties' borders and thus prevented Sámi reindeer herders to cross the frontiers and follow the natural migration patterns of their herds.[27] In 1931, non-Sámi academics and others felt compelled to create the first Finnish organization dealing with Sámi issues in Scandinavia, namely, the Lapin Sivistysseura. However, a system of boarding schools for Sámi children was operative from the 1940s to the 1970s.[28]

In Russia, the rise and fall of communism heavily affected Indigenous Peoples' (including the Sámi's) culture, subsistence means and societal

---

the assimilation policies led many Sámi to reject their Indigenous identity in order to succeed in Norwegian society (28).

23 Josefsen, 'The Saami and the National Parliaments – Channels for Political Influence', 9.

24 This research centre did not obviously produce any scientific evidence of such racial assumption. Its budget was drastically reduced in 1938. It was then renamed and incorporated within the Uppsala University in 1958. National Sámi Information Centre et al., *The Sámi. An Indigenous People in Sweden*, 11 and 15.

25 National Sámi Information Centre et al., *The Sámi. An Indigenous People in Sweden*, 63.

26 Saamelaiskäräjät/Sametinget/The Sámi Parliament, *The Sámi in Finland* (Inari: Sámi Parliament Publications, 2008), 5.

27 Riekkinen and Suksi, 'The Sámi Assembly in Finland'.

28 Riekkinen and Suksi, 'The Sámi Assembly in Finland'.

structures, first through 'collectivization' and later by the abrupt transition to a market economy.[29] During the Soviet period, the government forced Indigenous Peoples to give away their own reindeer and to create and work in collective reindeer farms, which clashed with the world view of reindeer nomads.

After the end of the Second World War and the adoption of the Universal Declaration on Human Rights in 1948, the public attitude vis-à-vis the Sámi started to change, at least in the three Nordic countries.[30] At the same time, the Sámi started self-organizing and creating their own associations.[31] The Sámi in Finland established their organization (Saami Litto) in 1945. The joint efforts of this as well as the above-mentioned Lapin Sivistysseura of 1931 eventually led to the creation of the first Commission on Sámi Issues in 1949.

In Sweden, the national organization Same Ätnam (regarding general Sámi issues) was established in 1945, and the Svenska Samernas Riksförbund (dealing with issues involving Sámi herders) was founded in 1950.[32]

In Norway, the national Sámi organization Norske Reindriftssamers Landsforbund was created in 1948. In the following decades, two more organizations promoting Sámi rights started working: Norske Samers Riksforbund was established in 1968, and Samenes Landsforbund in 1979. The latter was connected to the 'Alta-Kautokeino' controversy, the so-called Alta case (on this case see further below).[33]

---

29 Alexander Pika, 'The Small Peoples of the North: From Primitive Communism to "Real Socialism"', in Alexander Pika, Jens Dahl and Inge Larsen (eds), *Anxious North. Indigenous Peoples in Soviet and Post-Soviet Russia* (Copenhagen: IWGIA, 1996), 15–35, 17.

30 Josefsen, 'The Saami and the National Parliaments – Channels for Political Influence', 9.

31 Josefsen, 'The Saami and the National Parliaments – Channels for Political Influence', 18.

32 Josefsen, 'The Saami and the National Parliaments – Channels for Political Influence', 20.

33 Josefsen, 'The Saami and the National Parliaments – Channels for Political Influence', 21.

Instead, in Russia, from the late 1950s until 1990, the Soviet state adopted an incisive resettlement policy that eventually forcibly relocated approximately 232,000 people.[34] This meant that the Indigenous Peoples, including the Sámi, were prevented from pursuing their traditional way of life. In the 1980s, Indigenous Peoples created their first associations in an attempt to revitalize their languages and cultures. When the Soviet Union collapsed in 1989, the welfare programmes set up by the state to support the co-operative farms, which the Indigenous Peoples also benefitted from, were curtailed. By introducing the market economy, co-operative farms entered open competition or were eventually replaced by private companies. As a result, a large number of Indigenous Peoples returned to a subsistence way of life, which was regulated by the Law No. 104-FS of 2000 'On General Principles of Organisation of Obshchina of Numerically Small Indigenous Peoples of the North, Siberia and the Far East of the Russian Federation' ('On Obshchina').[35]

The changes since the 1970s

In the three Nordic countries, Norway in particular, a turning point was the above-mentioned 'Alta-Kautokeino' controversy, namely, the so-called Alta case. This case concerned the construction of a 110-metre-high dam close to the town of Alta-Kautokeino to serve as a hydroelectric plant. The construction was approved by the Norwegian Parliament in 1978. The Sámi and other civil society organizations held demonstrations, hunger strikes and campaigns, thereby making the Alta-Kautokeino controversy a symbol of the fight for the Sámi rights and for ending discrimination against them.[36] Nevertheless, the Norwegian Supreme Court eventually ruled in favour of the dam, which was completed in 1987.

---

34   Galina Diatchkova, 'Indigenous Peoples of Russia and Political History', *Canadian Journal of Native Studies* 21/2 (2001), 217–33, 220.
35   Olga Povoroznuk, 'Evenks of Chitinskaya Province. Society and Economy (Still) in Transition', *Indigenous Affairs* 2/3 (2006), 68–74, 69.
36   Minde, 'Assimilation of the Sámi – Implementation and Consequences', 7.

The 'Alta-Kautokeino' controversy led to a number of meetings and consultations between the Norwegian government and the Sámi organizations between 1980 and 1981 and also echoed widely in Sweden and Finland. This prompted the adoption of different Sámi Acts and constitutional recognitions.

Article 108 of the reformed Norwegian Constitution recognized that 'the authorities of the state shall create conditions enabling the Sami people to preserve and develop its language, culture and way of life'.[37] The 1999 (new) Finnish Constitution introduced a constitutional recognition of the Sámi by stating that 'the Sami, as an indigenous people, as well as the Roma and other groups, have the right to maintain and develop their own language and culture. Provisions on the right of the Sami to use the Sami language before the authorities are laid down by an Act' (section 17, para. 3), and that 'provisions on self-government in administrative areas larger than a municipality are laid down by an Act. In their native region, the Sami have linguistic and cultural self-government, as provided by an Act' (section 121, para. 3).[38] The 2011 reform of the Constitution of Sweden introduced in its article 2, para. 6 that 'the opportunities of the Sami people and ethnic, linguistic and religious minorities to preserve and develop a cultural and social life of their own shall be promoted', and in article 17, para. 2, that 'the right of the Sami population to practise reindeer husbandry is regulated in law.'[39]

The Constitution of the Russian Federation of 1993 acknowledged Indigenous Peoples in its article 69, which states that 'the Russian Federation shall guarantee the rights of indigenous small peoples in accordance with the universally recognised principles and norms of international law and

37 *Kongeriket Norges Grunnlov*/The Constitution of the Kingdom of Norway, LOV-1814-05-17, Ministry of Justice and Public Security, last consolidated FOR-2020-05-29-1088 from 14 May 2020, last updated 15 June 2020, <https://lovdata.no/dokument/NLE/lov/1814-05-17?q=grunnloven>, accessed 11 January 2022.

38 The Constitution of Finland, 11 June 1999, Act 731/1999, amendments up to 817/2018 included, <https://finlex.fi/en/laki/kaannokset/1999/en19990731.pdf>, accessed 11 January 2022.

39 The Constitution of Sweden, The Fundamental Laws and the Riksdag Act, as reformed in 2016, <https://www.riksdagen.se/globalassets/07.-dokument--lagar/the-constitution-of-sweden-160628.pdf>, accessed 11 January 2022.

international treaties of the Russian Federation.'[40] This article was meant to be implemented by the adoption of three following federal laws: 'On Guarantees' (1999), 'On Obshchina' (2000) and 'On Territories' (2001). These laws did include a number of Indigenous rights but are systematically unapplied and ignored.[41]

At the international level, Norway ratified the 'Convention concerning Indigenous and Tribal Peoples in Independent Countries' (International Labour Organization, ILO No. 169). None of the other three countries has it ratified yet.[42] The three Nordic countries have ratified the Framework Convention for the Protection of National Minorities (FCNM)[43] and the European Charter for Regional or Minority Languages (ECRML).[44] The Russian Federation had ratified the FCNM and only signed the ECRML,[45] but it eventually ceased to be a member of the Council of Europe due to its attack on Ukraine.[46] Finally, Protocol 3 of the Accession Treaty to the

---

40 The Constitution of the Russian Federation, <http://www.constitution.ru/en/10003000-01.htm>, accessed 11 January 2022.

41 See further in Nikolaevna Averyanova, Pavlovich Anisimov and Nikolaevna Komkova, 'Debatable Issues on Land Rights Protection'.

42 Ratifications of C169 – Indigenous and Tribal Peoples Convention, 1989 (No. 169), <https://www.ilo.org/dyn/normlex/en/f?p=NORMLEXPUB:11300:0::NO::P11300_INSTRUMENT_ID:312314>, accessed 12 January 2022.

43 State Parties to the Framework Convention for the Protection of National Minorities, <https://www.coe.int/en/web/minorities/etats-partie>, accessed 13 January 2022.

44 Signatures and Ratifications of the European Charter for Regional or Minority Languages, <https://www.coe.int/en/web/european-charter-regional-or-minority-languages/signatures-and-ratifications>, accessed 13 January 2022.

45 Chart of signatures and ratifications of Treaty 148, European Charter for Regional or Minority Languages (ETS No. 148), <https://www.coe.int/en/web/conventions/full-list?module=signatures-by-treaty&treatynum=148>, accessed 13 January 2022.

46 Committee of Ministers of the Council of Europe, Resolution CM/Res(2022)2 on the cessation of the membership of the Russian Federation to the Council of Europe (Adopted by the Committee of Ministers on 16 March 2022 at the 1428ter meeting of the Ministers' Deputies), <https://search.coe.int/cm/Pages/result_details.aspx?ObjectID=0900001680a5da51>, accessed 31 March 2022.

EU of Finland and Sweden (and Austria) contains specific provisions regarding the Sámi people by recognizing the existing exclusive rights on reindeer husbandry (articles 1 and 2).[47]

Notwithstanding this, the Sámi traditional territories (or homeland) continue to be affected by industrialization policies, particularly those aimed at promoting the wind power industry but that do not take into consideration the needs of Sámi reindeer herders or have destroyed sacred sites.[48] Moreover, the Sámi are still discriminated against and face many other challenges linked to their Sámi Parliaments and their cross-border co-operation. This is discussed in detail below.

The peculiar 'Sámi Parliaments' in the three Nordic countries and other national laws

The Norwegian Parliament's 'Sámi Act' (Act No. 56, chapters 1–2) of 1987 established the Sámi Parliament (Sámediggi) in 1987, which was inaugurated on 9 October 1989.[49] This Sámediggi[50] is composed of 39 members who are elected by those Sámi enrolled in the Sámi Electoral Register.[51] Elections are held every four years in concomitance with the elections of the Norwegian Parliament (Storting). The Sámi may vote in the seven districts that are foreseen in accordance with articles 2–4 of the recently reformed 'Sámi Act'.[52]

---

47 Protocol 3 on the Sámi People, concerning the accession of the Republic of Austria, the Kingdom of Sweden, the Republic of Finland and the Kingdom of Norway to the European Union, Official Journal C 241, 29 August 1994.

48 Vars (2021), 'Sápmi', 512.

49 Hocking, 'Evaluating Self-Determination of Indigenous People through Political Process and Territorial Rights', 299.

50 See the Norwegian Sámi Parliament, <www.samediggi.no>, accessed 14 January 2022.

51 Norwegian Sámi Parliament.

52 *Lov om Sametinget og andre samiske rettsforhold (sameloven)*/Sami Act, LOV-1987-06-12-56, *Kommunal- og moderniseringsdepartementet*, last reformed by LOV-2021-06-11-76 fra 1 July 2021, <https://lovdata.no/dokument/NL/lov/1987-06-12-56>, accessed 14 December 2021.

Formally, the Sámediggi is an independent body that deals with issues of special concern for the Sámi people. It exercises a limited power of decision-making on issues not covered by national law, promotes political initiatives and carries out administrative tasks that may be delegated to it in accordance with national laws and authorities. The overall policy *vis-à-vis* the Sámi falls under the competencies of the Department of Sámi and Minority Affairs in the Norwegian Ministry of Labour and Social Inclusion,[53] while the Sámediggi deals with those initiatives aimed at preserving the Sámi culture, the protection of Sámi cultural heritage and Sámi teaching aids.[54] Governmental authorities have to consult the Sámediggi on issues concerning the Sámi, but the opinions expressed by the Sámediggi are not binding.[55]

In Finland, on a proposal made by the Commission on Sámi Issues, the first ever Sámi Parliament (then called 'Sámi Delegation') was created in 1973.[56] The main goal of this body was to promote a dialogue between the Sámi and the Finnish government. The Sámi Parliament replaced the Sámi Delegation in 1996 after the adoption of the 'Act on the Sámi Parliament' that entered into force that year.[57] Section 1 of this act retakes the Sámi 'cultural' autonomy with regard to language and culture as stated also by the above-mentioned constitution. Section 9 imposes a duty to negotiate with the Sámi Parliament with regard to those relevant measures that are likely to involve, for example, traditional Sámi occupations, community planning, use and teaching of the Sámi language and 'the status of the Sámi

53   Resource Centre for the Rights of Indigenous Peoples, *The Sámi People. A Handbook.*
54   Resource Centre for the Rights of Indigenous Peoples, *The Sámi People. A Handbook.*
55   Resource Centre for the Rights of Indigenous Peoples, *The Sámi People. A Handbook.*
56   Josefsen, 'The Saami and the National Parliaments – Channels for Political Influence', 18.
57   Act No. 974/1995, amended by Act No. 1279/2002; Hocking, 'Evaluating Self-Determination of Indigenous People through Political Process and Territorial Rights', 297–8.

as an indigenous people'.[58] The Sámi Parliament in Finland was thus created to officially guarantee to the Sámi people their 'cultural' autonomy as well as to represent the Sámi *vis-à-vis* third parties at the national and international level and embody their highest political body.[59] It is formally independent but it falls within the administration of the Finnish Ministry of Justice.[60] It is composed by 4 deputies and 21 members who are elected every four years by those Sámi enlisted in the electoral register. Among its competences are the status of the Sámi language and culture in addition to the submission of initiatives, proposals, and statements to the Finnish authorities.[61]

In Sweden, the Sámi Parliament[62] was set up in 1993[63] on the basis of the Sámi Assembly Act of 1989.[64] The Swedish Sámi Parliament has no representative powers, and it is conceived as a state administrative body with regulatory tasks, and it is thus considered a 'compromise solution'.[65] In principle, it may exercise some limited decision-making powers on Sámi culture, language and schooling. It is composed by 31 members who are also elected by those Sámi registered on a specific electoral roll.[66]

58   Section 9 of the Act on the Sámi Parliament (974/1995), unofficial translation published by the Finnish Ministry of Justice, <http://www.finlex.fi/en/laki/kaannok set/1995/en19950974.pdf>, accessed 17 January 2022.

59   Hocking, 'Evaluating Self-Determination of Indigenous People through Political Process and Territorial Rights', 298.

60   The Sámi Parliament – The Representative Self-Government Body of the Sámi, <https://www.samediggi.fi/task/?lang=en>, accessed 14 December 2021.

61   The Sámi Parliament – The Representative Self-Government Body of the Sámi.

62   Josefsen, 'The Saami and the National Parliaments – Channels for Political Influence', 20.

63   Act No. 1433/1992. See also the Swedish Sámi Parliament, <www.samediggi.se>, accessed 14 December 2021.

64   Act No. 41/1989. See Josefsen, 'The Saami and the National Parliaments – Channels for Political Influence', 20.

65   Hocking, 'Evaluating Self-Determination of Indigenous People through Political Process and Territorial Rights', 301.

66   National Sámi Information Centre et al., *The Sámi. An Indigenous People in Sweden*, 63.

There is no Sámi Parliament in Russia, and Indigenous participation is generally very low.[67]

In 2000, the three Sámi Parliaments established the Sámi Parliamentary Council, which is a joint council of representatives from all three bodies.[68] In 2015, the three Sámi Parliaments attempted to unify, but this process eventually failed.[69]

At the national level, a few more acts and legislative initiatives are worth mentioning. The (first) Norwegian Reindeer Husbandry Act of 1996 introduced the right of the Sámi people to own and breed reindeer.[70] Importantly, the Norwegian Parliament adopted the Finnmark Act in 2005. This act created the Finnmark Estate (Finnmarkseiendommen), which is an autonomous organization in charge of administering the land, the water and the other natural resources of Finnmark, a territory that expands to 46,000.00 square kilometres (i.e. approximately the size of Denmark). This land was traditionally inhabited by the Sámi in Norway. This act thus officially aimed at 'securing Sámi culture, reindeer husbandry, rough pasturing, economic activity and community life'.[71] The (Norwegian) Sámediggi appoints half of the members of the Finnmark Estate's board and oversees the provision of guidelines and suggestions on the changes that shall be made in the use of uncultivated areas. These indications should be mandatorily taken into consideration by the state, the county and the

---

67   See further in Nikolaevna Averyanova, Pavlovich Anisimov and Nikolaevna Komkova, 'Debatable Issues on Land Rights Protection'.

68   Vars (2021), 'Sápmi', 507.

69   Hannikainen and Nuorgam, 'Cross-Border Cooperation of the Northern Indigenous Saami People', 92.

70   A new Reindeer Husbandry Act was adopted in 2007. Malgosia Fitzmaurice, 'The New Developments Regarding the Saami Peoples of the North', *International Journal on Minority and Group Rights* 17 (2009), 67–156, 86.

71   Johan Mikkel Sara, 'Indigenous Governance of Self-Determination: The Saami Model and the Saami Parliament in Norway', paper presented in the Symposium on 'The Right to Self-Determination in International Law', organized by Unrepresented Nations and Peoples Organization (UNPO), Khmers Kampuchea-Krom Federation (KKF), Hawai'i Institute for Human Rights (HIHR), 29 September-1 October 2006, The Hague, Netherlands, 2–3 and note 78, <http://www.unpo.org/downloads/JohanMikkelSara.pdf>, accessed 17 January 2022.

municipal authorities.[72] Nevertheless, this act has been criticized for not having taken into consideration previous consultations on this estate and for having opened Finnmark also to non-Sámi users.[73]

In Finland, the new Sámi Language Act of 2003 proved to be a good basis for promoting the use of the Sámi languages with local and national authorities.[74]

In Sweden, the first Reindeer Husbandry Act (Act No. 437/1971) was enacted in 1971 and it recognized the eternal right of the members of the Sámi villages (*Sameby*) to herd within the area of their *Sameby*.[75] The 'act concerning the right to use the Sámi language in dealings with public authorities and courts' was adopted in 1999 and it is applicable in Sámi administrative areas (Arjeplog, Gällivare, Jokkmokk and Kiruna municipalities).[76] While new tasks regarding reindeer husbandry and the management of *Sameby* were given to the Swedish Sámi Parliament in 2007, the county administrative boards retained land management and the overall supervision of reindeer herding.[77] A (second) Language Act of 2009[78] recognized the Sámi as one of the national minority languages and regulated the use of the Sámi and other minority languages in courts.[79]

72 Mikkel Sara, 'Indigenous Governance of Self-Determination', 3.

73 Peter Jull, 'Finnmarksloven [The Finnmark Act]: A Brief Commentary', *Australian Indigenous Law Reporter* 8/3 (2003), 69–70.

74 Act No. 1986/2003, Decree No. 108/2004. See the Advisory Committee, Second Opinion on Finland (opinion adopted 2 March 2006, published on 20 April 2006), paras 9, 14 and 110.

75 See International Centre for Reindeer Husbandry, 'Reindeer Husbandry in Sweden – Rights to Own Reindeer and "Sameby"', <http://icr.arcticportal.org/index.php?option=com_content&view=article&id=176&Itemid=118&lang=en&limitstart=1>, accessed 17 January 2022.

76 Swedish Code of Statutes (*Svensk författningssamling* – SFS) 1999, 1175.

77 Advisory Committee, Second Opinion on Sweden (opinion adopted on 8 November 2007, published on 30 January 2008), para. 164.

78 *Språklag*, Swedish Code of Statutes (*Svensk författningssamling* – SFS) 2009, 600.

79 *Lag 2009:724 Om nationella minoriteter och minoritetsspråk* (only available in Swedish), <https://www.regeringen.se/informationsmaterial/2010/01/lag-om-nationella-minoriteter-och-minoritetssprak-pa-romani-kale>, accessed 21 December 2021.

The impact of the creation of the states and current challenges

The legal status of the Sámi people in the three Nordic countries has undeniably improved in the past 30 years. This is particularly evident in comparison with the situation during the twentieth century and the assimilation policies that were pursued back then. Nowadays, the Sámi are very much present and active in both the local and national arenas as well as in international organizations,[80] especially the UN.[81] The three Sámi Parliaments are unquestionably a rather unique system worldwide, but they still have only limited powers. Moreover, the Sámi people still face much discrimination, which has been further exacerbated by the pandemic and other crucial challenges related to their cross-border co-operation, which has been further hindered by border closures due to Covid-19 travel restrictions (discussed below). This section thus points at how these three main hurdles may partly, if not totally, embody an inheritance of the creation of the states and of the imposition of national frontiers on territories that were ancestrally and wholly inhabited by the Sámi people before. Also, it flags how these three hurdles perpetuate a colonial approach.

The limited powers of the Sámi Parliaments

The Sámi Parliaments tend to have an advisory function rather than granting full participatory rights: as Oskal put it, the 'political inclusion

80   For example, the Sámi have a seat at the Arctic Council as joint representatives of the Nordic Sámi Council in the category of 'Permanent Participant', <https://arctic-council.org/about>, accessed 20 November 2023.

81   The Arctic area's seat in the United Nations Permanent Forum on Indigenous Issues (UNPFII) usually rotates between Sámi and Inuit representatives. The holder of this seat for the term 2020–2 was Anne Nuorgam, a member of the Finnish Sámi Parliament since 2000. The current member (2023–25) is the (Russian) Sámi Valentina Sovkina. Membership of Permanent Forum on Indigenous Issues, <https://www.un.org/development/desa/indigenouspeoples/unpfii-sessions-2/newmembers.html>, accessed 20 November 2023.

of Sámi, via the Sámi Parliament, requires far more than a granting of a right to be heard'.[82]

The Sámi Parliaments have eventually become mere consultative mechanisms and their hearings tend not to result in mandatory actions. Despite their unique political status, they have limited decision-making powers, which weakens their authority over the cultural, economic and social issues faced by the Sámi people.[83] For instance, in Norway, despite the 2006 'Agreement on Consultation Procedures', the mandate of the ministries who are in charge of consulting the Sámi Parliament is still unclear. This has often resulted in slow consultation processes and has created confusion.[84] In Finland, as mentioned above, the government authorities have an obligation to negotiate with the Sámi Parliament on any act that may affect – directly or indirectly – the (listed) Sámi issues in accordance with section 9 of the Finnish Sámi Act, as mentioned above. This case should thus be different. However, the praxis has shown that even in Finland this procedure is yet to be totally guaranteed.[85] A recent attempt to amend and clarify what such 'negotiation' implies (government bill HE 167/2014) failed in 2015.[86] In particular, the Sámi Parliament complains that many of their proposals are ultimately ignored and not inserted in the final documents.[87] This holds particularly true with regard to Sámi land

---

82   Nils Oskal, 'Political Inclusion of the Saami as Indigenous People in Norway', *International Journal on Minority and Group Rights* 8 (2001), 235–61, 256.

83   John B. Henriksen, 'Sámi Self-Determination – Scope and Implementation', *Gáldu Čála – Journal of Indigenous Peoples Rights* 2 (2008), 1–48, 30.

84   Gunn-Britt Retter, 'Sápmi Norway', in International Work Group for Indigenous Affairs, *The Indigenous World 2008* (Copenhagen: IWGIA, 2008), 24–8, 27.

85   Advisory Committee, Second Opinion on Finland (opinion adopted on 2 March 2006, published on 20 April 2006), para. 178; Advisory Committee, Third Opinion on Finland (opinion adopted on 14 October 2010, published on 13 April 2011), paras 56 and 158; Advisory Committee, Fourth Opinion on Finland (opinion adopted on 24 February 2016, published on 6 October 2016), para. 95; Advisory Committee, Fifth Opinion on Finland (opinion adopted on 27 June 2019, published on 31 October 2019), para. 175.

86   Advisory Committee, Fourth Opinion on Finland, para. 95.

87   Advisory Committee, Second Opinion on Finland, para. 155.

and water use.[88] Moreover, there is no clear interlocutor at the state level, and the various ministries and state officials tend to have different understandings and agendas vis-à-vis the Sámi people and their affairs, which shows that a genuine and mutual dialogue between the Sámi Parliament and the state bodies is yet to be established.[89] Lastly, there is an ongoing harsh debate on who can be considered a Sámi and thus allowed to enrol in the electoral register to vote for the Sámi Parliament's members.[90] On this, the UN Human Rights Committee recently confirmed that the current criteria violate article 25 (in conjunction with article 27 and as interpreted in light of article 1) of the International Covenant on Civil and Political Rights.[91]

In Sweden, the Sámi Parliament's powers are limited and tend to focus mainly on reindeer husbandry.[92] Like Finland, the resolution of Sámi issues is ultimately in the hands of state authorities: the Ministry of Agriculture holds the overarching responsibility over Sámi matters, and one of its departments – the Sámi and Educational Department (*Same-och utbildningsenheten*) – oversees most Sámi subjects.[93]

While Norway ratified the ILO Convention No. 169 back in 1990, Sweden and Finland are yet to ratify it and the debate over such ratification has been ongoing for several years without any result.

Finally, it may be argued that the Sámi Parliaments in Finland and in Norway embody some (limited) forms of 'cultural' autonomy,[94] but in Sweden, despite several attempts by Sámi organizations and national

---

88   Advisory Committee, Fifth Opinion on Finland, para. 175.
89   Advisory Committee, Third Opinion on Finland, paras 53 and 159; Advisory Committee, Fifth Opinion on Finland, para. 175.
90   Advisory Committee, Fifth Opinion on Finland, paras 37–53.
91   Advisory Committee, Fifth Opinion on Finland, para. 41.
92   Advisory Committee, Second Opinion on Sweden (opinion adopted on 8 November 2007, published on 30 January 2008), para. 24 et seq.; Advisory Committee, Fourth Opinion on Sweden (opinion adopted on 22 June 2017, published on 16 January 2017), para. 9; Josefsen, 'The Saami and the National Parliaments – Channels for Political Influence', 20.
93   Josefsen, 'The Saami and the National Parliaments – Channels for Political Influence', 11. See also Advisory Committee, Second Opinion on Sweden, para. 195.
94   On the Sámi cultural autonomy system, see further in Riekkinen and Suksi, 'The Sámi Assembly in Finland'.

committees, the Sámi Parliament is still far from being considered a system of 'cultural' autonomy.[95]

All in all, the Sámi people are not given effective decision-making powers over their matters, and state influence over their affairs is still extremely strong. This indicates that in the case of the Sámi people, among others, the logic of colonialism and state supremacy persists to this day.[96]

Discrimination vis-à-vis the Sámi people and the new TRCs

Despite all the efforts and recent developments, the Sámi continue to be subject to racial discrimination as well as hate speech, especially on social media, along with other minorities and immigrants. This is particularly evident in Finland.[97]

In Sweden, the Sámi face daily discrimination, while their culture and traditions are little known, and the folkloric stereotypes tend to prevail among the mainstream society.[98] More problematically, very few know about the past atrocities that the Sámi had to face throughout Swedish history.[99]

95 Advisory Committee, Fourth Opinion on Sweden, para. 9.
96 George Steinmetz, 'Colonialism, Modern, and Race', in John Stone, Rutledge M. Dennis, Polly S. Rizova, Anthony D. Smith and Xiaoshuo Hou (eds), *The Wiley Blackwell Encyclopedia of Race, Ethnicity, and Nationalism* (Wiley online), 1–3, 3, <https://onlinelibrary.wiley.com/doi/book/10.1002/9781118663202>, <https://onlinelibrary.wiley.com/doi/full/10.1002/9781118663202.wberen641>, accessed 13 January 2022.
97 Advisory Committee, Fourth Opinion on Finland, paras 47, 52, and 59; Advisory Committee, Fifth Opinion on Finland, paras 46 and 96.
98 Lee Roden, 'Campaign Launched to Highlight 'Everyday Racism' against Sámi People', *The Local* (28 March 2017), <www.thelocal.se/20170328/campaign-launched-to-highlight-everyday-racism-against-sami-people>, accessed 18 January 2022.
99 'Opinion: 'Why Is What Happened to the Sami in Sweden Not Common Knowledge?'', *The Local* (21 March 2017), <https://www.thelocal.se/20170321/opinion-why-is-what-happened-to-the-sami-in-sweden-not-common-knowledge>, accessed 18 January 2022.

Another source of frustration and discrimination concerns the 'status' of the Sámi people. Only the Finnish Constitution has explicitly acknowledged the Sámi as an 'Indigenous People', while, as reported above, Norway and Sweden refer to them only as 'Sámi people'. Notwithstanding this, as mentioned, there is a harsh ongoing debate in Finland on who may eventually be recognized as Sámi. Recently, the Sámi Parliament in Finland has proposed to separate the definition of who is a Sámi from those who wish to register in the Sámi electoral roll.[100]

To be identified as 'Indigenous Peoples' and not (or not only) as a 'national minority' is extremely important for the Sámi. Indeed, the Norwegian Sámi Parliament, in the first state report pursuant to article 25 of the FCNM submitted by Norway, communicated that they refused to accept the fact that the FCNM applies to the Sámi people, since 'as an indigenous people the Sámi have legal and political rights that exceed those covered by the provisions of the Convention'.[101]

During the pandemic, the uncertainty regarding data on the Sámi population had widespread repercussions. The lack of aggregated data on the Sámi people, among other Indigenous Peoples across the world, has heavily challenged the monitoring of the Sámi people's health conditions in addition to understanding the impact of Covid-19 on them.[102] During the pandemic, the Nordic countries did not publish information leaflets in any of the Sámi languages – a task which was taken over by the Sámi Parliaments.[103]

In this regard, a positive development is the recent establishment of Sámi Truth and Reconciliation Commissions (TRC) in the three Nordic countries. These commissions, which look at similar processes in Canada and Latin America, aim to pursue reconciliation and conduct public

---

100   Advisory Committee, Fifth Opinion on Finland, para. 39.
101   Advisory Committee, First State Report by Norway, 2 March 2001. Nevertheless, the FCNM may apply to Sámi peoples and serve as an additional guarantee of their rights.
102   Vars (2021), 'Sápmi', 509–10.
103   Vars (2021), 'Sápmi', 510.

investigations into the effects that colonial policies, discrimination and oppression have had on the Sámi peoples (and others).[104]

In Norway, the Commission to Investigate the Norwegianization policy and Injustice against the Sámi and Kven/Norwegian Finnish Peoples (TRC) was established in June 2017 and entrusted with carrying out three main tasks. First, historical mapping, that is, researching and reporting on the policy decisions and activities carried out by the Norwegian authorities against the Sámi and Kvens/Norwegian Finns at the local, regional and national levels, from around 1800 to date. Second, investigating the impacts of the Norwegianization policy today, which looks at repercussions that this policy may have in this day with regard to the Sámi and Kven/Finnish language and culture in terms of social, health-related or identity-related impacts for groups and for individuals as well as episodes of hate crime and discrimination. Last, proposing measures for both continued reconciliation, which focuses on providing greater equality for the Sámi and Kven/Norwegian Finnish peoples, and dissemination of these peoples' culture and history among the majority population.[105]

The Finnish Sámi Parliament proposed to establish a similar commission in December 2019. By May 2020, the Sámi Parliament, together with the Siida Assembly of the Skolt Sámi in Finland, had consulted various Sámi organizations and communities in Finland and collected 16 candidatures to be nominated as experts as part of this TRC.[106] However, the pandemic and difficulties in finding appropriate psychological support for those who would participate in the commission's endeavours have delayed its establishment until late 2021.[107]

In Sweden, too, there were preparatory works to establish a TRC. As in Finland, the Sámi Parliament opted for a participatory pre-phase.

---

104 Vars (2021), 'Sápmi', 510–11.
105 The Commission to Investigate the Norwegianization Policy and injustice against the Sámi and Kven/Norwegian Finnish Peoples (The Truth and Reconciliation Commission), 'Mandate', <https://uit.no/kommisjonen/mandat_en>, accessed 18 January 2022.
106 Vars (2021), 'Sápmi', 510.
107 Vars (2021), 'Sápmi', 511. See also Vars, Laila Susanne, 'Sápmi', in International Work Group for Indigenous Affairs (ed.), The Indigenous World 2023 (IWGIA: Copenhagen, 2023), 465–72.

First, the Sámi Parliament initially organized physical meetings with only a limited number of Sámi representatives due to the pandemic. Second, it set up a steering group and a reference group with members from different Sámi organizations. Finally, it sent out a letter to those Sámi who are registered on the electoral roll of the Sámi Parliament eliciting their views on the creation of such a TRC in late 2020. After this consultation phase, the Sámi Parliament proposed to enter into discussions with the Swedish government on how to establish the Swedish TRC. It was eventually set up in 2021, started collecting testimonies in 2023 and should finalize by the end of 2025.[108]

Cross-border co-operation and the exacerbating effects of Covid-19

Although the Sámi are divided by borders, they have always been used to crossing the Nordic states' frontiers for both livelihood purposes (related to reindeer grazing, husbandry and herding) and family reasons. Hannikainen and Nuorgam state that 'in the three Nordic States nearly half of the Sámi live elsewhere outside the recognised Sámi territories'.[109]

The first official meeting that brought together the Sámi from the southern and the northern areas of the three Nordic countries took place in Trondheim (Norway) back in 1917. A Sámi conference was then held in Jokkmokk (Sweden) in 1953 to discuss language and land rights. Three years later, they founded the Nordic Sámi Council (Sámiráđđi)[110] which brought together the Sámi from all four countries (including Russia) in order to establish a liaison body. The highest organ of this council, the so-called Sámi Conference, meets every four years, and one of its main tasks was elaborating the Nordic Sámi Convention.[111] After many years of discussions, a draft Nordic Sámi Convention ('Draft Convention') was

---

108   Vars (2021), 'Sápmi', 511; Vars (2023), 'Sápmi', 468.
109   Hannikainen and Nuorgam, 'Cross-Border Cooperation of the Northern Indigenous Saami People', 90.
110   Nordic Sámi Council, <https://www.saamicouncil.net/en/home>, accessed 19 January 2022.
111   Saamelaiskäräjät/Sametinget/The Sámi Parliament, The Sámi in Finland, 5.

approved by the three Sámi Parliaments and submitted to the three Nordic governments in 2005.[112] Negotiations regarding the text ended in 2017, but its final approval is still pending.[113]

Another source of cross-border disruptions was the reindeer grazing agreements between Norway and Sweden. Since 2005, a dispute has been going on between the two states as to which legal instrument is applicable. The (previous) convention between the two states on reindeer grazing of 1972 expired that year. Hence, Sweden argued that – in the absence of another convention – the 'Lapp Codicil' of 1751 should apply, but Norway disagreed.[114] Hence, Norway began to put up fences along its border with Sweden.[115] These tensions generated mistrust among the Sámi peoples across this border, who resorted to marches and protests.[116] Tensions reduced when Norway and Sweden signed a new convention on 7 October 2009. However, Sweden eventually refused to ratify it. Finally, only in Spring 2021, in the absence of an ad hoc agreement among the two states, some measures were agreed upon, and conditions for reindeer grazing improved.[117]

Last, but not least, the pandemic has exacerbated the existing difficulties in the Sámi cross-border co-operation. Emergency measures, as elsewhere, ultimately led to family disruptions that particularly affected Sámi elders and children. Sámi organizations and non-Indigenous individuals

112   Hannikainen and Nuorgam, 'Cross-Border Cooperation of the Northern Indigenous Saami People', 93–4; see further in Koivurova, 'The Draft for a Nordic Saami Convention'.

113   IWGIA, 'Sápmi', <https://iwgia.org/en/sapmi.html>, accessed 19 November 2023.

114   Koivurova, 'The Draft for a Nordic Saami Convention', 135; National Sámi Information Centre et al., *The Sámi. An Indigenous People in Sweden*, 35.

115   Paul O'Mahony, 'Swedish Reindeer Herders Defy Norwegian Authorities', *The Local* (21 June 2007), <http://www.thelocal.se/7676/20070621>, accessed 19 January 2022.

116   Paul O'Mahony, 'Reindeer Herders March on Stockholm', *The Local* (23 November 2007), <http://www.thelocal.se/9188/20071123>, accessed 19 January 2022.

117   Christian Fernsby, 'Norway and Sweden Finally Agree on Reindeer Herders in Border Areas', *Post Online Media* (1 April 2021), <https://lite.poandpo.com/agrifish/norway_and_sweden_finally_agree_on_reindeer_herders_in_border_areas>, accessed 18 January 2022.

mobilized to reach those who were self-isolated in order to provide them with goods, medicines and food.[118] The Sámi complained that the security measures and the closure of borders had a significant impact on their communities, particularly with regard to the availability of health and social care, cross-border Sámi education and, most importantly, Sámi reindeer industry. Conversely, the Sámi also reported that the lockdowns have been a positive experience as they provided the Sámi people the opportunity to practice their own culture as well as return to and reconnect with their traditional lands.[119]

Conclusion

This chapter has challenged belonging and borders from a decolonial perspective by focusing on the impact of the creation of states on the Sámi peoples in Northern Europe and Russia. It has offered an overview, albeit brief and concise, of the main facts, data and historical events that have shaped the relationship between the Sámi peoples and the four states they are now divided into – Norway, Sweden, Finland and the Russian Federation. It also looked at the peculiar system of the Sámi Parliaments and their limitations, the discrimination against the Sámi and the current issues they face mainly with regard to their cross-border co-operation – all of which have been further exacerbated by the pandemic. This analysis indicated that these three factors may be identified, on the one hand, as consequences of the creation of the states and the imposition of their national borders upon ancestral Sámi lands and, on the other hand, as evidence of how the colonial approach vis-à-vis the Sámi persists nowadays. The relationship between the Sámi and the three Nordic states has undeniably improved in the past 30 years. On the one hand, there have been recently some unexpected and very positive steps, such as the so-called

118   Vars (2021), 'Sápmi', 508.
119   Vars (2021), 'Sápmi', 509.

'Girjas case' and the Swedish Supreme Court's landmark decision of January 2020.[120] This sentence put an end to a ten-year dispute between the Girjas Sámi District and the Swedish state regarding the Girjas Sámi's right to manage fishing and hunting in their traditional areas. The unanimous verdict of the court – which referred to the ILO Convention No. 169 and which Sweden, as mentioned, has not ratified as yet – finally ruled that the Sámi from the Girjas District can exercise small-scale game and fishing rights without the state's approval. At the same time, the state cannot grant such rights to anybody else. This decision has certainly expanded the understanding of the Sámi rights, and it has had a significant impact not only in Sweden but also across the other two Nordic countries.[121]

On the other hand, there have been negative developments, such as the persistent industrial activities (especially mining and forestry) that Finland, for instance, pursues also in the Sámi territories and that hinders their traditional herding and fishing activities. On this, the Sámi tried to appeal to the UN Human Rights Committee (cases *Länsman et al v. Finland*, No. 1 and No. 2), complaining about the adverse effects of quarrying, the transportation of stones through territories that were dedicated to reindeer herding, and of logging and road construction in their traditional lands. However, they were not successful.[122] Moreover, as mentioned, there is a harsh ongoing debate on who is a Sámi and on who may eventually register on the Sámi Parliament's electoral roll.

In this frame, this chapter underlines the persistent colonial structure that still exists within the three Nordic countries, and most prominently in Russia. The Sámi Parliaments, despite some recent positive developments, are still unable to fully exert influence in their affairs, which ultimately continue to be governed by the state bodies. At the same time, the Sámi continue to be discriminated against, which highlights how much still needs

---

120 Vars (2021), 'Sápmi', 513.
121 Vars (2021), 'Sápmi', 514. For an in-depth analysis of this case, see Christina Allard and Malin Brannstrom, '*Girjas Reindeer Herding Community v. Sweden*: Analysing the Merits of the Girjas Case', *Arctic Review on Law and Politics* 12 (2021), 56–79.
122 Riekkinen and Suksi, 'The Sámi Assembly in Finland'.

to be done in terms of deconstructing prejudices and stereotypes among the rest of the population. Finally, their cross-border co-operation, which embodies both an essential part of their traditional lifestyle and their only access to their whole traditional homeland, is severely affected by national borders and regulations – legal frontiers that can suddenly become 'impenetrable walls' as shown by the Covid-19 pandemic and the consequent travel restrictions.

The Sámi people, as an Indigenous People who have inhabited, since time immemorial, the territory that is now divided between four states, should thus be given greater access to participation, consultation and decision-making powers, including the obligation to obtain their *free, prior and informed consent* any time a measure is likely to affect them. This would be in line with the international law standards in the field of Indigenous rights.[123] Most importantly, they should finally be freed from the logic of colonialism that still governs their affairs. This requires genuine dialogue and mutual trust, and it is a process that certainly requires time. There is thus the hope that the three TRC that have been set up will finally rebalance the state supremacy on Sámi affairs.

Bibliography

Act on the Sámi Parliament (974/1995), Unofficial Translation Published by the Finnish Ministry of Justice, <http://www.finlex.fi/en/laki/kaannokset/1995/en19950974.pdf>, accessed 17 January 2022.

Advisory Committee, Fifth Opinion on Finland (opinion adopted on 27 June 2019, published on 31 October 2019).

---

123   On the Free, Prior and Informed Consent, inter alia, see Cathal Doyle, *Indigenous Peoples, Title to Territory, Rights and Resources. The Transformative Role of Free Prior and Informed Consent* (London: Routledge, 2015); on the Indigenous right to political participation, see, among others, Alexandra Tomaselli, *Indigenous Peoples and their Right to Political Participation. International Law Standards and Their application in Latin America* (Baden-Baden: Nomos, 2016).

————, First State Report by Norway (2 March 2001).

————, Fourth Opinion on Finland (opinion adopted on 24 February 2016, published on 6 October 2016).

————, Fourth Opinion on Sweden (opinion adopted on 22 June 2017, published on 16 January 2017).

————, Second Opinion on Finland (opinion adopted 2 March 2006, published on 20 April 2006).

————, Second Opinion on Sweden (opinion adopted on 8 November 2007, published on 30 January 2008).

————, Second Opinion on Sweden (opinion adopted on 8 November 2007, published on 30 January 2008).

————, Third Opinion on Finland (opinion adopted on 14 October 2010, published on 13 April 2011).

Allard, Christina and Brannstrom, Malin, '*Girjas Reindeer Herding Community v. Sweden*: Analysing the Merits of the Girjas Case', *Arctic Review on Law and Politics* 12 (2021), 56–79.

Arctic Council, 'Permanent Participant', <https://arctic-council.org/about>, accessed 20 November 2023.

Baer, Lars-Anders, 'The Rights of Indigenous Peoples. A Brief Introduction in the Context of the Sámi', *International Journal on Minority and Group Rights* 8 (2001), 245–67.

Committee of Ministers of the Council of Europe, Resolution CM/Res(2022)2 on the Cessation of the Membership of the Russian Federation to the Council of Europe (adopted by the Committee of Ministers on 16 March 2022 at the 1428ter meeting of the Ministers' Deputies), <https://search.coe.int/cm/Pages/result_details.aspx?ObjectID=0900001680a5da51>, accessed 31 March 2022.

The Constitution of Finland, 11 June 1999, Act 731/1999, amendments up to 817/2018 included, <https://finlex.fi/en/laki/kaannokset/1999/en19990731.pdf>, accessed 11 January 2022.

The Constitution of Sweden, The Fundamental Laws and the Riksdag Act, as reformed in 2016, <https://www.riksdagen.se/globalassets/07.-dokument--lagar/the-constitution-of-sweden-160628.pdf>, accessed 11 January 2022.

The Constitution of the Russian Federation, <http://www.constitution.ru/en/10003000-01.htm>, accessed 11 January 2022.

Diatchkova, Galina, 'Indigenous Peoples of Russia and Political History', *Canadian Journal of Native Studies* 21/2 (2001), 217–33.

Doyle, Cathal, *Indigenous Peoples, Title to Territory, Rights and Resources. The Transformative Role of Free Prior and Informed Consent* (London: Routledge, 2015).

Fernsby, Christian, 'Norway and Sweden Finally Agree on Reindeer Herders in Border Areas', *Post Online Media* (1 April 2021), <https://lite.poandpo.com/agrifish/norway_and_sweden_finally_agree_on_reindeer_herders_in_borde r_areas>, accessed 18 January 2022.

Fitzmaurice, Andrew, 'The Genealogy of Terra Nullius', *Australian Historical Studies* 38/129 (2007), 1–15.

Fitzmaurice, Malgosia, 'The New Developments Regarding the Saami Peoples of the North', *International Journal on Minority and Group Rights* 17 (2009), 67–156, 86.

———, 'The Sámi People: Current Issues Facing an Indigenous People in the Nordic Region', *Finnish Yearbook of International Law* 8 (1997), 201–42.

Geisler, Charles, 'New *Terra Nullius* Narratives and the Gentrification of Africa's "Empty Lands"', *Journal of World Systems Research* 28/1 (2012), 15–29.

Gilbert, Jérémie, *Indigenous Peoples' Land Rights under International Law: From Victims to Actors* (Ardsley: Transnational Publishers, 2006).

Hannikainen, Lauri and Nuorgam, Anne, 'Cross-Border Cooperation of the Northern Indigenous Saami People', *Europa Ethnica* 3/4 (2008), 82–9.

Henriksen, John B., 'Sámi Self-Determination – Scope and Implementation', *Gáldu Čála –Journal of Indigenous Peoples Rights* 2 (2008), 1–48.

High Court of Australia, *Mabo and Others v. Queensland (No. 2)*, 175 CLR 1 F.C. 92/014 (3 June 1992), <http://www.austlii.edu.au/au/cases/cth/HCA/1992/23.html>, accessed 13 January 2022.

Hocking, Barbara Ann, 'Evaluating Self-Determination of Indigenous People through Political Process and Territorial Rights: The Status of the Nordic Saami from an Australian Perspective', *Finnish Yearbook of International Law* 12 (2002), 289–323.

International Centre for Reindeer Husbandry, 'Reindeer Husbandry in Sweden – Rights to Own Reindeer and "Sameby"', <http://icr.arcticportal.org/index.php?option=com_content&view=article&id=176&Itemid=118&lang=en&limitstart=1>, accessed 17 January 2022.

International Court of Justice, *Western Sahara*, Advisory Opinion, 16 October 1975, ICJ Reports 1975.

International Work Group for Indigenous Affairs (IWGIA), 'Sápmi', <https://iwgia.org/en/sapmi.html>, accessed 19 November 2023.

Josefsen, Eva, 'The Saami and the National Parliaments – Channels for Political Influence', *Gáldu Čála – Journal of Indigenous Peoples Rights* 2 (2007), 1–28.

Jull, Peter, 'Finnmarksloven [The Finnmark Act]: A Brief Commentary', *Australian Indigenous Law Reporter* 8/3 (2003), 69–70.

Koivurova, Timo, 'The Draft for a Nordic Saami Convention', *European Yearbook of Minority Issues* 7 (2006/7), 103–36.

Kongeriket Norges Grunnlov [The Constitution of the Kingdom of Norway], LOV-1814-05-17, Ministry of Justice and Public Security, last consolidated FOR-2020-05-29-1088 from 14 May 2020, last updated on 15 May 2020, <https://lovdata.no/dokument/NLE/lov/1814-05-17?q=grunnloven>, accessed 11 January 2022.

Lag 2009:724 Om nationella minoriteter och minoritetsspråk (only available in Swedish), <https://www.regeringen.se/informationsmaterial/2010/01/lag-om-nationella-minoriteter-och-minoritetssprak-pa-romani-kale>, accessed 21 December 2021.

Lov om Sametinget og andre samiske rettsforhold (sameloven) [Sami Act], LOV-1987-06-12-56, *Kommunal- og moderniseringsdepartementet*, last reformed by LOV-2021-06-11-76 from 1 July 2021, <https://lovdata.no/dokument/NL/lov/1987-06-12-56>, accessed 14 December 2021.

Minde, Henry, 'Assimilation of the Sámi – Implementation and Consequences', *Gáldu Čála – Journal of Indigenous Peoples Rights* 3 (2005), 6–33.

National Sámi Information Centre, *The Sámi. An Indigenous People in Sweden* (Västerås: Edita Västra Aros, 2007).

Nikolaevna Averyanova, Natalia, Pavlovich Anisimov, Aleksey and Nikolaevna Komkova, Galina, 'Debatable Issues on Land Rights Protection of Indigenous Small-numbered Peoples of the North, Siberia and the Far East of the Russian Federation', *International Journal on Minority and Group Rights* 28/2 (2021), 331–50.

The Nordic Sámi Council, <https://www.saamicouncil.net/en/home>, accessed 19 January 2022.

The Norwegian Sámi Parliament, <www.samediggi.no>, accessed 14 January 2022.

O'Mahony, Paul, 'Reindeer Herders March on Stockholm', *The Local* (23 November 2007), <http://www.thelocal.se/9188/20071123>, accessed 19 January 2022.

——, 'Swedish Reindeer Herders Defy Norwegian Authorities', *The Local* (21 June 2007), <http://www.thelocal.se/7676/20070621>, accessed 19 January 2022.

Oskal, Nils, 'Political Inclusion of the Saami as Indigenous People in Norway', *International Journal on Minority and Group Rights* 8 (2001), 235–61.

Permanent Forum on Indigenous Issues – Membership, <https://www.un.org/development/desa/indigenouspeoples/unpfii-sessions-2/newmembers.html>, accessed 20 November 2023.

Pika, Alexander, 'The Small Peoples of the North: From Primitive Communism to "Real Socialism"', in Alexander Pika, Jens Dahl and Inge Larsen (eds), *Anxious North. Indigenous Peoples in Soviet and Post-Soviet Russia* (Copenhagen: IWGIA, 1996), 15–35.

Povoroznuk, Olga, 'Evenks of Chitinskaya Province. Society and Economy (Still) in Transition', *Indigenous Affairs* 2/3 (2006), 68–74.

Protocol 3 on the Sámi People, Concerning the Accession of the Republic of Austria, the Kingdom of Sweden, the Republic of Finland and the Kingdom of Norway to the European Union, Official Journal C 241 (29 August 1994).

Resource Centre for the Rights of Indigenous Peoples, *The Sámi People. A Handbook. We Are the Sámi – Fact Sheets: An Introduction to Indigenous Issues of Norway* (Karasjok: Resource Centre for the Rights of Indigenous Peoples, 2006).

Retter, Gunn-Britt, 'Sápmi Norway', in International Work Group for Indigenous Affairs (ed.), *The Indigenous World 2008* (Copenhagen: IWGIA, 2008), 24–8.

Riekkinen, Mariya and Suksi, Markku, 'The Sámi Assembly in Finland', *Online Compendium Autonomy Arrangements in the World* (2019), <www.worldaut onomies.info>, accessed 11 January 2022.

Roden, Lee, 'Campaign Launched to Highlight 'Everyday Racism' against Sami people', *The Local* (28 March 2017), <www.thelocal.se/20170328/campaign-launched-to-highlight-everyday-racism-against-sami-people>, accessed 18 January 2022.

Saamelaiskäräjät/Sametinget [The Sámi Parliament], *The Sámi in Finland* (Inari: Sámi Parliament Publications, 2008).

The Sámi Parliament (The Representative Self-Government body of the Sámi), <https://www.samediggi.fi/task/?lang=en>, accessed 14 December 2021.

Samson, Colin, 'The Rule of *Terra Nullius* and the Impotence of International Human Rights for Indigenous Peoples', *Essex Human Rights Review* 5/1 (2008), 1–12.

Sara, Johan Mikkel, 'Indigenous Governance of Self-Determination: The Saami Model and the Saami Parliament in Norway', paper presented in the Symposium on 'The Right to Self-Determination in International Law', organized by Unrepresented Nations and Peoples Organization (UNPO), Khmers Kampuchea-Krom Federation (KKF), Hawai'i Institute for Human Rights (HIHR), 29 September–1 October 2006, The Hague, Netherlands, 2–3 and note 78, <http://www.unpo.org/downloads/JohanMikkelSara.pdf>, accessed 17 January 2022.

Sedholm, Oscar, 'Why Is What Happened to the Sami in Sweden Not Common Knowledge?', *The Local* (21 March 2017), <https://www.thelocal.se/20170 321/opinion-why-is-what-happened-to-the-sami-in-sweden-not-common-knowledge>, accessed 18 January 2022.

Steinmetz, George, 'Colonialism, Modern, and Race', in John Stone, Rutledge M. Dennis, Polly S. Rizova, Anthony D. Smith and Xiaoshuo Hou (eds), *The Wiley Blackwell Encyclopedia of Race, Ethnicity, and Nationalism* (Wiley online), 1–3, <https://onlinelibrary.wiley.com/doi/book/10.1002/9781118663 202>, <https://onlinelibrary.wiley.com/doi/full/10.1002/9781118663202. wberen641>, accessed 13 January 2022.

Swedish Code of Statutes (*Svensk författningssamling* – SFS) 1999, 1175.

Swedish Code of Statutes (*Svensk författningssamling* – SFS) 2009, 600.

The Swedish Sámi Parliament, <www.samediggi.se>, accessed 14 December 2021.

Toivanen, Reetta, 'From Ignorance to Effective Inclusion: The Role of National Minorities within the Finnish Consensus Culture', in Peter A. Kraus and Peter Kivisto (eds), *The Challenge of Minority Integration: Politics and Policies in the Nordic Nations* (Warsaw: De Gruyter, 2015), 110–40.

Tomaselli, Alexandra, *Indigenous Peoples and Their Right to Political Participation. International Law Standards and Their Application in Latin America* (Baden-Baden: Nomos, 2016).

The Truth and Reconciliation Commission (Commission to investigate the Norwegianization policy and injustice against the Sámi and Kven/Norwegian Finnish peoples), 'Mandate', <https://uit.no/kommisjonen/mandat_en>, accessed 18 January 2022.

Vars, Laila Susanne, 'Sápmi', in International Work Group for Indigenous Affairs (ed.), *The Indigenous World 2021* (IWGIA: Copenhagen, 2021), 506–18.

——, 'Sápmi', in International Work Group for Indigenous Affairs (ed.), The Indigenous World 2023 (IWGIA: Copenhagen, 2023), 465–72.

Wiessner, Siegfried, 'Indigenous Sovereignty: A Reassessment in Light of the UN Declaration on the Rights of Indigenous Peoples', *Vanderbilt Journal of Transnational Law* 41 (2008), 1141–76.

Map of Dobrudja, indicating the changes of the Romanian-Bulgarian borderline between 1913 and 1940. © Tobias Weger.

TOBIAS WEGER

Borders, Demography, Politics and Pragmatism: The Case of Dobrudja/Dobrogea/Dobrudža since 1878

Before the lower Danube River pours its waters into the Black Sea, after floating through the large Danube Delta, the course of the river is diverted northwards by the high plateau of the Dobrudja (*Dobrogea* in Romanian, *Добруджа/Dobrudža* in Bulgarian). The steppe region between the river and the sea has been inhabited by different ethnic groups since ancient times.[1] It was part of the Ottoman Empire from the fourteenth/fifteenth centuries to 1878. Following the Berlin Peace Congress that put conditions in South-East Europe on a new footing after the Russo-Turkish War of 1877–8, Northern Dobrudja – with the major towns of Constanţa, Medgidia, Hârşova, Măcin, Babadag and Tulcea – was ceded by the Sublime Porte to the Principality of Romania. Southern Dobrudja, including the towns of Silistra, Bazargic (*Добрич/Dobrič* in Bulgarian) and Balcic, was incorporated into the Bulgarian Principality. The Romanian representatives at the Berlin Congress, headed by Prime Minister Ion C. Brătianu and Foreign Minister Mihail Kogălniceanu, would have preferred the Districts of Cahul, Ismail (Ізмаїл in Ukrainian) and Bolgrad (Болград in Ukrainian) in Southern Bessarabia, then a province of the Russian Empire, to Northern Dobrudja. However, they were unable to assert themselves diplomatically in the Peace Treaty signed on 13 July 1878,

---

1   The author of this contribution is currently working on a more encompassing project on the history and culture of the German ethnic group in Dobrudja. On closer inspection, the term 'group' proves to be inadequate, in this as well as in other cases, since it assumes an inner homogeneity that never existed in historical reality. For pragmatic reasons, however, this term is retained in this as in other examples.

which also secured Romania's and Bulgaria's full sovereignty and political independence from the Ottoman Empire.[2]

This chapter outlines the various territorial adjustments of Dobrudja since 1878. It considers demographic, territorial and political changes as well as the 'everyday pragmatism' of its inhabitants. An attempt is made here to reconcile bottom-up and top-down perspectives on a European border area at the continent's periphery. This study considers aspects of social, political and cultural histories, presenting Dobrudja as a generally neglected example of a fluctuating borderland since the late nineteenth century. Indeed, it deserves greater attention in general historiography and ethnology.

Demography: A flowing population

The possession of Northern Dobrudja granted Romania direct access to the Black Sea. The newly acquired territory had a surface area of 15,776 square kilometres and counted, according to different sources, a population of between 170,000 and 290,000 inhabitants.[3] The numbers vary as demographic data were unreliable in this transitional period following heavy conflict. However, all statistics agree that the Muslim population – Turks and Tatars – was majoritarian at the time Northern Dobrudja became Romanian.[4] The following compilation of census results displays at first glance already blatant demographic shifts in the ethnic configuration of Northern Dobrudja from the Berlin Congress of 1878 to the present day.[5] During that time the overall population of Northern Dobrudja has quadrupled:

2   Sorin Liviu Damean, *România și Congresul de pace de la Berlin (1878)* (București: Editura Mica Valahie, 2011), 55–7, 70, 73–5.
3   Nathalie Clayer and Xavier Bongarel, *Les musulmans de l'Europe du Sud-Est. Des Empires aux États balcaniques* (Paris: Karthala, 2013), 118.
4   Lucian Boia, *Cum s-a românizat România* (București: Humanitas, 2015), 26.
5   Mictat Gârlan, 'Turcii si ucrainenii din România. Cercetări de etnopsihologie', in Jakab Albert Zsolt and Peti Lehel (eds), *Procese și contexte social-identitare la*

Table 1. Demography and ethnic groups in Northern Dobrudja, 1878–2011

	1878	1913	1930	1956	1992	2011
All	225,692	380,430	437,131	593,659	1,019,766	897,165
Romanians	46,504	216,425	282,844	514,331	926,608	751,250
Bulgarians	30,177	51,149	42,070	749	311	58
Turks	48,763	20,092	21,748	11,994	27,685	22,500
Tatars	71,146	21,350	15,546	20,239	24,185	19,720
Russians	12,748	35,859	26,210	29,944	26,154	13,910
Greeks	3,480	9,999	7,743	1,399	1,230	1,447
Germans	1,134	7,697	12,023	735	677	166
Armenians	438	3,194	3,627	1,371	568	321
Jews	781	4,573	2,988	971	122	43
Roma	341	3,263	3,831	1,176	5,983	11,977
Other	10,180	6,829	18,501	10,750	6,243	75,773

At the same time, although the population developed much more slowly in Southern Dobrudja, its internal structure was noticeably modified:[6]

---

minorităţile din România (Cluj-Napoca: Editura ISPMN, 2009), 385–518, 395; Vasile Alexandru-Marian, 'Statistici ale populaţiei dobrogene 1850–1878', *Revista Philohistoriss* 7/11 (2011), 37–51, 49.

6   G. A. Dabija, *Cadrilaterul bulgar*, 2nd edition (Bucureşti: Atelierele Grafice Sorec & Cie., 1913), 198; Valentin Ciorbea, 'Dinamica şi structura socio-profesională a populaţiei dobrogene (decembrie 1918–septembrie 1940)', in Stela Cheptea, Marusia Cîrstea and Horia Dumistrescu (eds), *Istoria şi societate*. Vol. II (Bucureşti: Editura Mica Valahie, 2011), 195–228, 201.

Table 2. Demography and ethnic groups in Southern Dobrudja, 1913–2011

	1913	1930	2011
All	259,957	378,344	283,395
Romanians	6,259	77,728	947
Bulgarians	116,324	143,209	192,698
Turks	105,765	129,025	72,963
Tatars	11,734	6,546	808
Russians	?	1,219	698
Greeks	?	1,280	20
Germans	?	558	?
Armenians	?	1,740	?
Jews	?	717	?
Roma	11,024	7,615	12,163
Other	?	8,707	?

Hidden behind these numbers are several alterations in the proportion of the regional population. Initially because of numerous atrocities committed by Russian soldiers against Muslims during the Russo-Turkish War of 1877–8, Turks and Tatars started to migrate to other Balkan territories or to the remaining lands of the Ottoman Empire.

For various political and economic reasons, the relocation of Muslims from Dobrudja continued in the interwar period. Between 1930 and 1938 alone, approximately 45,000 Turks and Tatars left Dobrudja.[7] In order to steer the voluntary resettlement of Turks and Tatars in an orderly manner, the Romanian and the Turkish governments signed a convention on 4 September 1936, after which another 70,000 individuals emigrated to Turkey from 1937 onwards.[8] A visible effect of the Muslims leaving Dobrudja was the falling number of Islamic

7   Ciorbea, 'Dinamica și structura socio-profesională a populației dobrogene', 210.
8   Ciorbea, 'Dinamica și structura socio-profesională a populației dobrogene'.

places of worship. They totalled 195 in 1900, but only 80 of them are left today.[9] The oldest and culturally most prominent buildings – the Esmahan-Sultan-Mosque in Mangalia (1573–5) or the Gazi-Ali-Pascha Mosque at Babadag (1610) – are currently well-maintained, honoured landmarks and tourist attractions. In various towns and villages, minarets continue to be an element of the local silhouette, and the daily call of the muezzin echoes the sound of Christian church bells. However, many smaller mosques have forever vanished from the Dobrudjan cultural landscape.

After the Muslim mass exodus, the subsequent resettlement of the Bulgarians also deeply shaped the region. Ethnic Bulgarians formed an important proportion of the regional population at the end of the Ottoman Empire (13.4%, according to official sources). Nationalist politicians in independent Bulgaria after 1878 did not accept the fact that Northern Dobrudja was assigned to Romania, as they claimed the area was an 'ancient Bulgarian land', while official Romanian politics pretended Dobrudja belonged to the antique Roman-Dakian sphere. The annexation of Southern Dobrudja (called the 'New Dobrudja' or the *Cadrilater*,[10] due to its shape) by Romania as an effect of the Second Balkan War in 1913 was therefore perceived as a 'national trauma'. Bulgarian troops took part in the occupation of Northern Dobrudja by the Central Powers from 1916 to 1918; Sofia and its political representatives in the area hoped for an extension of their national territory, merging both parts of Dobrudja under Bulgarian rule. The Bulgarian military authorities even arranged a pseudo-democratic representation of 247 Bulgarian deputies in December 1917, the so-called Dobrudjan Congress of Babadag, emphasizing Sofia's claims for the entire region. The outcome of the Paris Peace Conference which had been escorted by a Romanian-Bulgarian propaganda rivalry deceived the leadership in Sofia in a double sense: not only did Northern Dobrudja remain Romanian, but Southern Dobrudja was also returned to Romania, as the

---

9   Nuredin Ibram, 'Die Muslime in Rumänien', in Jürgen Henkel (ed.), *Halbmond über der Dobrudscha. Der Islam in Rumänien* (Bonn: Schiller Verlag, 2015), 37–69, 52.

10   The Romanian word *cadrilater* means 'square'.

border question had been settled in 1913.[11] The international press of the interwar period was filled with articles on "Bulgarian irredentism" and permanent acts of terror. These incidents were not performed by members of the local Bulgarian population, basically working in agriculture and viticulture, but by agents from outside the region. The Bulgarian government maintained its claims for at least a re-evaluation of the 1913 borderline and received support in the 1930s from the Nazi authorities in Germany. Under their diplomatic pressure, Romania and Bulgaria concluded the Treaty of Craiova on 7 September 1940, giving the *Cadrilater* back to Bulgaria.[12] This shift in territory was followed by a Romanian-Bulgarian population exchange: roughly 110,000 Romanians and Aromanians[13] had to move from Southern to Northern Dobrudja, whereas 77,000 Bulgarians moved from Northern to Southern Dobrudja. When Romania had taken over the *Cadrilater* in 1913, the proportion of the ethnic Romanian population had been primarily very low (2.4%), but a systematic strategy of Romanian interior colonization had changed this setting to the benefit of the Romanians from 1918 to 1940.[14] In 1940, an estimated number of 115,000 Romanians and 145,000 Bulgarians lived in the area. Most Bulgarians who remained in Northern Dobrudja after 1940 were persons living in mixed couples.[15] In Northern Dobrudja, certain religious edifices of Bulgarian-Orthodox

11   For details, see Constantin Iordachi, 'Diplomacy and the Making of a Geopolitical Questions: The Romanian-Bulgarian Conflict over Dobrudja, 1878–1947', in Rouman Daskalov and Tchavdar Marinov (eds), *Entangled Histories of the Balkans*. Vol. 4: *Concepts, Approaches, and (Self)Representations* (Leiden: Brill, 2017), 291–393.

12   'Tratat din 7 septembrie 1940 între România şi Bulgaria', *Monitorul oficial*, No. 212 (12 September 1940).

13   The Aromanians or Balkan Romanians are a diversified ethnic group originally living in parts of Albania, Greece, Macedonia, Bulgaria and Serbia. In its attempt to 'romanize' Southern Dobrudja, the Romanian government resettled many of them in special colonies in the *Cadrilater* during the interwar years. In Northern Dobrudja, many of them found a new home in places where German settlers had lived prior to autumn 1940.

14   Boia, *Cum s-a românizat România*, 29.

15   Mihai Milian, *Dobrogea ca mozaic etnic*. Ediţie revizuită şi adăugită (Brăila: Ediţie Lucas, 2018), 86.

denomination persisted, which were taken over by the Romanian Orthodox Church. One of them was the famous 'Buried Church' (Biserica îngropată) or Church of the Holy Trinity (Biserica 'Sfânta Treime') at Istria[16] and the other was the small Church of St Kirill and Method at Constanța, which in autumn 1941 became the provisory Romanian-Orthodox Cathedral under the new, non-Slavic patronage of St Nicholas (Sfântul Nicolae), after the Romanian Orthodox St Peter and Paul Cathedral (*Catedrala Sfinții Petru și Pavel*) had been bombed by Soviet airplanes on 3 August 1941.[17]

Trucks of Romanian and Bulgarian farmers and their families were still on the roads of Dobrudja, heading north- or southwards, respectively, when the next population transfer was already deliberated in this region. On 22 September 1940, Nazi-German diplomats and representatives of the Romanian Foreign Ministry signed a bilateral Romanian-German Agreement on the resettlement of the ethnic German population from Southern Bucovina and Dobrudja.[18] On the one hand, this was a direct response to the Soviet annexation of Bessarabia and Northern Bucovina. On the other hand, this was an additional step of Berlin's pan-German attempts to create a homogeneous German ethnic space in Central and Eastern Europe through the resettlement of the 'splinters of Germandom', as Adolf Hitler had called them in his famous Reichstag speech of 9 October 1939. Within only a couple of weeks, almost 15,000 ethnic Germans left Dobrudja

16 The name 'Buried Church' derives from the fact that it was built in 1860 as a tolerance church under the Ottoman rule; the Ottoman authorities did concede, in the nineteenth century, the construction of Christian churches under the premise that it should not tower over the local mosque. The inhabitants of the village of Istria (close to the archaeological site of Histria, on the Black Sea coast) made do with lowering the church, placing the ground one metre below street level.

17 After the Second World War, St Peter and Paul Cathedral was restored, and between 1961 and the late 1970s, St Nicholas served temporarily as a Lutheran Church for the remaining small German Protestant community, after the Lutheran Church on Bulevardul Tomis had been demolished by order of the communist municipality, as it stood in the way of the local political mass manifestations.

18 See Dirk Jachomowski, *Die Umsiedlung der Bessarabien-, Bukowina- und Dobrudschadeutschen. Von der Volksgruppe in Rumänien zur 'Siedlungsbrücke' an der Reichsgrenze* (Munich: Oldenbourg, 1984); Josef Sallanz, *Dobrudscha. Deutsche Siedler zwischen Donau und Schwarzem Meer* (Potsdam: Deutsches Kulturforum östliches Europa, 2020), 77–98.

on the Danube River, most of them ending not 'back in the homeland', as the Nazi officials had promised, but as colonial game pieces in occupied Poland and Czechoslovakia. In those places formerly inhabited by Germans, there were churches of different denominations, which were now transferred to the Romanian Orthodox Church. To this end, the original church furnishings were removed, an iconostasis was installed and the church walls were often decorated with depictions of saints in the 'Byzantine style'. This was especially the case with former Protestant churches, whereas Roman Catholic churches (e.g. in the villages of Caramurat/Mihail Kogălniceanu[19] and Malcoci) remained under the ecclesiastic administration of the Catholic Archdiocese of Bucharest.[20]

The exodus of Muslims, Bulgarians and Germans outnumbered that of all other ethnic groups that left Dobrudja during the first half of the twentieth century. Nevertheless, the fate of the Jewish population must not be forgotten in this context. Jews became victims of the violent and arbitrary politics of General Ion Antonescu's totalitarian regime during the Second World War. With the launch of the German-Romanian joint invasion of the Soviet Union in June 1941, most Jews from the towns in Dobrudja were concentrated in a central camp in the village of Cobadin. After five weeks, dysentery broke out in that camp, and the inmates were deported to forced labour sites in other municipalities of Dobrudja. These were closed in November 1941, and the Jews could move to a ghettoed area of Constanța, while some of them were deported to Transnistria. After the end of the Second World War, the number of Jewish inhabitants of Constanța rose temporarily to 2,400 in 1947, as the Black Sea port functioned until 1951 as an important point of departure for Holocaust

19   The German population used the old Turkish name 'Caramurat'.
20   St Anthony's Church (Biserica Sfântul Anton de Padova) at Mihail Kogălniceanu, used today by Catholics of the Csango minority, is perfectly restored, whereas St George's Church (Biserica Sfântul Gheorghe) at Malcoci has fallen into ruins. Another famous ruin was for decades what was left of the former German parish church at Colelia (Culilia), a village completely destroyed by bulldozers in the 1960s in the context of the communist 'land systematization'. Beginning in 2005, the ruin was repaired and constitutes now the centre of the new Romanian-Orthodox Monastery of Our Lady at Jerusalem (Mănăstirea 'Intrarea în Biserică a Maicii Domnului').

survivors seeking a better future and a new home in Eretz Israel. By 1956, the number of Jewish residents in Constanța had shrunk to 586, continuing to decrease to 104, in 2003.[21] The regional metropolis had had a Sephardic and an Ashkenazi Synagogue before the Second World War – the first being shattered by the 1977 earthquake, the second being gradually abandoned and becoming a despairing ruin at the centre of the Old Town.[22] The Jews of the city of Tulcea originally had eight different synagogues. The extremely small number of community members in the post-war period gave the communist regime a pretext to raze seven of them during an "urban renewal" programme. Templul Coral, a reno-vated art déco building in Tulcea, is the only functioning Jewish place of worship in Dobrudja.

One of the last ethnic groups with a decreasing population in Dobrudja is the Armenians. In the first wave, many of them left for Armenia, then a republic of the Soviet Union, after the Romanian-Soviet alliance of August 1944. A second wave from 1960 to 1965 took a significant number of Armenians to West European countries, where numerous Armenian emigrants had been living since the First World War.[23] Two Armenian-Gregorian churches – St Mary's at Constanța and St Grigore at Tulcea – are still in use.

Politics: Civil rights, advance and destruction

In 1878, while Romanian politicians were still considering whether they would have preferred to see Southern Bessarabia as part of Romania in-stead of Dobrudja, international agreements on the country's border shift

21   Lucian-Zeev Herșcovici, 'Constanța', *The YIVO Encyclopedia of Jews in Eastern Europe* (2010), <https://yivoencyclopedia.org/article.aspx/Constanta>, accessed 22 December 2021.

22   'Sinagoga din Constanța: Poveste despre întunericul urii și al indiferenței', <https://www.info-sud-est.ro/sinagoga-din-constanta-poveste-despre-intunericul-urii-si-al-indiferentei/>, accessed 22 December 2022.

23   Milian, *Dobrogea ca mozaic etnic*, 57.

towards the Black Sea had long since fallen and were irreversible. The situation required, therefore, a pragmatic approach. Before Romanian troops crossed the Danube River in order to take possession of the new province, on 14 November 1878, the Romanian prince, Carol I. of Hohenzollern-Sigmaringen, spoke to these soldiers, trying to find historical arguments for Romania's amplification but also calling for a tolerant behaviour towards the otherness of the new province:

> Soldiers! In accordance with the Treaty of Berlin, the big European Powers have united Dobrudja, the old possession of our forefathers, to Romania. Today you are entering this soil, which is becoming Romanian again! But you are not entering Dobrudja as conquerors, but as friends, as the brothers of the local residents, who become today our compatriots. Soldiers! In this new Romania you will encounter a primarily Romanian population. But you will also meet inhabitants of different origin or different faith. All those who become members of the Romanian state have the same rights to be protected and estimated by you. [24]

In an article published five days later in the daily *Timpul* on 19 August 1878, the famous Romanian poet Mihai Eminescu considered Dobrudja to be a 'natural continuation of the Romanian land.' 'From a historical perspective', he saw Romania to be entitled to own it, but he did not advocate for a forced assimilation of its population. To preserve 'this orient in miniature', Eminescu claimed that all people living there should be treated lawfully and with human compassion.[25]

The Romanian historian Constantin Iordachi has described the period between the moment Romania took possession of Dobrudja and the Balkan wars of 1912–13 as a constellation of ethnic colonization, cultural homogenization and economic modernization.[26] According to Iordachi, the integration of Dobrudja – with its ethnic

---

24 Quoted after Sînziana Ionescu, 'Regele Carol I, domnitorul providenţial pentru Dobrogea: "Azi veţi pune piciorul pe acest pământ care devine din nou românesc!"', *Adevărul* (19 January 2016).

25 M. Eminescu, 'Anexarea Dobrogei', *Timpul* (19 August 1882), 1–2.

26 Constantin Iordachi, *Citizenship, Nation- and State-Building: The Integration of Northern Dobrogea into Romania, 1878–1913* (Pittsburgh: Center for Russian and East European Studies, 2002), 32.

and cultural diversity – challenged Romania's tendencies of political centralization and of ethno-political homogenization. Therefore, the Romanian political elites installed a specific administration in the new region: on 2 March 1880, the Romanian National Assembly passed the Organizational Law for Dobrudja (*Legea pentru organizarea Dobrogei*), which shaped the two districts of Tulcea and Constanța. All residents of the area, who on 11 April 1877 had been subjects of the Ottoman Empire, were to become Romanian citizens (article 3). Another clause placed Dobrudja and its inhabitants under a provisory status or 'exceptional regime' *(regimul excepțional)*.[27] This extraordinary situation lasted until 11 April 1909, when full civil rights were finally granted to all former Ottoman citizens in Dobrudja.[28] Before this date, the inhabitants of that region enjoyed very few political rights on the local level but lacked full civil rights.[29] Starting from 1909, their status equated to that of the Romanian citizens in Valahia and Moldova, and Dobrudja began to have its parliamentary representation in Bucharest.

During the period between 1878 and 1909, Romania considered itself the successor and heir of the Ottoman Empire and nationalized all areas in Dobrudja that in 1878 had belonged to the sultan. These lands were redistributed to new settlers, Romanians and Aromanians,[30] with the Property Regulation Law of 3 April 1882 (*Legea pentru regularea proprietății imobiliare în Dobrogea din 3 aprilie 1882*) giving a legal foundation for this practice.[31] This provision also restricted the right of the inhabitants to acquire land property which de facto favoured ethnic Romanians. During this period, roughly 90,000 Turks and Tatars emigrated from Romanian

---

27 Enache Tușa, 'Cultura politică în Dobrogea. Scurtă incursiune privind drepturile politice ale grupurilor etnice din Dobrogea, la sfârșitul secolului al XIX-lea și începutul secolului XX', in Adriana Cupcea (ed.), *Turcii și tătarii din Dobrogea* (Cluj-Napoca: Editura ISPMN, 2015), 17–30, 23.

28 Luigi Luzzatti, *God in Freedom. Studies in the Relations between Church and State.* Translated by Alfonso Abib-Costa (New York: Cosimo Classics, 2005), 458.

29 Clayer, and Bongarel, *Les musulmans*, 72.

30 Clayer, and Bongarel, *Les musulmans*.

31 Tușa, 'Cultura politică', 24.

Dobrudja.[32] In 1899, the Romanian authorities counted 41,700 Muslims in the region.[33] The exodus was due to the generally disadvantageous legal status and not because of any discriminatory behaviour on the part of the Christian neighbours in everyday life. The former German inhabitants of the village of Caramurat, mostly Roman Catholics, describe the common life with their Turkish neighbours as "relatively harmonious",[34] as did many others in their personal accounts.

In order to emphasize his religious tolerance in this tense situation, King Carol I offered to allow a huge mosque to be built for the Muslim community in Dobrogea. Its construction lasted from 1910 to 1913. On 31 May 1913, the royal couple, high-ranking Romanian politicians, the Ottoman ambassador to Romania and high dignitaries of both Muslim and Christian denominational groups were all present at the opening of the biggest mosque in Dobrudja, with its 70-metre-high minaret – a material symbol of the integration of the Muslims into Romania.[35]

Rivalries over territorial disputes between different post-Ottoman states led to the Balkan Wars in 1912. Romania, which was in an observer position during the first conflict, entered into the Second Balkan War against Bulgaria, and on 10 August 1913, it gained Southern Dobrudja through the Peace of Bucharest. In the 'New Dobrudja' or the *Cadrilater*,

---

32   Nathalie Clayer, *Mystiques. État & Société. Les Halvetis dans l'aire balkanique de la fin du XVᵉ siècle à nos jours* (Leiden: Brill, 1994), 292.

33   Eugen Oberhummer, *Die Türken und das osmanische Reich* (Leipzig: Teubner, 1917), 14; 'Dobruca', *Türk Ansiklopedisi*. Vol. XIII (Ankara: Milli Eğitim Basımevi, 1966), 405–6.

34   Cornelius Wagner, 'Karamurat (Ferdinand I.)', *Heimatbuch der Dobrudscha-Deutschen 1840–1940* (Heilbronn: Landsmannschaft der Dobrudscha- und Bulgariendeutschen e. V., 1986), 133–46, 133. See also Maria Bara, 'Relaţii interetnice dintre creştinii ortodocşi şi musulmani în Dobrogea. Studiu de caz: Medgidia şi Cobadin', *Philologia Jassyensis* 2/1 (2006), 93–104.

35   *Turcii şi Tătarii din România. Lăcaşuri de cult musulmane din România – Dobrogea* (Constanţa: Muftiatul Cultului Musulman din România, s. a.), 27–31; Doina Păuleanu, and Virgil Coman, *Moscheea Regală 'Carol I' Constanţa 1910–2010/ Köstence 'I. Carol' Kraliyet Camii 1910–2010/'Carol I' Royal Mosque Constanta 1910–2010* (Constanţa: Editura Ex Ponto 2010).

the Romanian element was rather weak.[36] The naming of the two new districts – Durostor and Caliacra – after antique places can be seen in the context of the myth of Roman-Romanian continuity and should symbolically underline the legitimacy of possessing this land.

After the turbulent years of the First World War, with a four-fold occupation regime of Dobrudja by German, Austrian, Bulgarian and Turkish troops, the Paris Peace Conference restored the status quo ante with the *Cadrilater* being returned to Romania. Through new territorial gains in Transylvania, the Banat, Bucovina, Bessarabia, the Maramureş and the Crişan Area, Romania had become "Greater Romania" (*România Mare*). Despite the permanent governmental crisis in Bucharest and vehement interior conflicts in Romanian politics, the regional modernization of Dobrudja continued during the interwar period with the improvement of the infrastructure – communication, schools and the economy gave new opportunities for the regional population. The Second World War, which saw Romania as an ally of the Third Reich from 1940 to 1944, obstructed many of these social improvements, while the terror of the fascist legionary regime established new mental and real borders between different social and ethnic portions of the population. The immediate post-war years were marked by ferocious conflicts between communists and former legionnaires and other anti-communist forces.

The Paris Peace Agreements of February 1947 confirmed the 1940 border regulations in the East Balkan zone: Bulgaria remained in possession of Southern Dobrudja, while Romania kept Northern Dobrudja. With the communist takeover in 1948, ethnic and national minorities as well as religious groups were placed under observance by Romania's secret service, the Securitate. From the files of the Constanţa Secret Service Branch, preserved at the CNSAS Archives in Bucharest, we know that Turks, Jews and Germans were specific objects of infiltration and surveillance by secret

---

36   Toader Popescu, 'On the Nation's Margins. Territorial and Urban Policies during the Romanian Administration of Southern Dobrudja (1913–1940)', *Studies in History and Theory of Architecture* 4 (2016): Marginalia. Architecture of Uncertain Margins, 103–21.

agents.[37] Contact between Turks with relatives in Turkey, Jews in Israel or the US as well as with Germans in West Germany were particularly "suspicious" from the standpoint and the logic of the communist state. It can only be doubted, and the 1956 and 1977 census data suggest this supposition, that state pressure forced members of the various ethnic and religious groups to deny their identity in official communication and in many situations. These circumstances of concealment would explain the new 'growth' of minorities after 1989.

Dobrudja was the first region in Romania to achieve the full collectivization of agricultural production by the end of the 1950s, standardizing the diversified rural life in "collective agricultural production units" (Gospodăria agricolă colectivă, GAC), following the Soviet model. The rural population in Dobrudja used to have a complex system of division of labour which was now effaced, as every individual was reduced to the status of an agricultural worker of the collectivized state companies. This system proved to be economically highly inefficient and contributed to the end of the communist regime in 1989, accompanied by bloody conflicts in towns such as Constanța and Tulcea.

In the newly born Republic of Romania, minority rights are granted by the constitution and by international agreements which the country had to sign before adhering to the European Union in 2008. The different ethnic groups have their political representations, their own institutions and media.

---

37 The CNSAS (Consiliul Național pentru Studierea Arhivelor Securități/National Council for the Study of the Securitate Archives) is the official Romanian institution for the collection, analysis and legal evaluation of secret service files. For an overview of available sources, see Inventar Fond Documentar, <http://www. cnsas.ro/documente/arhiva/Inventar%20Fond%20Documentar.pdf>, accessed on 5 January 2022.

Everyday pragmatism

Although, it appears as a widespread stereotype that the various ethnic and denominational groups in Dobrogea were and are on good terms and that the region is generally characterized by a tolerant relationship with one another in everyday life, in fact, a deeper inspection of the historical sources, both official and private, reveals that mutual understanding belonged to the practices, despite nationalist tendencies in different periods of Romania's history. In this sense, people traversed mental borders, against possible educational and ideological prejudices. The inhabitants of Dobrudja identified themselves with the Romanian state and its leadership (the Royal Family, prior to 1948). They were loyal citizens, but ordinary people were seldom involved in daily political debates: largely, they were politically abstinent and did not automatically share the values of the politicians from Bucharest. Their priority was the well-being of their local community, and this had to be factual for all its inhabitants, regardless of their religion, their language and their nationality. This attitude could be characterized as 'everyday pragmatism'. In other words, the practical activities of the local protagonists outweighed theoretical objections and obstacles. This also included the necessity to learn, on top of the mother tongue and Romanian as the official state language, some elements of other neighbouring languages – a communicative minimum which was needed to work, to live and to negotiate.[38] People also integrated estimated elements of neighbouring cultures into their own cultural repertoire – for instance, collection of recipes of traditional dishes.[39]

38   In function of where they had lived in Dobrudja, many Germans resettled from this area remembered some Turkish, Tatar, Bulgarian or Russian words that had helped them in everyday situations. From their early childhood on they had been playing with children of other linguistic backgrounds – the street was their best school.

39   See, for instance, Irmgard Gerlinde Stiller-Leyer, *Zu Gast bei der schwarzmeerdeutschen Kolonistenfrau. Eine Dokumentation über ihre Arbeit in Haus, Hof und Feld. Die Küche der dobrudschadeutschen Bäuerin 1840–1940* (Heilbronn: Heilbronner Stimme, 1987). This collection of recipes is based on the interrogation of German women from Dobrudja; the result shows a strong

The daily menu of the Dobrudjans was not organized along ethnic borders, but could be called a creole or 'fusion' cuisine, which integrated many different tastes.

During the last quarter of the nineteenth century, the new Romanian settlers in Dobrudja quickly adapted to living with the autochthonous Turkish and Tatar populations. Historical sources provide insights into occasions of mutual tolerance and encouragement. The following episode took place at Medgidia (Mecidiye in Turkish), a town established in 1856 by the Ottoman Sultan Abdülmecid after the previous settlement of Karasu had been devastated during the Crimean War. Medgidia had a Tatar majority population, but after 1878 many Romanians settled there. In 1890, the Romanian ethnic community decided to build an orthodox church dedicated to St Peter and Paul. After a couple of months, the construction work was interrupted for want of money: the local Romanians depended on the sum of 10,000 lei to finish building their place of worship. Medgidia's Muslim mayor, Kemal Hagi Ahmet, decided to travel to Bucharest and ask the National-Liberal politician Take Ionescu, then Romanian minister of cultural affairs, for some financial support for his fellow Christian citizens. Kemal Hagi Ahmet wore a 'European' suit, but his head was covered with a traditional fez. Ionescu first refused to meet with him, as he was very much astonished that a Tatar was begging for money for a Christian community, arguing that the Romanian state budget was already exhausted. Yet, the mayor remained stubborn and obstinately asked the minister how he could, as a Romanian patriot and as a Christian, reject peace between the inhabitants of the town of Medgidia. This angered Ionescu; however, he later agreed to support the construction of the orthodox church.[40] The edifice was consecrated on 15 March 1899, and Kemal Hagi Ahmet has since then been held in high esteem by the town's Muslim and Christian citizens.[41] Indeed, the Romanian authorities acted with general tolerance

---

impact of traditional Romanian, Russian, Turkish and Bulgarian food traditions. The book demonstrates the daily cultural border-crossing in the kitchens of average Dobrudjans.

40   I. Dumitrescu-Frasin, 'Kemal', *Analele Dobrogei* 16 (1935), 135–6.

41   Adrian Ilie, 'Biserica ortodoxă cu hramul "Sf. Apostoli Petru şi Pavel" din Medgidia – o biserică a creştinilor ridicată de un musulman', *Ziua de Constanţa*

towards the different religions and places of worship in Dobrudja where, in 1878, Islam still outnumbered all other faiths.[42]

What was true for the Romanian population could also be said about other ethnic groups of various Christian faiths. When Dobrudja was occupied by forces of the Central Powers during the years 1916–18, German soldiers noted the good relations between German farmers and their Turkish and Tatar neighbours.[43] Other sources illustrate the everyday practices of interreligious dialogue. In some villages, Christians brought homemade sweets to the houses of their Muslim fellow citizens when they celebrated the 'Feast of Breaking the Fast' (*Ramazan Bayramı*), popularly also called 'Feast of the Sweets' (*Şeker Bayramı*), which ended the Ramadan. Turks and Tatars would return the favour, bringing baklava to their Christian neighbours for Christmas or Easter. A photograph from the archives of the Baptist community of Mangalia taken in the interwar period shows the local German Baptist pastor together with the religious leaders of the local Muslim community in front of the old Mangalia Mosque.[44] The Christian pastor and the Muslim imam were such good friends that this rapport extended beyond their personal relationships in that they even practiced a kind of interreligious dialogue *avant la lettre*.

These everyday practices were actually based, among other things, on a relatively tolerant, respectful attitude of the respective clergy. After the Second World War, Abdülhakim Aktas, a native of the village of Cobadin, which was characterized by an ethnically and religiously diverse population, remembered that one day he was called to say the morning prayer in the local school. This was a daily ritual, and so the Tatar student had long since memorized the text of the prayer. He was able to recite it in front of his class without any difficulty. The text was a call to God, the 'heavenly

---

(27 February 2018). One of the town's main streets bears his name: strada Kemal Agi Amet.

42 Tuşa, 'Cultura politică în Dobrogea', 17–30, 27.

43 Gustav Rühl, 'Als deutscher Soldat während des Ersten Weltkrieges in der Dobrudscha', *Jahrbuch 1973 der Dobrudscha-Deutschen*, 112–118, 115.

44 Biserica Creştină Baptistă Emanuel din Mangalia, 'Mărturii din Istoria unei Biserici Binecuvântate!', <https://bisericacrestinabaptistaemanuelmangalia.files.wordpress.com/2011/03/20.png>, accessed on 5 January 2022.

Father', to enlighten the students' minds to do good. When Abdülhakim
came home after school on that day, his parents got angry that their son
had said a Christian prayer. They contacted the local hodja who asked
Abdülhakim to repeat the text in front of him. Since the hodja had nothing
to complain about in terms of the prayer text and considered it compatible with Muslim principles, he refused to impose any sanction, teaching
everyone an important lesson in religious tolerance.[45]

Tolerance is grounded on interest in openness towards and, ultimately,
acceptance of 'the Other' and of 'Otherness'. The Romanian culture during
the interwar period, the years when the *Cadrilater* belonged to Romania,
provides a good example of inclusion. The harbour town of Balcic became
a kind of 'Romanian Nice' with the Villa and Royal Garden laid out by
Queen Maria after 1924, a trendy meeting place for intellectuals and artists.
Hundreds of paintings from this period adorn Romanian art museums,
depicting scenes of the 'Romanian Riviera'. Ion Theodorescu-Sion, Ştefan
Dimitrescu, Gheorghe Petraşcu, Nicolae Tonitza, Iosif Iser and many other
artists were especially attracted by Muslim monuments. Minarets, mosques,
cemeteries, Ottoman *konaks* (townhouses), coffee houses, water fountains
and 'exotic' folk costumes figure in many of their artworks.[46] This specific
Romanian 'orientalism' drew its motivation from a recognizable ethno-
graphic interest. Artists from the core provinces of Valahia and Moldova
travelled to this part of Greater Romania in search of unusual sceneries,
as they also did to Transylvania, Bucovina, the Banat or Maramureş. Their
works referred to postcards produced in Northern Dobrudja two or three
decades earlier illustrating regional 'types of people'.[47] They sometimes

---

45   Abdülhakim Aktas, 'Völkerverständigung im Kleinen', *Mitteilungsblatt des
     Bessarabiendeutschen Vereins e. V.* 65 (2010) 1, 13–14.
46   Lucian Boia, *Balcic. Micul paradis al României Mari* (Bucureşti: Humanitas, 2014);
     Roland Prügel, ' "Unser kleiner Orient". Balchik und die südliche Dobruscha aus
     der Perspektive Rumäniens (1913–1940)', in Robert Born and Sarah Lemmen
     (eds), *Orientalismen in Ostmitteleuropa. Diskurse, Akteure und Disziplinen vom
     19. Jahrhundert bis zum Zweiten Weltkrieg* (Bielefeld: Transcript, 2014), 313–4.
47   A representative selection of these postcards can be found in Oana Ilie, Alexandra
     Mărăşoiu and Laura Lăptoiu, *Dobrogea. Locuri şi oameni/Dobruja. Places and
     People* (Bucureşti: Muzeul Naţional de Istorie a României, 2016).

challenged the traditional Muslim life with new Romanian landmarks such as Constanța's Ovidiu statue (1887), the railroad bridge of Cernavodă (1895) or the Casino of Constanța (1909–10). Both the artistic and the popular iconography demonstrate an inclusive tendency. They show that the producers of these depictions started to appreciate the people of different origins, cultured and religions as a normal part of their homeland.

Conclusion and perspectives

This chapter focuses on 150 years of regional history of Dobrudja, a borderland at the European periphery. In the case of this specific region, the term 'border' has to be premeditated at different levels:

1. Prior to the end of the Ottoman rule in that part of Europe, Dobrudja had been a shatter zone of Turkish-Russian conflict. Dobrudja had been a staging area for military conflicts since the late eighteenth century – conflicts that aimed to redraw the borderline between two huge rivals in South-East Europe. Ultimately these conflicts were fought out on the battlefields but decided and resolved on the international diplomatic stage. The victims of the clashes were primarily the civilians living here who were affected by destruction, abuse, disease and the loss of livelihoods. The Ottoman Empire's response was a settlement policy which contributed to the emergence of a multi-ethnic society.
2. Dobrudja existed only temporarily as a territorial entity. After the independence of Romania and Bulgaria, the course of the Romanian-Bulgarian border in this area was disputed. This corresponded to the implementation of national interests, whereby both sides did not back down from their total demands – the claim to the entire Dobrudja region. This created new potential for conflicts in Dobrudja, which ignited at national borders.
3. Loyalty to the Romanian state was a high good for the civilian population, regardless of its ethnic, religious or social self-definition.

The countless war memorials for the fallen of the First World War speak for themselves in an unmistakable way: they contain names from all ethnic groups represented in Dobrudja. In peace times, these ethnic groups lived a sort of 'everyday pragmatism', based on a practical approach to life. In general, it is evident that the sense of 'community' outweighed petty arguments. In this way, existing differences were neither denied nor ignored, but they were not instrumentalized as divisive obstacles in everyday life.

4. This situation was 'disturbed' by external factors: both the Ottoman Empire and the Turkish Republic promising a better life to the Muslim population, which led to a mass exodus; and the geopolitical approaches of the Third Reich, which not only imposed the Bulgarian-Romanian population exchange of 1940 but also the resettlement of the small German ethnic group from Dobrudja in the same year. It was also the Third Reich that, through its alliance with the totalitarian Antonescu regime, enhanced the persecution of the Jewish population. In that particular case, nationalist Romanian interests overlapped with the political and military axis between Berlin and Bucharest.

5. Despite all the consequences of both totalitarian systems of the twentieth century, fascist and communist, some elements of the tolerant and pragmatic coexistence of various groups in Dobrudja continue to prevail until the present day. This means that the bottom-up perspective of the overall population seems to be stronger than the top-down politics imposed by whoever in that region.

European politics today places an emphasis on the establishment of "Euroregions" as cross-border actors in transregional and trans-border cooperation. In the case of Dobrudja, the 'Euroregionalization' occurred regardless of historical allusions. Indeed, the District of Constanţa has been since 2004 part of the 'Euroregion Danube-Dobrudja' (Euroregiunea Dunăre-Dobrogea), together with the Wallachian Districts of Călăraşi and Ialomiţa and the Bulgarian Provinces of Silistra and Dobrič. The District of Tulcea was united in 2009 in the 'Euroregion Lower Danube'

(Euroregiunea Dunarea de Jos) with the Moldavian District of Galați and the Wallachian District of Brăila in Romania, the Rayons of Cahul and Cantomir in the Republic of Moldova as well as the Ukrainian Oblast Odessa. These newly created artificial regional organisms may offer opportunities for trans-border solutions in many practical ways; their risk is to create a new mental dividing line in the historical entity of Dobrudja. The Romanian-Bulgarian border from Vama Veche on the Black Sea coast westwards to Ostrov near Silistra on the banks of the Danube still plays the role of a perceptual dividing line, not only for linguistic purposes, being the de facto Romanian-Bulgarian language border. In the course of the twentieth century, both Romania and Bulgaria pursued a homogenization of their respective population. Many cross-border ties that had existed prior to the Second World War due to family, ethnic, denominational or social ties have been minimized or entirely cut since the mid-twentieth century. Historians and ethnologists are aware of Dobrudja as a historical entity on both sides of today's state border. In the daily life of the residents on the Romanian and the Bulgarian side of the border, this historical 'togetherness' has only a subordinate significance. In contrast to other divided regions in Europe – for instance, Tyrol, Silesia or Frisia – a common regional consciousness in Dobrudja is only faintly developed. Is this because of a territorial entity called 'Dobrudja' that existed only momentarily in history? The Despotate of Dobrudja was mentioned in different sources between the beginning of the fourteenth and the start of the fifteenth centuries. Under Ottoman domination, Dobrudja continued to exist as a distinct space on mental maps but, in terms of administrative realities, was part of the Eyalet Silistra and the Tuna (Danube) Vilayet from 1864 to 1878. As a part of Romania, Northern Dobrudja somehow "faded' in the context of the Old Kingdom (Vechiul Regat) prior to the First World War. When the northern and southern parts of Dobrudja were united from 1913 to 1916 and from 1918 to 1940, the Romanian-Bulgarian antagonism over the area might have been too strong to promote a true common regional identity. Therefore, Dobrudja is and remains a striking field of research, an experimental setting for regional developments on the periphery that often differs in many ways from those in the core of the continent.

Bibliography

Aktas, Abdülhakim, 'Völkerverständigung im Kleinen', *Mitteilungsblatt des Bessarabiendeutschen Vereins e. V.* 65/1 (2010), 13–14.

Boia, Lucian, *Balcic. Micul paradis al României Mari* (Bucureşti: Humanitas, 2014).

——, *Cum s-a românizat România* (Bucureşti: Humanitas, 2015).

Clayer, Nathalie, *Mystiques. État & Société. Les Halvetis dans l'aire balkanique de la fin du XVe siècle à nos jours* (Leiden: Brill, 1994).

Clayer, Nathalie and Bongarel, Xavier, *Les musulmans de l'Europe du Sud-Est. Des Empires aux États balcaniques* (Paris: Karthala, 2013).

Dabija, G. A., *Cadrilaterul bulgar*, 2nd edition (Bucureşti: Atelierele Grafice Sorec, 1913).

Damean, Sorin Liviu, *România şi Congresul de pace de la Berlin (1878)* (Bucureşti: Editura Mica Valahie, 2011).

Dumitrescu-Frasin, I. 'Kemal', *Analele Dobrogei* 16 (1935), 135–36.

Eminescu, M., 'Anexarea Dobrogei', *Timpul* (19 August 1882), 1–2.

Gârlan, Mictat, 'Turcii si ucrainenii din România. Cercetări de etnopsihologie', in Jakab Albert Zsolt and Peti Lehel (eds), *Procese şi contexte social-identitare la minorităţile din România* (Cluj-Napoca: Editura ISPMN, 2009), 385–518.

Herşcovici, Lucian-Zeev, 'Constanţa', *The YIVO Encyclopedia of Jews in Eastern Europe* (2010), <https://yivoencyclopedia.org/article.aspx/Constanta>, accessed 22 December 2021.

Ibram, Nuredin, 'Die Muslime in Rumänien', in Jürgen Henkel (ed.), *Halbmond über der Dobrudscha. Der Islam in Rumänien* (Hermannstadt, Bonn: Schiller Verlag, 2015), 37–69.

Ilie, Adrian, 'Biserica ortodoxă cu hramul "Sf. Apostoli Petru şi Pavel" din Medgidia – o biserica a creştinilor ridicată de un musulman', *Ziua de Constanţa* (27 February 2018).

Ilie, Oana, Mărăşoiu, Alexandra and Lăptoiu, Laura, *Dobrogea. Locuri şi oameni/ Dobruja. Places and People* (Bucureşti: Muzeul Naţional de Istorie a României, 2016).

Ionescu, Sînziana, 'Regele Carol I, domnitorul providenţial pentru Dobrogea: "Azi veţi pune piciorul pe acest pământ care devine din nou românesc!"', *Adevărul* (19 January 2016).

Iordachi, Constantin, 'Diplomacy and the Making of a Geopolitical Questions: The Romanian-Bulgarian Conflict over Dobrudja, 1878–1947', in Rouman Daskalov and Tchavdar Marinov (eds), *Entangled Histories of the Balkans*. Vol. 4: *Concepts, Approaches, and (Self)Representations* (Leiden: Brill, 2017), 291–393.

Jachomowski, Dirk, *Die Umsiedlung der Bessarabien-, Bukowina- und Dobrudschadeutschen. Von der Volksgruppe in Rumänien zur 'Siedlungsbrücke' an der Reichsgrenze* (Munich: Oldenbourg, 1984).

Păuleanu, Doina and Coman, Virgil, *Moscheea Regală 'Carol I' Constanța 1910–2010/ Köstence 'I. Carol' Kraliyet Camii 1910–2010/'Carol I' Royal Mosque Constanța 1910–2010* (Constanța: Editura Ex Ponto 2010).

Popescu, Toader, 'On the Nation's Margins. Territorial and Urban Policies during the Romanian Administration of Southern Dobrudja (1913–1940)', *Studies in History and Theory of Architecture* 4 (2016), 103–21.

Prügel, Roland, '"Unser kleiner Orient". Balchik und die südliche Dobruscha aus der Perspektive Rumäniens (1913–1940)', in Robert Born and Sarah Lemmen (eds), *Orientalismen in Ostmitteleuropa. Diskurse, Akteure und Disziplinen vom 19. Jahrhundert bis zum Zweiten Weltkrieg* (Bielefeld: Transcript, 2014), 313–34.

Rühl, Gustav, 'Als deutscher Soldat während des Ersten Weltkrieges in der Dobrudscha', *Jahrbuch 1973 der Dobrudscha-Deutschen*, 112–18.

Sallanz, Josef, *Dobrudscha. Deutsche Siedler zwischen Donau und Schwarzem Meer* (Potsdam: Deutsches Kulturforum östliches Europa, 2020).

Stiller-Leyer, Irmgard Gerlinde, *Zu Gast bei der schwarzmeerdeutschen Kolonistenfrau. Eine Dokumentation über ihre Arbeit in Haus, Hof und Feld. Die Küche der dobrudschadeutschen Bäuerin 1840–1940* (Heilbronn: Heilbronner Stimme, 1987).

'Tratat din 7 septembrie 1940 între Romania şi Bulgaria', *Monitorul oficial*, 212 (12 September 1940).

Turcii şi Tătarii din România. Lăcaşuri de cult musulmane din România – Dobrogea (Constanța: Muftiatul Cultului Musulman din România, s. a.).

Tuşa, Enache, 'Cultura politică în Dobrogea. Scurtă incursiune privind drepturile politice ale grupurilor etnice din Dobrogea, la sfârşitul al XIX-lea şi începutul secolului XX', in Adriana Cupcea (ed.), *Turcii şi tătarii din Dobrogea* (Cluj-Napoca: Editura ISPMN, 2015), 17–30.

ENIKŐ DÁCZ

Changing Political Landscapes – Adapting Biographies: Three Ideologically Engaged Transylvanian Saxon Writers before and after 1945 in Brașov, Vienna and Munich

This chapter analyses different positioning strategies of German-speaking authors from Transylvania in relation to power before and after 1945. In this sense, it adopts the perspective from below in exploring the views and responses of authors regarding major political changes. Adolf Meschendörfer (1877–1963), Egon Hajek (1888–1963) and Heinrich Zillich (1898–1988) shaped the cultural and literary field of the Transylvanian city of Brașov in both imperial and post-imperial contexts and, thus, the field of the German literature in Romania.[1] Understanding the literary field as a relational and practice-oriented social space,[2] this study selectively touches also upon the fields of politics and religion where the authors gained temporary influence and made interdependencies visible.

Meschendörfer and Zillich are considered the two most well-known Transylvanian Saxon authors in the first half of the twentieth century, while Hajek was regarded an outsider.[3] Living in various centres – Brașov,

---

1   For a detailed analysis of the imperial and postimperial literary field of Brașov, see Enikő Dácz and Réka Jakabházi, 'Der Kronstädter Literaturbetrieb im imperialen und postimperialen Machtfeld', Enikő Dácz and Réka Jakabházi (eds), *Literarische Rauminszenierungen in Zentraleuropa. Kronstadt/Brașov/Brassó in der ersten Hälfte des 20. Jahrhunderts* (Regensburg: Pustet, 2020), 35–59.

2   Based on Pierre Bourdieu, *Die Regeln der Kunst. Genese und Struktur des literarischen Feldes* (Frankfurt am Main: Suhrkamp, 2001).

3   Hermann Schlandt, 'Egon Hajek. Lebensbild eines Außenseiters', *Südostdeutsche Vierteljahresblätter* 12/3 (1963), 212–15.

Vienna and Starnberg near Munich – all three actors of the literary field expanded their radius of action during the National Socialist period and were, to different extents, involved in the ideological propaganda. Hajek's, Meschendörfer's and Zillich's ideological commitment has already been underlined in literary studies. However, it has been emphasized that a more in-depth analysis is still to be done,[4] which this chapter aims to provide based on the personal fonds of the writers.[5]

The first part of the chapter focuses on the individual strategies of the authors during the 1930s and answers the question posed by Stefan Sienerth as to whether Meschendörfer and Zillich had expressed themselves 'in a way that deviated from the public guidelines' or 'even gave hidden insubordination or sympathy signals for a time after National Socialism'.[6] Thereby it needs to be emphasized that there is a very thin dividing line between the 'völkisch'-nationalist, that is National Socialist literature, and a clear delimitation which might obscure continuities.[7] A young group of 'genuinely National Socialist authors' did not emerge until 1929–30, and

4   Stefan Sienerth, 'Adolf Meschendörfer und Heinrich Zillich im Literaturbetrieb des "Dritten Reiches"', in Michael Markel and Peter Motzan (eds), *Deutsche Literatur in Rumänien und das 'Dritte Reich'. Vereinnahmung – Verstrickung – Ausgrenzung* (Munich: IKGS, 2003), 83–118, 87; Enikő Dácz, 'Vom "gottbegnadeten Schriftsteller" zum Schriftleiter. Heinrich Zillichs literarisches Netzwerk im Nationalsozialismus', <https://halbjahresschrift.de/heinrich-zillich-netzwerk-nationalsozialismus/>, accessed 10 December 2021.

5   The personal fonds are in the archives of the Institute for German Culture and History of South-Eastern Europe at LMU Munich (Institut für deutsche Kultur und Geschichte Südosteuropas; IKGS) and the Transylvanian Institute (in Gundelsheim). Some further correspondences are to be found in other holdings of Monacensia Munich, the German Literature Archive Marbach, the Brenner Archive of the University of Innsbruck and the International Youth Library Munich. The personal fonds of Zillich is at the time being selected and does not have signatures.

6   Sienerth, 'Adolf Meschendörfer und Heinrich Zillich', 87.

7   1890–1918, 1918–33, 1933–45 and the period after the war. See Guy Tourlamain, *Völkisch Writers and National Socialism. A Study of Right-Wing Political Culture in Germany, 1890–1960* (Bern: Peter Lang, 2014), 9.

according to Uwe-Karsten Ketelsen, there was no 'literary implementation of a genuine National Socialist programme'.[8]

Actors in the literary field of the ideological mission

Adolf Meschendörfer had the reputation of having renewed the Transylvanian-Saxon literature, establishing modern standards in his journal *Karpathen* (1907–1914) and of being a 'lone wolf pursuing a dreamy muse on quiet side paths'.[9] After studying in Strasbourg, Vienna, Budapest, Heidelberg, Cluj and Berlin, he worked as a teacher, school director and writer as well as a journal editor in his native town Braşov. Co-founding a library and a cultural society further raised his cultural capital. His canonical *Die Stadt im Osten* (The City in the East) was the first Transylvanian-Saxon novel published in 1932 in the Reich and received over a thousand reviews.[10] Between 1933 and 1938 – like other foreign German authors – Meschendörfer also contributed to ideologically conceived anthologies such as *Rufe über Grenzen* (Calls over Borders).[11]

The National Socialist literary historian Hellmuth Langenbucher, an authoritative actor in the National Socialist literary field,[12] considered him to be one of the most important 'volksdeutsch' poets who were willing to fill the gap left by the emigration of many writers.[13] After the book

8   Tourlamain, *Völkisch Writers and National Socialism*, 64.

9   Alfred Gust, 'Adolf Meschendörfer (Ein Lebensbild)', *Neue Literatur* 8/2 (1957), *Adolf Meschendörfer zum 80. Geburtstag*, 65–82, 66.

10   Adolf Meschendörfer, *Siebenbürgen, Land des Segens* (Leipzig: Reclam, 1937), 36.

11   Adolf Meschendörfer, 'Die Stimme der Auslandsdeutschen', in Heinz Kindermann (ed.), *Des deutschen Dichters Sendung in der Gegenwart* (Leipzig: Reclam, 1933), 138–46.

12   Sebastian Graeb-Könneker, *Autochthone Modernität. Eine Untersuchung der vom Nationalsozialismus geförderten Literatur* (Opladen: Westdeutscher Verlag, 1996), 85–8.

13   Hellmuth Langenbucher, *Volkhafte Dichtung der Zeit* (Berlin: Jünker und Dünnhaupt, 1937), 362.

burnings, Meschendörfer was one of the 160 authors recommended by the Reichsschrifttumskammer for lending libraries.[14] He considered the awards of the Nazi literary establishment as a recognition of his many years of literary activity. For his novel *Büffelbrunnen* (Buffalofountain), published in Munich, he was awarded an honorary doctorate from the Silesian Friedrich Wilhelm University in Wrocław in 1936, and on his sixtieth birthday, he was honoured with the German Goethe Medal for Art and Science.

Despite Gerhardt Csejka's emphasis that Meschendörfer 'did not accommodate National Socialism in essential points',[15] a more detailed analysis reveals that the writer's criticism mainly referred to the interference of the Nazi apparatus in local affairs and not fundamentally or generally to National Socialism. Edith Konradt also interprets Meschendörfer's criticism of the central interference in local affairs as a turning away from the regime and speaks of the author's 'fatal' error, which he himself tried to explain by differentiating between 'völkisch' and 'national'.[16] Indeed, Meschendörfer criticized the power struggle that defined public life in Braşov and also affected him as head of the Honterus School.[17] What he avoided as headmaster in a school belonging to the church, he did as a writer by fulfilling the expectations of the National Socialist literary policy in his *Büffelbrunnen*, which he began writing in 1933 and completed in 1935. The political novel summarized what 'a young professor must learn from life as a German abroad on a dangerous post'.[18] Moreover, in the new edition of *Die Stadt im Osten* in 1937, he willingly adopted the vocabulary to the current ideological expectations[19] – a step sometimes overlooked in specialist

14   Section of the 'Reichskulturkammer' regarding all book-related professions, Chamber of Literature.

15   Gerhardt Csejka, 'Vorwort', in Bernd Kolf (ed.), *Adolf Meschendörfer: Gedichte, Erzählungen, Drama, Aufsätze* (Bucharest: Kriterion, 1978), 5–28, 26.

16   Edith Konradt, *Grenzen einer Inselliteratur. Kunst und Heimat im Werk Adolf Meschendörfers (1877–1963)* (Frankfurt am Main: Peter Lang, 1987), 290–4.

17   Meschendörfer, *Land des Segens*, 39.

18   Meschendörfer, *Land des Segens*, 36.

19   The book had eight editions by Langen Müller between 1932 and 1942. The 1937 edition was dedicated to the University of Wrocław. See Sienerth, 'Adolf Meschendörfer und Heinrich Zillich', 116.

literature.[20] The novel manuscript *Erneuerung* (Renewal)[21] leaves no doubt about the ideology-compliant and propagandistic content.[22]

Meschendörfer's anticipatory obedience turned over time into a willingness to actively support National Socialism, culminating in 1941 in a propagandistic reading tour to the Banat on behalf of the Reichsschrifttumskammer. He was also one of the five members on the board of trustees of the annual Eichendorff Prize in 1935 and 1936,[23] alongside prominent, ideologically committed, literary figures such as Hanns Johst, Bruno Brehm, Herbert Cysarz and Erwin Guido Kolbenheyer. In 1936, he opened the 'Week of the German Book' as the keynote speaker at the Celebration of the Reichsdeutsch Colony in Bucharest legitimizing the regime and strengthening his own position in the cultural field in Romania.

Meschendörfer's contacts in the literary field of the Reich remained, in the light of his correspondence, quite limited. In 1934, he, like Heinrich Zillich, received a scholarship for several months from the Deutsches Ausland-Institut (DAI; German Foreign Institute) in Stuttgart,[24] but had to return home and cancel several readings and radio contributions because of family reasons. This missed opportunity of breaking his 'Transylvanian isolation' is mirrored in his correspondence with major actors of the field such as Hans Grimm[25] or Gustav Pezold.[26] They were part of his network but

---

20 For example, István Gombocz, ' "Eine knorrige Eiche mit [...] gebogenen Ästen": Zukunftsängste in Adolf Meschendörfers siebenbürgischem Roman "Die Stadt im Osten" '. *Jahrbuch der ungarischen Germanistik* (2017), <http://jug.hu/images/2017/04-istvan_gombocz.pdf>,125–39, 137, accessed 12 December 2021.

21 NL Adolf Meschendörfer, box 34.

22 Sienerth, 'Adolf Meschendörfer und Heinrich Zillich', 116–18. His correspondence with the Eugen Diederichs publishing house, to which he wanted to go because its National Socialist spirit suited him, is also to be mentioned.

23 Biografie, Manuscript, NL Adolf Meschendörfer, box 1, folder 1, 2. See also Jan Zimmermann, *Die Kulturpreise der Stiftung F.V.S. 1935–1945. Darstellung und Dokumentation* (Hamburg: Christians, 2000), 266.

24 The Transylvanian Saxon Germanist and cultural politician Richard Csaki led it beginning with 1933.

25 Uwe K. Ketelsen, *Literatur und Drittes Reich* (Schernfeld: SH-Verlag, 1992), 199–215.

26 NL Adolf Meschendörfer, box 5.

not close friends. He maintained the most intensive contact with Langen Müller Publishing House and corresponded from 1932 with Langenbucher, who reviewed and promoted *Die Stadt im Osten*,[27] signalizing, for example, great interest for the colonization theme that became the central topic of *Büffelbrunnen*.[28]

Meschendörfer's reading tours abroad took him from Sweden to northern and southern Germany in 1937 – from Berlin,[29] Leipzig,[30] and Cologne to Nürnberg or Stuttgart. He was present at the Raabe Days (Memorial Days for Wilhelm Raabe) in Braunschweig and a guest on the radio in Cologne or in Vienna. In 1938, he read in Piła at a poetry evening organized by the local National Socialist German Workers' Party (NSDAP) leaders[31] as well as in Flensburg,[32] Lunden,[33] Kiel,[34] Dessau[35] or Halle.[36] Such undertakings strengthened his position in the literary field back in Romania more than in the Reich, where he remained a representative of the Germans abroad.

Egon Hajek[37] belonged to the circle around both Meschendörfer's *Karpathen* and Zillich's *Klingsor*.[38] He studied in Berlin, Kiel and Budapest.

27   Letter from Hellmuth Langenbucher to Adolf Meschendörfer (8 September 1932 and 14 September 1932), NL Adolf Meschendörfer, box 5.

28   Letter from Hellmuth Langenbucher to Adolf Meschendörfer (8 September 1932 and 14 September 1932).

29   'Vortragsreise Meschendörfers durch Schweden, Nord- und Süddeutschland', *Bukarester Tageblatt* (31 January 1938).

30   *Neue Leipziger Zeitung* (8 January 1936 and 15 January 1936); *Leipziger Neuste Nachrichten* (14 January 1936); *Leipziger Tagesnachrichten* (14 January 1936).

31   *Der Gesellige* (8 November 1938).

32   *Flensburger Nachrichten* (20 October 1938).

33   *Dithmarscher Zeitung* (7 November 1938).

34   *Nordische Rundschau* (7 November 1938).

35   *Anhalter Anzeiger* (3 November 1938).

36   *Hallesche Nachrichten* (2 November 1938).

37   For a first overview, see Hermann A. Hienz (ed.), *Schriftsteller-Lexikon der Siebenbürger Deutschen*. Vol. VII H–J (Köln: Böhlau, 2000), 6–27.

38   Walter Myss, *Fazit nach achthundert Jahren* (Munich: Südostdeutsches Kulturwerk, 1968), 115. For a list of his works, see Uwe Baur and Karin Gradwohl-Schlacher (eds), *Literatur in Österreich 1938–1945*. Vol. 4. *Literarisches System in Österreich* (Wien: Vandenhoeck-Ruprecht, 2018), 31–313.

Later, he returned to Braşov and worked as a teacher and pastor and was active in the music field, among others, as a choirmaster. Similar to Meschendörfer, literature was only one of his many fields of activity. In 1929, he moved to Vienna and became a pastor after a few years in the largest Protestant congregation, working there until his retirement in 1956. In addition, he was a senior church councillor for the reorganization of Protestant musical life in Austria'[39] and became a professor of Protestant church music at the Academy for Music in Vienna in 1938.

In contrast to Meschendörfer and Zillich, Hajek initially published only short literary texts between 1933 and 1937. In the following three years, three novels followed – all of them being committed to the 'volksdeutsch' ideology and religious topics. Not fitting the Zeitgeist – an accusation he had been confronted with[40] – explains both the modest success he found among the public and the reserved reactions of prominent literary actors such as Walter von Molo or Hans Grimm.[41] Reviews of the well-known Austrian Nazi author Carl Hans Watzinger's[42] work remained the exception.[43] Hajek's protestant network – he was a collaborator for *Der Evangelische Heimbote* (Evangelic Herald) and *Das evangelische Wien* (Evangelic Vienna)[44] – also explains the review of an evangelic bishop from Transylvania in one of his novels.[45]

Although Hajek actively supported National Socialism, as a protagonist in the religious field he could not join the NSDAP, but was a member of the National Socialist People's Welfare Association (NSV) and, from

---

39   Rotraut Sutter, 'Egon Hajek', in Rotraut Sutter (ed.), *Siebenbürger Sachsen in Österreichs Vergangenheit und Gegenwart. Eine Auswahl* (Innsbruck: Universitätverlag Wagner 1976), 66–8.

40   'Neuere siebenbürgische Literatur', *Der Auslandsdeutsche. Halbmonatsschrift für Auslanddeutschtum und Auslandskunde. Mitteilungen des Deutschen Ausland-Instituts* 5 (1922–6), 2, 187.

41   See personal fond Egon Hajek, B I 31, A-711, Vols 1 and 3, Letters from Egon Hajek to Walter von Molo and Grimm from 1938.

42   Carl Watzinger, 'Der siebenbürgische Dichter Egon Hajek', *Der Augarten* 2/ 6 (1936), 175.

43   See personal fond Egon Hajek, B I 31, A-711, folder with reviews/performances.

44   Hajek was the editor in 1933 and 1939–40.

45   Viktor Glondys, 'Meister Johannes', *Kirchliche Blätter* 31/ 49 (1939), 623.

1938, a supporting member of the NSDAP's Schutzstaffel (SS).[46] His Gau file documents his commitment to the regime.[47] He supported the SA (Sturmabteilung/Assault Division) in the illegal period by actively helping their members in the Sixteenth and Nineteenth Viennese and being a supporter of Martin Luther People's Home, which was entirely in the hands of the SA.[48] Further, in 1938 he refused to backdate the baptism of the well-known writer Egon Friedell[49] out of a 'sense of duty':

> Ich mußte aus Pflichtbewusstsein diese Zumutung ablehnen. Es hätte ihm auch nicht geholfen, er trug die nichtarischen Merkmale in seinem Gesicht zu deutlich zur Schau. Aber ich bemitleidete ihn von Herzen.[50]
>
> [I had to refuse this unreasonable demand out of a sense of duty. It would not have helped him either, he had the non-Aryan features much too clearly written in his face. But I pitied him from the bottom of my heart.]

Martina Fuchs attests Hajek's 'not unproblematic' affinity towards greater 'German-völkisch ideas'[51] and goes on to emphasize that the author and his wife had distanced themselves from National Socialism formally,

---

46   See, for more, Franz Graf-Stuhlhofer, 'Wiener Evangelische Professoren der Theologie im Spiegel der Gau-Akten. Dokumentation zu Beth, Egli, Entz, Hajek, Hoffmann, Koch, Kühnert, Opitz, Schneider und Wilke', *Jahrbuch für die Geschichte des Protestantismus in Österreich* 116 (2000/1), 191–222, 197–205. See also Leonhard Jungwirth, 'Politische Vergangenheiten Entpolitisierungs- und Politisierungsprozesse im österreichischen Protestantismus 1933/34 bis 1968', <http://othes.univie.ac.at/63952/1/67784.pdf>, accessed 9 September 2021, 122.

47   48 pages, in the Archives of the Republic in Vienna, No. 2404.

48   Graf-Stuhlhofer, 'Wiener Evangelische Professoren der Theologie im Spiegel der Gau-Akten', 199.

49   Friedell had already converted in 1897.

50   Egon Hajek, *Wanderung unter Sternen. Erlebtes, Erhörte und Ersonnenes* (Stuttgart: J. F. Steinkopf 1958), 269. For more on the incident, see Jungwirth, 'Politische Vergangenheiten Entpolitisierungs- und Politisierungsprozesse im österreichischen Protestantismus 1933/34 bis 1968', 163.

51   Martina Fuchs, 'Egon Hajek – ein Pfarrer aus Siebenbürgen als Reformationsschriftsteller', *Jahrbuch des Bundesinstituts für Kultur und Geschichte der Deutschen im östlichen Europa*. Vol. 22: *Reformation* (Berlin: De Gruyter Oldenbourg 2015), 325–74, 325.

without fulfilling an inner turn.[52] Hajek's memoirs show that even in the 1950s he considered himself an 'exponent of the anti-Nazi opposition'.[53] The denunciation of the chairman of the Association of Transylvanian Saxons in 1942 supported his claim. The Gau file states that Hajek's ideological orientation cannot be assumed because of his position in the church, but the denunciation had no consequences.[54]

Hajek's brief correspondences with actors of the literary field in the 1930s, in contrast to that of the religious one, reveal loose connections to Hans Grimm or E. G. Kohlbenheyer and show a network mainly limited to Austria, and friends such as Carl Hans Watzinger, Robert Hohlbaum and Walter von Molo were an exception. Hajek's symbolic capital and position in the Viennese literary field was signalled by readings with Watzinger, Hohlbaum and Josef Weinheber in Vienna or lectures and evenings elsewhere in Austria (e.g. in Graz), where his wife read selected texts during such sessions, which were frequently held in Transylvania.[55] He published some texts in propagandistic publications in the Reich,[56] but never won any prizes in the National Socialist literary field. On the Viennese radio, his role in the 1930s was only as a composer and conductor.

Heinrich Zillich became known in the Romanian-German literature of the interwar period as the founder and editor of the journal *Klingsor*, which illustrates that a modern literary concept and an anti-modern interpretation of history were not mutually exclusive,[57] and how rapidly ideological positions could change. Considering the number of publications

---

52 Fuchs, 'Egon Hajek – ein Pfarrer aus Siebenbürgen als Reformationsschriftsteller', 372.
53 Jungwirth, 'Politische Vergangenheiten Entpolitisierungs- und Politisierungsprozesse im österreichischen Protestantismus 1933/34 bis 1968', 245.
54 Fuchs, 'Egon Hajek – ein Pfarrer aus Siebenbürgen als Reformationsschriftsteller', 342.
55 Personal fond Egon Hajek, B I 31, A-711, Vol. 3.
56 For example, Heinz Kindermann (ed.), *Rufe über Grenzen. Antlitz und Lebensraum der Grenz- und Auslandsdeutschen in ihrer Dichtung* (Berlin: Junge Generation, 1938), 454; Langenbucher, *Volkhafte Dichtung der Zeit*, 373; Uwe Baur, *Karin Gradwohl-Schlacher: Literatur in Österreich 1938–1945*. Vol. 5: *Literarisches System in Österreich* (Wien: Vandenhoeck-Ruprecht 2021), 20.
57 For more on the relationship between National Socialism and modernism, see Jeffrey Herf, *Reactionary Modernism. Technology, Culture and Politics in Weimar and the Third Reich* (Cambridge: Cambridge University Press, 1984).

and awards he obtained in the period between 1933 and 1938, this time marks the beginning of Zillich's most successful literary phase. In contrast to Meschendörfer and Hajek, he earned his living, after having finished his studies in Berlin and returning to Braşov, exclusively by writing and working for newspapers such as the local *Kronstädter Zeitung*.

As a scholarship holder of the DAI in 1934, he had already given numerous readings and made radio contributions in the Reich – not only in Marburg, Münster or Kassel but also in Graz. In this period, he enthusiastically reported to his wife: 'One can see our books in all the bookshops [...] I also saw our books in the shop windows in Tübingen [...] It is quite different from the previous year.'[58] He was equally satisfied with the payments he earned as well as the publicity received by Transylvanian authors in the newspapers. Regarding his standing among scholarship holders in Jena, he expressed great satisfaction and was touched by his own 'celebrity' status.[59] He was particularly glad about Gustav Pezold's offer to move to the Reich: 'For me, an unexpected and great prospect of life arises [that] I have never had before.'[60] The plans were realized (for financial reasons) only in 1936 but his letters written during the scholarship in 1934–5 attest a clear reorientation to the expectation of representing Germans abroad in the literary field of the Reich. He regularly consulted with his friend Pezold about his future political novel and followed his recommendations. Zillich got also closer to authors such as Agnes Miegel or Ina Seidel, and although he was enthusiastic about Ernst Wiechert, who later went into internal exile, he instructed his wife not to publish any reviews of 'democratic newspapers' on the back page of *Klingsor*.[61] In line with his success, his writings were included in representative propagandistic anthologies.[62]

58   Letter from Heinrich Zillich to Maria Zillich, 9 September 1934, in NL Heinrich Zillich in the archive of the IKGS.

59   Among other letters from Heinrich Zillich to Maria Zillich, 15 September 1934 and 27 October 1934, NL Heinrich Zillich.

60   Letter from Heinrich Zillich to Maria Zillich, 27 November 1934, NL Heinrich Zillich.

61   Letter from Heinrich Zillich to Maria Zillich, 14 November 1934, NL Heinrich Zillich.

62   For example, Kindermann, *Rufe über Grenzen*.

After moving to the Reich, Zillich repositioned himself in the Nazi cultural field in many ways: he reached a broad public as a writer and commentator via radio,[63] a representative example is the radio play *Die Zinnenschlacht* (The Battle of the Tâmpa).[64] He continued to contribute to literature in Romania but used the acquired cultural capital and information for strengthening his position in the Reich.[65]

In 1934, he received the Storyteller Prize from the magazine *die neue linie* for the second time.[66] He won the very same prize once again in 1935 for *Der baltische Graf* (The Baltic Count), the film version that Meteorfilm was planning to produce in 1937. In 1936, his first widely known political novel *Zwischen Grenzen und Zeiten* (Between Borders and Times) received the 'Literaturpreis der Reichshauptstadt Berlin' and in 1937, the 'Volksdeutsche Schrifttumspreis' from the City of Stuttgart and the DAI, as well as the Book Prize from the Wilhelm Raabe Society. In the same year, he was one of the authors that Hitler met during the seventh Berlin Poetry Week.[67] Likewise in 1937, a special parchment edition of *Zwischen Grenzen und Zeiten* was gifted to Hitler on his birthday, and Zillich received an honorary doctorate from Göttingen University.[68]

A total of 37 books by Zillich were distributed, with 1.5 million copies circulated in the market. *Zwischen Grenzen und Zeiten* was regarded as the south-eastern counterpart to Hans Grimm's *Volk ohne Raum* (People

---

63 Zillich was a returning guest in several radio programmes. For an overview, see *Radio Wien*, <https://anno.onb.ac.at/anno-suche#searchMode=complex&text=Heinrich+Zillich&title=Radio+Wien&dateMode=period&yearFrom=1933&yearTo=1938&from=1>, accessed 10 September 2021.

64 'Die Zinnenschlacht. Hörspiel aus der Vorkriegszeit Siebenburgens von Heinrich Zillich', *Deutschlandsender* (28 March 1936), 10:15–44.

65 Jan-Pieter Barbian, *Literaturpolitik im 'Dritten Reich'. Institutionen, Kompetenzen, Betätigungsfelder* (Munich: dtv, 1995), 458–69.

66 The first time in 1932.

67 Next to Erwin Wittstock, Robert Hohlbaum, Bruno Brehm, Graf Bossi Fedrigotti and Karl H. Waggerl.

68 Klaus Popa Böhm, 'Heinrich Zillich', in Klaus Popa Böhm (ed.), *Vom NS-Volkstum zum Vertriebenenfunktionär. Die Gründungsmitglieder des Südostdeutschen Kulturwerks München und der Landsmannschaften der Deutschen aus Rumänien, Ungarn und Jugoslawien* (Frankfurt am Main: Peter Lang, 2014), 37–40.

without Space) with 120,000 copies published. Besides a school edition of selected fragments, he presented the novel in the province[69] and major centres such as Vienna, Berlin and Hamburg.

Like Meschendörfer, Zillich also belonged to the Marienburg Circle of Poets, which placed 'German writers from the East' in the service of National Socialist propaganda.[70] In 1938, he was present at the Weimar Poets' Meeting dedicated to the 'Anschluss', together with authors such as Josef Weinheber and Robert Hohlbaum.[71] Zillich's position in the National Socialist literary field was further strengthened by his activity as a juror for literary awards and his presence at the Salzburg Festival in 1938. His cultural and political commitment also included his engagement with the German Labour Front, which he demonstrated, for example, by giving 'suitable lectures' on a cruise trip to Lisbon and Madeira.[72]

Zillich's extensive correspondence illustrates – in contrast to that of Meschendörfer or Hajek – his strategically built literary network. On the one hand, he acted as 'a genius of friendship'[73] by taking care of his friends – the most prominent example being Josef Weinheber,[74] with whom he had been friends since 1926 and who had contributed several first publications in *Klingsor*. He forwarded some of Weinheber's poems to Will Vesper,[75] who published them in *Neue Literatur* (New Literature), the

69   In July 1937, Zillich was on a three-week lecture tour, including Belgium.

70   'Berufung in den Marienburger Dichterkreis', *Deutsche Allgemeine Zeitung*, 27 August 1942.

71   Ketelsen, *Völkisch-nationale und nationalsozialistische Literatur in Deutschland 1890–1945*, 438.

72   Letters from the Deutschen Arbeitsfront, NL Heinrich Zillich.

73   Hajek, *Wanderung unter Sternen*, 165.

74   See Heinrich Zillich, 'Uns wird er immer geheimnisvoller werden', in Heinrich Zillich (ed.), *Bekenntnis zu Josef Weinheber. Erinnerungen seiner Freunde* (Salzburg: Akad. Gemeinschaftsverlag, 1950), 247. For more on Weinheber in National-Socialism, see, for example, Albert Berger, 'Josef Weinheber und der Nationalsozialismus. Zur politischen Biographie des Dichters', in Uwe Baur and Helga Mitterbauer (eds), *Macht Literatur Krieg. Österreichische Literatur im Nationalsozialismus* (Wien: Böhlau, 1998), 185–201.

75   Walther Methlagl, 'Josef Weinheber: Zwei Briefe an Heinrich Zillich', *Südostdeutsche Semesterblätter* 17/20/21 (1968), 1–14.

first prominent journal loyal to the regime that published Weinheber's poetry and dedicated its issue in January 1935 to the poet. On the other hand, Zillich also proved to be a 'callous nerd'[76] as he criticized authors from Romania particularly harshly, accusing them of being envious of his success.[77] He further corresponded in the 1930s, beyond his Transylvanian colleagues, with prominent literary actors such as Edwin Erich Dwinger, political activists such as Anton Count Bossi Fedrigotti and, later, 'God-blessed writers' such as Hans Grimm, Josef Weinheber, Hanns Johst, Hans Carossa, Bruno Brehm, Hans Friedrich Blunck and Robert Hohlbaum. The extensive correspondence with Brehm shows that he was among Zillich's closest friends while his detailed letters to Hans Grimm illustrate that not only was Zillich a welcome guest in Lippoldsberg and collaborated with Grimm in the Causa Pezold[78] but also that Grimm supported him by organizing readings.[79]

Zillich was in contact with well-known Germanists such as Heinz Kindermann, Hellmuth Langenbucher, Herbert Cysarz, Will Vesper and, later, Innsbruck University professor Karl Kurt Klein. The fact that Zillich met Joseph Goebbels as early as 1935 shows how well his networking strategy worked.[80] Zillich's prominent position in the cultural field was illustrated in a letter from Harald Krasser, to whom he handed over the *Klingsor* editorship in 1936. In his correspondence to Zillich, Krasser reported on both the current editorial issues and the conflicts between Fritz Fabritius and Alfred Bonfert; Zillich took this issue further and informed Will Vesper.[81] He also intervened on another occasion during

---

76 Werner Bergengruen about Zillich. See Ernst Klee, *Das Kulturlexikon zum Dritten Reich. Wer war was vor und nach 1945* (Frankfurt am Main: S. Fischer, 2007), 684.

77 Letter from Heinrich Zillich to Harald Krasser, 28 February 1937, NL Heinrich Zillich.

78 Zillich corresponded not only with Grimm, but also with other authors such as Robert Hohlbaum and wrote even to Dr Joseph Goebbels on 18 January 1938.

79 Grimm asks Zillich to replace Carossa at a reading with Wehrmacht people. Letter from Hans Grimm to Heinrich Zillich, 20 June 1937, NL Heinrich Zillich.

80 Letter to Maria Zillich, 2 March 1935, NL Heinrich Zillich.

81 Letter from Heinrich Zillich to Harald Krasser, 7 February 1939; Harald Krasser to Heinrich Zillich, 31 January 1936 or 10 February 1937, NL Heinrich Zillich.

the conflict between Meschendörfer and Pezold over the publication of *Büffelbrunnen*.[82]

As a recurrent guest on radio, Zillich had a major influence on its Transylvanian discourse. His role in shaping the public narratives about the Germans abroad in the Reich is mirrored in his contributions to journals such as *Nation und Staat* (Nation and State), *Das Innere Reich* (The Inner Reich) and in inquiries such as those published in *Deutsche Frömmigkeit* (German Piety).[83] That he was regarded as an expert on South-East Europe is shown, among other things, by the request of the Amt für Schrifttumspflege (Office for Promotion of Publications) in 1938. Citing his own lack of language skills as a reason, Zillich recommended K. K. Klein and Harald Krasser as potential reviewers.[84] His position in the literary and cultural field is also evidenced by his letters to Richard Csaki (head of the DAI), to whom he gives suggestions on paying more attention to other Germans abroad in addition to the Sudeten Germans.[85]

Adolf Meschendörfer, Heinrich Zillich and Egon Hajek all co-operated – as shown – to varying degrees with the National Socialist apparatus: the fact that Zillich was ideologically the most committed is un-doubtedly also related to his financial situation and his ambition to finance his growing family exclusively from his writing.[86] All three examples state what Sarkowicz concluded for writers in general:

> Jede Schriftstellerpersönlichkeit ist ihren Weg gegangen, hat ihre Kompromisse und Konzessionen gemacht. Wie stark man sich dabei mit dem nationalsozialistischen Apparat einließ, zu wieviel Widerstand man in der Lage war, hing von persönlichen Umständen und von der eigenen Stärke ab.[87]

---

82   Heinrich Zillich to Harald Krasser, 7 February 1939; Harald Krasser to Heinrich Zillich, 31 January 1936 or 10 February 1937, NL Heinrich Zillich.

83   Letter of the editors to Heinrich Zillich, 26 March 1938, NL Heinrich Zillich.

84   Heinrich Zillich to Heinz Kindermann, 25 March 1938, NL Heinrich Zillich.

85   Letters from Heinrich Zillich to Richard Csaki, 4 September 1937 and 21 April 1937, NL Heinrich Zillich.

86   He wrote about this several times to his wife Maria Zillich, NL Heinrich Zillich.

87   Hans Sarkowicz and Alf Mentzer, *Literatur in Nazideutschland. Ein biografisches Lexikon* (Hamburg: Europa Verlag, 2000), 29.

[Every writer personality went his or her own way, made compromises and concessions. How much one got involved with the National Socialist apparatus, how much resistance one was capable of, depended on personal circumstances and one's own strength.] (my translation)

Adapting biographies

Adolf Meschendörfer was said to have distanced himself in the early 1940s from National Socialism and, by 1943, to have started to withdraw from public life.[88] This is contradicted by the fact that, after his retirement in 1940, he intended to devote himself entirely to literature and tried to co-operate with the Universum-Film Aktiengesellschaft/Universe-Film Limited Company (UFA).[89] He also signalized his ideological convictions by choosing a new publishing house and engaging actively in cultural propaganda: in January 1942, he spoke at the local opening ceremonial of the Schrifttumskammer.[90] He was a member of the Marienburg Poets' Circle and received the honorary certificate of a *Kulturrat* (cultural council) in 1943.[91]

Konradt interpreted the three short stories published in the second half of the 1940s together with the unpublished essays *Völkisch und national*[92] and *Dichterisches Glaubensbekenntnis*[93] as signs of a crisis of Meschendörfer's art conception and a turning away from all dogma.[94] This is, however, questionable when reading, for instance, the correspondence with Fritz Löffler,[95]

88 Konradt, *Grenzen einer Inselliteratur*, 292.
89 See screenplay *Prinzessin Omer*, NL Adolf Meschendörfer, and note in his 'Biografie', box 1, folder 1, 2.
90 *Südostdeutsche Tageszeitung* (21 January 1942).
91 The ethnic group leader honoured several cultural agents by appointing them as cultural councillors, see *Kronstädter Zeitung* (26 January 1943).
92 'Völkisch und national', manuscript, NL Adolf Meschendörfer, box 35.
93 'Dichterisches Glaubensbekenntis' (1945). Manuscript, NL Adolf Meschendörfer, box 35.
94 Konradt, *Grenzen einer Inselliteratur*, 298.
95 Fritz Löffler was the headmaster of a grammar school in Pforzheim and actively participated in the Gauleiter's De-Welshization campaign

who reports also about his Denazification – a procedure Meschendörfer was not confronted with in Romania. Meschendörfer was active even in 1949, organizing a Goethe Conference in Braşov and offered Mihail Sadoveanu, president of the Romanian Writers' Association at that time, to hold a conference also in Bucharest.[96] By the end of the 1940s and the beginning of the 1950s, he was also actively looking for publication possibilities, including in Germany, where he received feedback that *Büffelbrunnen* would be published as soon as 'the known circumstances' would allow for it.[97]

However, his fame, which is thought to have protected him against political attacks,[98] did not help him with public lectures abroad. In 1956, he sent Thusnelda Henning a few poems that she read at a literary event in Vienna.[99] In 1957, he read in Cluj in the Literary Circle of the German Students.[100] His nimbus as a lonely writer was further strengthened on his eightieth birthday (1957) as he stood in the literary spotlight and got the Order of Labour 1st Class,[101] despite having difficulties in publishing at this time. Meschendörfer stands proof of how making arrangements with the regime could function if the preconditions of belonging to an older generation and being known in the West were fulfilled. He was stylized as the figurehead of multi-ethnic literature in Romania on radio and in different

('Entwelschungs-Kampagne') in Alsace in the 1930s. Peter von Polenz, *Deutsche Sprachgeschichte I* (Berlin: Walter de Gruyter, 2000), 283.

96   Letter from Adolf Meschendöfer to Mihail Sadoveanu, 8 July 1949, NL Adolf Meschendörfer, box 2, folder 3.

97   For example, Letter from Dr Erwin Speck & Co, Düsseldorf, 21 October 1948, NL Adolf Meschendörfer, box 2, folder 3. Letters from Hellmuth Stöber.

98   He did not get involved in the political processes towards the end of the 1950s, which defined the public life of the German-speaking minority in Transylvania. Peter Motzan and Stefan Sienerth (eds), *Worte als Gefahr und Gefährdung. Fünf Schriftsteller vor Gericht (15. September 1959 – Kronstadt/Rumänien)* (Munich: Verlag Südostdeutsches Kulturwerk, 1993), 198.

99   Letter from Thusnelda Henning to Adolf Meschendörfer, 19 April 1956, NL Adolf Meschendörfer, box 2, folder 4.

100 Two letters from Kurtfelix Schlattner and Joachim Wittstock in November 1957, NL Adolf Meschendörfer, box 2, folder 4.

101 Gust, 'Adolf Meschendörfer (Ein Lebensbild)', 81.

German, Hungarian and Romanian journals.[102] The only unfavourable opinion that the author was being 'always a conscious German and had not even secretly resisted National Socialism' was published in Germany.[103]

On the contrary, collaborating with the regime did not necessarily exclude him from having difficulties in publishing. For instance, releasing a new edition of his work by Alfred Gustl took forever in the 1950s,[104] as the 'racial ideas' implied in his prose were repeatedly brought to focus. The publishers made their position clear: 'It goes without saying that we are not uncritical of Adolf Meschendörfer's work.'[105] They cited having a discussion with Ernst Breitenstein who emphasized 'the positive sides' of Meschendörfer's work together with 'limits of his world view and consequently of his art.'[106] This correspondence showed again that Meschendörfer was not opposed to a new interpretation of his work from a 'socialist world view' and actively looked for an arrangement with the regime.[107]

Contrastingly, Egon Hajek continued his career after the war in the field of music. In 1945, he received a teaching assignment for liturgy and hymnology[108] becoming a professor in the Faculty of Protestant Theology

---

102 'Medalionul literar' Adolf Meschendörfer", *Programul de Radio* (18 July 1957), 13:30; Adolf Meschendörfer, 'Wachsmann halotti tora'. Translated by Miess G. János, *Útunk* (18 May 1957), 5; Georg Scherg, 'Küldetés és helytállás', *Útunk* (18 May 1957); 'Ehrung Adolf Meschendörfers. Staatspreisträger Ferenc Szemlér überreicht dem Altmeister den Arbeitsorden', *Neuer Weg* (16 March 1957). Since 1954, he was a member of the Romanian Writers' Union.

103 Cristian Caspari, 'Der Deutsche stirbt nicht. Adolf Meschendörfer zum 80. Geburtstag am 8. Mai', *Nationale Rundschau. Zeitung für deutsche Politik* (4 May 1957).

104 'Correspondence with "Espla"' (Editura de stat pentru literatură și artă [State Publishing House for Literature and Art]), NL Adolf Meschendörfer, box 39.

105 'Correspondence with "Espla"', 30 January 1957, NL Adolf Meschendörfe, Letter No. 894.

106 *Contemporanul* (19 July 1957).

107 *Contemporanul* (19 July 1957).

108 Karl Schwarz (ed.), 'Quellentexte zur österreichischen evangelischen Kirchengeschichte zwischen 1918 und 1945', *Jahrbuch der Gesellschaft für die Geschichte des Protestantismus in Österreich* 104/105 (1988/9), 689. For his activity on musical field, see Thomas Reuter, 'Evangelische Kirchenmusik in Österreich. Studien zu ihren Organisationsformen und Persönlichkeiten im 20. Jahrhundert

at the University of Vienna in the following year. However, he was less successful in this field when compared to his literary endeavours. His memoirs *Wanderung unter Sternen* was mainly received by his countrymen. In the 1950s and 1960s, he published regularly in the supplement of the *Wiener Zeitung* and, as his correspondence shows, he was no longer able to find a renowned publisher, as a result of which protestant periodicals remained as the main medium of publication. However, in 1955, he became a member of the Schutzverband österreichischer Schriftsteller.[109] On his seventieth birthday in 1958, he received the Golden Medal of Honour from the federal president of Austria and the honorary membership of the Landsmannschaft in Germany. He perceived his public readings in Innsbruck and Upper Austria, organized by his countrymen, as successful.[110]

His correspondence also mirrors his network in protestant circles. Among writers in Austria, he continued corresponding, for instance, with Carl Hans Watzinger, who had lost his position in the literary field.

Zillich's American Denazification file illustrates how 'successful' he was in maintaining his literary network after 1945. Being accused of having 'glorified National Socialist tyranny and Adolf Hitler' based only on his poem 'Den Deutschen von Gott gesandt' (Sent to the Germans by God), Zillich invoked the right to political error made immediately after the 'Anschluss'.[111] The accusation failed to contextualize the poem or evoke the author's propagandistic activity.[112]

The expert opinion of the Commission for Cultural Workers reflects how overburdened this body was: regarding Gustav Pezold and Paul Fechter, it was noted that they had by no means been anti-fascist. The fact that recommendation letters by Hans Grimm and Ina Seidel could be submitted

---

(mit besonderer Berücksichtigung des Wirkens von Egon Hajek', Dissertation, Universität Wien, Wein, 1995, 23–145.

109   Egon Hajek and Professor Dr H. J. Moser, Wien, 12 January 1955, personal fond Egon Hajek B I 31, Vol. 6.

110   Letter from Egon Hajek to his relative Mare, 15 April 1958, personal fond Egon Hajek B I 31, Vol. 6.

111   See Zillich's declaration in front of the Spruchkammer, personal fond Egon Hajek B I 31, Vol. 6, 13.

112   Statement of Claim, 4 July 1947, American Denazification File, NL Zillich.

as exculpatory documents illustrates the consequences of clearly dividing völkisch-national-conservative and National Socialist literature. On the contrary, it also shows that the Spruchkammer in Starnberg had competence neither in the literary field nor on South-Eastern Europe. It even accepted the recommendation letter of the Transylvanian-Hungarian writer and main cultural ideologist József Nyírő, a member of the Hungarian Arrow Cross Parliament from October 1944 who had to flee to Germany. He was listed in Zillich's file as 'the best-known Hungarian poet living in Germany'.[113]

Except for Karl Kurt Klein,[114] his long-time friend and comrade-in-arms who should have continued editing *Klingsor* in 1940, Zillich had considerable difficulty in finding Germanists without a National Socialist past who could testify before the Spruchkammer or write an expert opinion. The defence lawyer initially did not want to submit Alexander Schröder's expert opinion because he wrote about Zillich's 'error',[115] and as the well-known German scholar Paul Kluckhohn from the University of Tübingen emphasized, he had met Zillich once.[116]

The affidavits of Franz Werneke and Jürgen Eggebrecht 'proved' Zillich's courage and resistance.[117] Conversely, the brief statement by G. A.

113　See request from the lawyer, Hermann Alletag, for the initiation of the Spruchkammer proceedings, 29 November 1946, NL Zillich.

114　See correspondence with Karl Kurt Klein and Alexander Schröder from the period 1946–7, NL Zillich.

115　Letter from Dr Rudolf Alexander Schröder to the Spruchkammer, 27 August 1947, 'Amerikanische Entnazifizierungsakte', NL Zillich.

116　Dr Paul Kluckhohn (Professor of German Language and Literature), Tübingen, 19 August 1947, NL Zillich. Kluckhohn was considered a national conservative who kept a certain distance from National Socialism, because of which he became the dean at the University of Tübingen in 1945. See Holger Dainat, 'Zur Berufungspolitik in der Neueren deutschen Literatur', in Dainat et al. (eds), *Literaturwissenschaft und Nationalsozialismus* (Tübingen: Max Niemeyer Verlag, 2003), 55–86, 59.

117　'Franz Werneke: Eidesstattiche Erklärung', 8 August 1947; 'Eidesstattiche Erklärung of Dr. jur. Jürgen Eggebrecht', 15 July 1946, 'Amerikanische Entnazifizierungsakte'; Erklärung of Dr. jur. Jürgen Eggebrecht', 15 July 1946; 'Amerikanische Entnazifizierungsakte', NL Zillich.

Giles of Durham University, who had to emigrate in 1933 for 'racial reasons', was supposed to have a particularly exculpatory effect:

> I know how gravely concerned Heinrich Zillich has been about the degrading of human nature which accompanied the Nazi-System, and that it was his ardent desire to restore thoughtfulness and decent behaviour among man [...] I am convinced that with his rare gifts he has a real contribution to make towards a re-shaping of the German mind.[118]

The Aid Committee of Transylvanian Saxons and Swabians also emphasized in a letter to the Spruchkammer that it was dependent on the work of the 'best-known poet of the South-East'. Zillich had taken in eight refugees and had already been working voluntarily for his refugee compatriots for two years.[119] In addition, the Munich headquarters of the Aid and Counselling Centre for Romanian Germans within the Protestant Aid Organization asked for speeding up the procedure so that they could employ Zillich.[120]

Zillich's Denazification, which proved to be a farce,[121] ended with classifying him as a *Mitläufer* (nominal supporter) – despite the public plaintiff's request for Level II of incrimination (*Stufe II der Belasteten*). He had to pay a fine (of 700 Reichsmark) and the legal costs.

---

118   G. A. Giles (Professor of Education, University of Durham), 6 February 1947, NL Zillich.

119   Letter from Hilfskomitee der Siebenbürger Sachsen und Banater Schwaben to Spruchkammer, 11 July 1947, NL Zillich.

120   Münchner Zentrale der Hilfs- und Beratungsstelle für Rumäniendeutsche im Evangelischen Hilfswerk to the Spruchkammer Starnberg, 7 November 1946, NL Zillich. The undersigned Otto Appel was a member of the Resettlement Commissions for Northern and Southern Bucovina in 1940–1, a front-line soldier from 1941 to 1945, an employee of the German Red Cross in 1945 as well as the managing director of the Aid and Counselling Centre for Southeast Germans in Munich from 1946 to 1949; he subsequently held numerous administrative and political positions in Bavaria.

121   As showed by Lutz Niethammer, *Entnazifizierung in Bayern. Säuberung und Rehabilitierung unter amerikanischer Besatzung* (Frankfurt am Main: S. Fischer, 1972).

Although Zillich could have worked in his profession after Denazification, he no longer managed to publish in renowned houses in the Federal Republic of Germany or to enjoy literary success. His manuscripts were rejected one after the other and he remained known only in a South-East European right-wing extremist niche. He also belonged to Hans Grimm's circle of friends but was reduced to attending the Lippoldsberg Poetry Days and later stayed away for strategic political reasons.[122] Indeed, between 1952 and 1963, he was federal chairman and then honorary chairman of the Landsmannschaft der Siebenbürger Sachsen for a quarter of a century. Nevertheless, his contacts with the extreme right-wing field did not cease, as he was an honorary member of Deutschen Kulturwerk Europäischen Geistes (German Cultural Association of the European Spirit). For example, in 1977, he gave a lecture at the Society for Free Journalism on the 'Germans in Southeastern Europe'.[123] At the same time, he considered himself a European and was proud of having contact with Otto von Habsburg and writing to Theodor Heuss regarding the anthem question.[124]

In spite of Zillich's shrinking literary network (especially when those who had remained in Transylvania dropped out), he remained friends with actors such as Hans Grimm, Bruno Brehm and Karl Kurt Klein. His correspondence shows how the old network was activated after 1945 and kept the 'Starnberg literary elite' together.[125] Zillich's reports about his literary activities are particularly revealing. For instance, he spoke positively about his visit to Bolzano and reported to Hans Grimm about the Styrian Poets' Day in 1954, at which many dilettantes appeared alongside von Blunck and Cysarz.[126] In 1956, when reading in Salzburg, he invited his compatriot Otto

122 Letter from Heinrich Zillich to Bruno Brehm, 29 July 1960, NL Zillich.
123 'Dossier Heinrich Zillich', <http://www.halbjahresschrift.homepage.t-online.de/zill.htm#Mosaik>, accessed 2 August 2019.
124 See the few letters to and from Otto von Habsburg and Theoder Heuss, NL Zillich.
125 Hanns Johst, Gustav Pezold or Ina Seidel were living here. See Sibylle Friedrike Hellerer, 'Die NSDAP im Landkreis Starnberg. Von den Anhängen bis zur Konsolidierung der Macht (1919–1938)', Inaugural dissertation, Ludwig-Maximilians-Universität, Munich, 2014, 10.
126 Letter from Heinrich Zillich to Hans Grimm, 31 July 1954, NL Zillich, 1.

Folberth, among others.[127] The correspondence with Karl Kurt Klein illustrates that this friendship became much closer after 1945.[128] Klein supported Zillich – by organizing readings and by recommending him to the position of the editor of the *Südostdeutsche Vierteljahresblätter* (South-East German Quarterly) to the board of the Südostdeutsches Kulturwerk (South-East German Cultural Society) – and was also an interlocutor when it came to Transylvanian-Saxon affairs. Thus, the Innsbruck professor received detailed reports on Zillich's visits to the Foreign Office in Bonn.[129] In this context, he bitterly remarked: 'I don't work on my own things anymore, I'm doing family reunification.'[130]

His engagement and work in the *Landsmannschaft* advanced his position, as he was considered to be an important player in the political field. The Securitate, the Romanian Secret Service, identified him as one of the leaders of the Saxon emigration and classified him as a 'fascist enemy and traitor' who was inciting Transylvanian authors. The file in which he was also accused of being a spy showcases the mechanism of the Securitate of overestimating the role of individuals in constructing political show trials.[131] Contacts to Zillich and his book *Wir Siebenbürger* became central in incriminating some authors in Romania who were convicted in 1959.[132]

127 Folberth was the head of department at the Research Institute of the German Ethnic Group in Romania before 1945 and director of the affiliated press organ Deutsche Forschungen im Südosten [German Research in the South-East].

128 See Hermine Pildner-Klein, *Karl Kurt Klein. Ein Gelehrtenleben im Umbruch. Versuch einer Darstellung* (Jassy, Konstanz: 'Alexandru Ioan Cuza', Hartung-Gorre Verlag, 1997), 532.

129 See, for example, Letter from Heinrich Zillich to Karl Kurt Klein, 22 December 1956, NL Zillich.

130 Letter from Heinrich Zillich to Karl Kurt Klein, 22 December 1956, NL Zillich.

131 CNSAS – Consiliul Naţional pentru Studierea Arhivelor Securităţii [The National Council for the Study of the Securitate Archives], Direcţia Cercetare, Expoziţii, Publicaţii, Dosar No. 2907, Vol. I, II, III, I 260208. Arhiva Operativă, Dosar: Acţiunea Operativă Heinrich Zillich, 03.03.1961, Regională Stalin, Serviciul II, Biroul I, No. 1319, Dosar individual, deschis la data de 17.10.1957 [Research, Exhibitions, Publications Directorate, File No. 2907, Vol. I, I 260208. Operational Archive, File: Heinrich Zillich Operational Action, 3. March 1961, Stalin Regional, Service II, Office I, No. 1319, Individual file, opened on 17 October 1957].

132 Motzan and Sienerth, *Worte als Gefahr und Gefährdung*.

Despite the differences, in the 1930s, all three authors showed a strong individual striving for power that was not disturbed by ideological content. This attitude can be, at least partly, attributed to their previously marginal position in the 'all-German' literary field where the writers in exile had several gaps to fill. Due to their habitus, as well as for geographical reasons, Meschendörfer, Hajek and Zillich got involved – to different extents – in the negotiation processes or the accompanying conflicts of the National Socialistic cultural field. Zillich, being the youngest and living near Munich, became most intensively involved. Hajek's position as a pastor allowed him to shape the literary field of the Nazi period only to a very limited extent, for example in protestant circles. Last, Meschendörfer had less room for getting involved owing to geographical reasons and thus, once retired, engaged more in the propaganda on the margins. This kind of co-operation was impossible for Hajek due to his profession, which, however, did not prevent him from participating in propagandist publications or supporting the illegal SA.

The great number of actors in the National Socialist literary field joined by a 'proliferating juxtaposition and opposition of cultural-political institutions'[133] gave room for different interpretations regarding ideological engagements. For example, the Lippoldsberg Poetry Days, which in 1934–9 were 'a silent protest against the rigid National Socialist cultural policy,'[134] could be listed as evidence of anti-National Socialist sentiments, as seen in the case of Heinrich Zillich during the course of the Denazification.[135] However, considering his activities – such as radio broadcasts, literary meetings, journalistic texts and other propagandistic events during the Second World War – and his retrospective explanatory efforts, the question posed by Stefan Sienerth was whether Meschendörfer's and Zillich's statements deviated from public guidelines or if they sympathized temporarily after the fall of the regime.[136] There were individual cases, for example, the

---

133   Ketelsen, *Völkisch-nationale und nationalsozialistische Literatur in Deutschland 1890–1945*, 83.
134   Sarkowicz and Mentzer, *Literatur in Nazideutschland*, 65.
135   Zillich's Denazification File, NL Zillich. The materials are predominantly transcripts.
136   Sienerth, 'Adolf Meschendörfer und Heinrich Zillich', 87.

Pezold's or Meschendörfer's local school issues, in which they disagreed with the official procedure, but there were no deviating statements or sympathetic signals for a post-National Socialist era. At this point, the problem of differentiating between völkisch-national-conservative and National Socialist literature becomes obvious once more.[137] Meschendörfer, Hajek and Zillich were clearly 'völkisch'-national-conservative and co-operated with the National Socialist regime, going as far as playing active roles in various fields: cultural, literary and religious. While Meschendörfer and Zillich actively engaged in the National Socialist propaganda, Hajek was hindered by his position in the religious field, which strengthened his cultural capital after 1945.

In conclusion, we can say that the three positioning 'strategies' exemplify how cultural capitals could be used in new fields under different political circumstances. Meschendörfer was the only one who could apparently profit from different political systems before and after 1945. Closer inspection, however, indicates that he made the requested compromise: he accepted the conditions for publishing and gave up, for example, the right to choose his texts. Hajek's strategy shows how interdependencies between the different fields (literary and religious) can be damaging or useful depending on the political system. His way of arranging proved to be successful in the long term in the musical field, while Zillich's strategy did pay off only temporarily in the literary field. Due to his excellent network, he was able to find success after 1945 in the public sphere and gained political relevance, even if this was limited to the sphere of the German refugees.

Adapting biographies – reinterpreting them – proved to be effective in all three cases, even if Zillich and Hajek lost their positions in the literary field.

137   Ketelsen, *Völkisch-nationale und nationalsozialistische Literatur*, 19–30.

Bibliography

Barbian, Jan-Pieter, *Literaturpolitik im 'Dritten Reich'. Institutionen, Kompetenzen, Betätigungsfelder* (Munich: dtv, 1995).

Baur, Uwe and Gradwohl-Schlacher, Karin (eds), Literatur in Österreich 1938–1945. Vol. 4: Literarisches System in Österreich (Wien: Vandenhoeck-Ruprecht, 2018).

——, *Literatur in Österreich 1938–1945*. Vol. 5: *Literarisches System in Österreich* (Wien: Vandenhoeck-Ruprecht, 2021).

Berger, Albert, 'Josef Weinheber und der Nationalsozialismus. Zur politischen Biographie des Dichters', in Uwe Baur and Helga Mitterbauer (eds), *Macht Literatur Krieg. Österreichische Literatur im Nationalsozialismus* (Wien: Böhlau, 1998), 185–201.

Böhm, Klaus Popa, 'Heinrich Zillich', in Klaus Popa Böhm (ed.), *Vom NS-Volkstum-zum Vertriebenenfunktionär. Die Gründungsmitglieder des Südostdeutschen Kulturwerks München und der Landsmannschaften der Deutschen aus Rumänien, Ungarn und Jugoslawien* (Frankfurt am Main: Peter Lang, 2014), 37–40.

Bourdieu, Pierre, *Die Regeln der Kunst. Genese und Struktur des literarischen Feldes* (Frankfurt am Main: Suhrkamp, 2001).

Csejka, Gerhardt, 'Vorwort', in Adolf Meschendörfer and Bernd Kolf (eds), *Gedichte, Erzählungen, Drama, Aufsätze* (Bukarest: Kriterion, 1978), 5–28.

Dácz, Enikő, 'Vom "gottbegnadeten Schriftsteller" zum Schriftleiter. Heinrich Zillichs literarisches Netzwerk im Nationalsozialismus', <https://halbja hresschrift.de/heinrich-zillich-netzwerk-nationalsozialismus/>, accessed 10 December 2021.

Dácz, Enikő and Jakabházi, Réka, 'Der Kronstädter Literaturbetrieb im imperialen und postimperialen Machtfeld', in Enikő Dácz and Réka Jakabházi (eds), *Literarische Rauminszenierungen in Zentraleuropa. Kronstadt/Brașov/Brassó in der ersten Hälfte des 20. Jahrhunderts* (Regensburg: Pustet, 2020), 35–59.

Dainat, Holger, 'Zur Berufungspolitik in der Neueren deutschen Literatur', in Dainat et al. (eds), *Literaturwissenschaft und Nationalsozialismus* (Tübingen: Max Niemeyer Verlag, 2003), 55–86.

'Dossier Heinrich Zillich', <http://www.halbjahresschrift.homepage.t-online.de/ zill.htm#Mosaik>, accessed 2 August 2019.

Fuchs, Martina, 'Egon Hajek – ein Pfarrer aus Siebenbürgen als Reformationsschriftsteller', *Jahrbuch des Bundesinstituts für Kultur und*

Geschichte der Deutschen im östlichen Europa. Vol. 22: *Reformation* (Berlin: De Gruyter Oldenbourg, 2015), 325–74.

Glondys, Viktor, 'Meister Johannes', *Kirchliche Blätter* 31/49 (1939), 623.

Gombocz, István, ' "Eine knorrige Eiche mit […] gebogenen Ästen": Zukunftsängste in Adolf Meschendörfers siebenbürgischem Roman "Die Stadt im Osten" '. *Jahrbuch der ungarischen Germanistik* (2017), <http://jug.hu/images/2017/04-istvan_gombocz.pdf>, 125–39, 137, accessed 12 December 2021.

Graeb-Könneker, Sebastian, *Autochthone Modernität. Eine Untersuchung der vom Nationalsozialismus geförderten Literatur* (Opladen: Westdeutscher Verlag, 1996).

Graf-Stuhlhofer, Franz, 'Wiener Evangelische Professoren der Theologie im Spiegel der Gau-Akten. Dokumentation zu Beth, Egli, Entz, Hajek, Hoffmann, Koch, Kühnert, Opitz, Schneider und Wilke', *Jahrbuch für die Geschichte des Protestantismus in Österreich* 116/191–222 (2000–1), 197–205.

Gust, Alfred, 'Adolf Meschendörfer (Ein Lebensbild)', *Neue Literatur* 8/2 (1957), *Adolf Meschendörfer zum 80. Geburtstag*, 65–82.

Hajek, Egon, *Wanderung unter Sternen. Erlebtes, Erhörte und Ersonnenes* (Stuttgart: J. F. Steinkopf, 1958).

Hellerer, Sibylle Friedrike, *Die NSDAP im Landkreis Starnberg. Von den Anhängen bis zur Konsolidierung der Macht (1919–1938)* (Munich: Inaugural dissertation an der Ludwig-Maximilians-Universität, 2014).

Herf, Jeffrey, *Reactionary Modernism: Technology, Culture and Politics in Weimar and the Third Reich* (Cambridge: Cambridge University Press, 1984).

Hienz, Hermann A. (ed.), *Schriftsteller-Lexikon der Siebenbürger Deutschen*. Vol. VII H–J (Köln: Böhlau, 2000).

Jungwirth, Leonhard, 'Politische Vergangenheiten Entpolitisierungs- und Politisierungsprozesse im österreichischen Protestantismus 1933/34 bis 1968', <http://othes.univie.ac.at/63952/1/67784.pdf>, accessed 9 September 2021.

Ketelsen, Uwe K., *Literatur und Drittes Reich* (Schernfeld: SH-Verlag, 1992).

Kindermann, Heinz (ed.), *Rufe über Grenzen. Antlitz und Lebensraum der Grenz- und Auslandsdeutschen in ihrer Dichtung* (Berlin: Junge Generation, 1938).

Klee, Ernst, *Das Kulturlexikon zum Dritten Reich. Wer war was vor und nach 1945* (Frankfurt am Main: S. Fischer, 2007).

Konradt, Edith, *Grenzen einer Inselliteratur. Kunst und Heimat im Werk Adolf Meschendörfers (1877–1963)* (Frankfurt am Main: Peter Lang, 1987).

Langenbucher, Hellmuth, *Volkhafte Dichtung der Zeit* (Berlin: Jünker und Dünnhaupt, 1937).

Meschendörfer, Adolf, 'Die Stimme der Auslandsdeutschen', in Heinz Kindermann (ed.), *Des deutschen Dichters Sendung in der Gegenwart* (Leipzig: Reclam, 1933), 138–46.

——, *Siebenbürgen, Land des Segens* (Leipzig: Reclam, 1937).

Methlagl, Walther, 'Josef Weinheber: Zwei Briefe an Heinrich Zillich', *Südostdeutsche Semesterblätter* 17/20/21 (1968), 1–14.

Motzan, Peter and Sienerth, Stefan (eds), *Worte als Gefahr und Gefährdung. Fünf Schriftsteller vor Gericht (15 September 1959 – Kronstadt/Rumänien)* (Munich: Verlag Südostdeutsches Kulturwerk, 1993).

Myss, Walter, *Fazit nach achthundert Jahren* (Munich: Südostdeutsches Kulturwerk, 1968).

'Neuere siebenbürgische Literatur', *Der Auslandsdeutsche. Halbmonatsschrift für Auslanddeutschtum und Auslandskunde. Mitteilungen des Deutschen Ausland-Instituts* 5/2 (1922–6), 187.

Niethammer, Lutz, *Entnazifizierung in Bayern. Säuberung und Rehabilitierung unter amerikanischer Besatzung* (Frankfurt am Main: S. Fischer, 1972).

Pildner-Klein, Hermine, *Karl Kurt Klein. Ein Gelehrtenleben im Umbruch. Versuch einer Darstellung* (Jassy, Konstanz: 'Alexandru Ioan Cuza', Hartung-Gorre Verlag, 1997).

Reuter, Thomas, 'Evangelische Kirchenmusik in Österreich. Studien zu ihren Organisationsformen und Persönlichkeiten im 20. Jahrhundert' (mit besonderer Berücksichtigung des Wirkens von Egon Hajek), Dissertation, Universität Wien, Wien, 1995.

Sarkowicz, Hans and Mentzer, Alf, *Literatur in Nazideutschland. Ein biografisches Lexikon* (Hamburg: Europa Verlag, 2000).

Schlandt, Hermann, 'Egon Hajek. Lebensbild eines Außenseiters', *Südostdeutsche Vierteljahresblätter* 12/3 (1963), 212–5.

Schwarz, Karl (ed.), 'Quellentexte zur österreichischen evangelischen Kirchengeschichte zwischen 1918 und 1945', *Jahrbuch der Gesellschaft für die Geschichte des Protestantismus in Österreich* (Wien: Evangelischer Presseverband, 1989), 104/105 (1988–9).

Sienerth, Stefan, 'Adolf Meschendörfer und Heinrich Zillich im Literaturbetrieb des "Dritten Reiches"', in Michael Markel and Peter Motzan (eds), *Deutsche Literatur in Rumänien und das 'Dritte Reich'. Vereinnahmung – Verstrickung – Ausgrenzung* (Munich: IKGS, 2003), 83–118.

Sutter, Rotraut, 'Egon Hajek', in R. Sutter (ed.), *Siebenbürger Sachsen in Österreichs Vergangenheit und Gegenwart. Eine Auswahl* (Innsbruck: Universitätverlag Wagner, 1976), 66–8.

Tourlamain, Guy, *Völkisch Writers and National Socialism. A Study of Right-Wing Political Culture in Germany, 1890–1960* (Bern: Peter Lang, 2014).

von Polenz, Peter, *Deutsche Sprachgeschichte I* (Berlin: Walter de Gruyter, 2000).

Watzinger, Carl, 'Der siebenbürgische Dichter Egon Hajek', *Der Augarten* 2/6 (1936), 175.

Zillich, Heinrich (ed.), *Bekenntnis zu Josef Weinheber. Erinnerungen seiner Freunde* (Salzburg: Akad. Gemeinschaftsverlag, 1950).
Zimmermann, Jan, *Die Kulturpreise der Stiftung F.V.S. 1935–1945. Darstellung und Dokumentation* (Hamburg: Christians, 2000).

Archive fonds

CNSAS (Consiliul Naţional pentru Studierea Arhivelor Securităţii) [The National Council for the Study of the Securitate Archives], Direcţia Cercetare, Expoziţii, Publicaţii, Dosar Nr. 2907, Vol. 1, II, III, I 260208. Arhiva Operativă, Dosar: Acţiunea Operativă Heinrich Zillich, 03.03.1961, Regională Stalin, Serviciul II, Biroul I, Nr. 1319, Dosar individual, deschis la data de 17.10.1957 [Research, Exhibitions, Publications Directorate, File No. 2907, Vol. 1, I 260208. Operational Archive, File: Heinrich Zillich Operational Action, 3. March 1961, Stalin Regional, Service II, Office I, No. 1319, Individual file, opened on 17 October 1957].
NL Adolf Meschendörfer, Archive of the Institut für deutsche Kultur und Geschichte Südosteuropas (IKGS), Munich.
NL Heinrich Zillich in the Archive of the Institut für deutsche Kultur und Geschichte Südosteuropas (IKGS), Munich.
Personal fond Egon Hajek, B I 31, Archive of the Siebebürgen-Institute, Gundelsheim [Transylvania-Institute].

Website

<https://anno.onb.ac.at/anno-suche#searchMode=complex&text=Heinrich+Zillich&title=Radio+Wien&dateMode=period&yearFrom=1933&yearTo=1938&from=1>, accessed 10 September 2021.

WINFRIED R. GARSCHA

Being Made Jewish: A Secular Jewish Girl Fleeing Hitler's Vienna – Identity Discourses through the Eyes of Ruth Maier's Diary

Ruth Maier (1920–42) grew up in Vienna as the elder of two daughters of Dr Ludwig Maier (1882–1933), a senior official in the Austrian postal service and leading social-democratic unionist, and Irma Maier, née Grossmann (1895–1964).[1] Her father's family was Jewish and lived in Southern Moravia, in villages south-east of Brno. Her mother's family, who lived in Vienna, had Jewish ancestors but had no relations with Judaism whatsoever. Her mother's brother, Oskar Grossmann, was an Austrian communist journalist and member of the French Résistance. Ruth's father left the Viennese Jewish Community before she started to go to school. After her father's premature death from an erysipelas infection, her grandmother Anna Grossmann moved into their apartment in a municipal housing complex in the Eighteenth District of Vienna, a solid middle-class neighbourhood. A few weeks after the decease of her father on 28 December 1933, Ruth started to keep a diary in

---

1 For more information about Ruth Maier and her family, see Winfried R. Garscha, 'Wien – Oslo – Auschwitz. Das kurze Leben der Ruth Maier' [Vienna – Oslo – Auschwitz. The Short Life of Ruth Maier], *DÖW Mitteilungen* 234 (December 2017), 1–8. Biographical details can be found also in the introductory remarks to the different chapters of Jan Erik Vold's edition of the diaries. Cf. for the English version, which was translated by Jamie Bulloch: Jan Erik Vold (ed.), *Ruth Maier's Diary. A Jewish girl's life in Nazi Europe* (London: Harvill Secker, 2009). All quotes from the diary follow the paperback edition (London: Vintage Books, 2010). In his 'Translator's Note', Buloch stressed that Ruth Maier's sister Judith Suschitzky had looked 'carefully through the English proofs' (viii).

which she continued to write until November 1942, a few days before her deportation to Auschwitz.

There are only two significant gaps in her entries: January until September 1938 and January 1939 until March 1940. Although there are no diary entries in the first 15 months of her stay in Norway, Ruth's letters to her sister Judith ('Dittl'), who was already in Great Britain at that time, can serve as a substitute which allows an assessment of her situation as a refugee in Norway before the invasion by the German Wehrmacht in April 1940. For the dramatic events preceding and following the 'Anschluss' in March 1938, however, no statement of Ruth Maier exists. We do not know to what extent she and her family were affected by the pogrom in March and by the introduction of the Nuremberg Laws in Austria in May of that year. Because the Nazi authorities only knew the late Ludwig Maier as 'Jewish' (according to the Nuremberg Laws of 1935), his daughters counted as 'half-Jewish'. Nevertheless, the family was affected by the June 1938 eviction order of the Vienna Housing Office against 2,000 tenants who were either Jews themselves or spouses of a Jew. A friend of her late husband offered Irma Maier a room in his small apartment in Obere Donaustraße 43, in the Second District – a rather poor neighbourhood with many inhabitants of Jewish descent. Ruth and Judith were thrown out of school; from 2 October 1938, they had to attend the Jewish grammar school nearby, the Chajes-Gymnasium. On 10 December, when the first 'Kindertransport' left Vienna,[2] Judith was among the 500 children who departed from Vienna for London. Ruth was already too old for a 'Kindertransport'. Among the contacts of her husband, who had been secretary general of the 'Postal, Telegraph and Telephone International' from 1919 until his death in 1933, Irma Maier found a helpful Norwegian postmaster in Lillestrøm, east of Oslo. Arne Strøm and his wife Dagmar were ready to accommodate Ruth for the two years she would need to finish grammar school. On 30 January 1939,

2   Sabine Bergler and Caitlin Gura-Redl (eds), *Jugend ohne Heimat – Kindertransporte aus Wien*. [Without a Home – Kindertransports from Vienna] (Vienna: Jüdisches Museum Wien, 2021).

Ruth arrived there. Eventually, in late April 1939, Irma Maier and her mother Anna Grossmann found a way to flee from Austria to England.

In late autumn of 1940, Ruth met a young woman, Gunvor Hofmo (1921–1995) – who, after the war, was to become one of the most out-standing figures of modern Scandinavian poetry. Gunvor was one year younger than Ruth. The two fell in love and became closely attached until the time of Ruth's deportation. They had got to know each other at the 'Arbeidstjenesten', the Norwegian Labour Service. When, in May 1941, Ruth was confronted with anti-Semitism by Norwegian officials for the first time in one of the Labour Service camps, Gunvor defended her in a furious manner, and both left the camp, together with other girls (as for fe-males the Labour Service was not compulsory). Gunvor's family was linked with the Norwegian resistance movement. After the German occupation, an uncle of hers was arrested and sent to the Sachsenhausen concentration camp. Other members of her family were socialists or communists, who were involved in smuggling weapons from Great Britain to Norway.[3] In May 1941, Gunvor herself was briefly arrested.

In January and February 1942, anti-Jewish legislation was introduced in Norway. All people who counted as 'Jews' according to the Nuremberg Laws had to register. Ruth filled out the questionnaire on 4 March 1942. As present religious affiliation, she stated 'none (since 1926)', while as previous affiliation, she wrote 'Mosaic by birth'. On 26 November 1942, she was ar-rested together with more than 500 Norwegian Jews. On the same day, she departed on the German troop carrier 'Donau' from Oslo to Stettin. From there the deportees were brought to Auschwitz-Birkenau and murdered upon arrival on 1 December 1942. Gunvor Hofmo preserved Ruth's diaries.

The diaries were discovered in the late 1990s by the Norwegian writer and jazz musician Jan Erik Vold, literary executor of Gunvor Hofmo.[4] Jan Erik Vold could establish contact with Ruth Maier's sister Judith Suschitzky

---

3   See David Howarth, *The Shetland Bus. A Classic Story of Secret Wartime Missions Across the North Sea* (Lerwick: The Shetland Times Ltd, 2017). The first edition of the book was published in 1951.

4   See Jan Erik Vold, *Mørkets sangerske. En bok om Gunvor Hofmo* [Songstress of the Darkness. A Book about Gunvor Hofmo] (Oslo: Gyldendal, 2000).

in England. That enabled him to substitute lost diaries by letters to the
family. In 2007, he published a Norwegian edition of diaries and letters.[5]
The first German version followed in 2008.[6] Editions in Danish, Dutch,
English, Estonian, French, Hebrew, Italian, Russian, Spanish and Swedish
followed.

On the hundredth birthday of Ruth Maier in November 2020, the
Norwegian Centre for Holocaust and Minority Studies facilitated online
access to Ruth Maier's diaries, letters, drawings and watercolours,[7] which
had been listed in the United Nations Educational, Scientific and Cultural
Organization's (UNESCO) Memory of the World Register since 2012.
Although the majority of the diary entries and all her letters are written
in German, Ruth Maier's literary remains became part of the Norwegian
Memory of the World Register ('Norges dokumentarv'; Norway's document legacy), acknowledging the fact that Ruth Maier had found refuge
in Norway, when she had to leave Austria in 1939. On the occasion of her
centenary, Jan Erik Vold published a re-edition of her diaries in Austria.[8]
One year later, a Czech translation[9] was released. Thus, information about
Ruth Maier became available in the country where survivors of her paternal
family still live (her father's family had lived in Žarošice, 40 kilometres
south-east of Brno, and other parts of Moravia).

The centennial induced memorial activities in Austria, Norway and
the Czech Republic. Due to restrictions during the Covid pandemic, some
of these activities had to be postponed to 2021 or even 2022. In Oslo, a

5   Jan Erik Vold (ed.), *Ruth Maiers dagbok. En jødisk flyktning i Norge* [Ruth Maier's
     Diary. A Jewish Refugee in Norway] (Oslo: Gyldendal, 2007–10).
6   Ruth Maier, *'Das Leben könnte gut sein'. Tagebücher 1933 bis 1942* [Life Could Be
     Good. Diaries 1933 until 1942]. Edited by Jan Erik Vold (Munich: DVA, 2008).
7   <https://www.hlsenteret.no/aktuelt/nyheter/2020/arkivet-etter-ruth-maier-digit
     alt-tilgjengelig-.html>, accessed 20 January 2022.
8   Ruth Maier, *'Es wartet doch so viel auf mich …'. Tagebücher und Briefe Wien 1933 –
     Oslo 1942* [There Is Still So Much Waiting for Me. Diaries and Letters Vienna 1933 –
     Oslo 1942]. Edited by Jan Erik Vold (Vienna: Mandelbaum, 2020).
9   Jan Erik Vold (ed.), *Deník Ruth Maierové. Příběh židovské dívky v Evropě pod
     nadvládou nacistů* [Ruth Maier's Diary. The Story of a Jewish Girl in Europe under
     Nazi Rule] (Brno: Edika, 2021).

place near her last address, before her deportation to Auschwitz, now bears her name. In Vienna, a park opposite the last Viennese address of Ruth's family in the Obere Donaustraße was named after her. A Czech version of the 2017 Austrian exhibition, which took place 75 years after her death in Auschwitz-Birkenau, was completed by an exhibition about Ruth Maier's family; both exhibitions have been shown in half a dozen of Czech cities, starting in 2021 in the Jewish cultural centre Vila Löw-Beer in Brno and the village museum of Žarošice – always accompanied by public events like readings from her diaries, which would, on occasion, be attended by the Norwegian ambassador. In late 2022 in Austria, an updated version of the exhibition with a 'translation' into simplified German was shown in institutions for adult vocational training, which offer their services especially for migrant workers and refugees. Since 9 November 2021, the name of Ruth Maier as well as of 64,500 other Austrian victims of the Holocaust can be seen on the Shoah Wall of Names in Vienna.

Some journalists called Ruth Maier 'Norway's Anne Frank' or 'Austria's Anne Frank', an attribution that does not meet historical reality. Ruth was nine years older than Anne Frank and was never forced to live in a hideout. Ruth Maier's reflection of Judaism was not – as it was for Anne Frank – a religious dispute but a question of identity. Ruth grew up in a completely assimilated, secular family; she had no ties to Judaism and re- garded herself, like the majority of the population in interwar Austria, as German. According to her diary, Ruth Maier attended a Jewish service in a Synagogue for the first time in June 1942, five months before she was murdered in Auschwitz-Birkenau.

Ruth Maier's father, Ludwig Maier, was the oldest son of Šimon Maier, who had run a grocery store in Žarošice. The store served also as a post office, which was run by Ludwig's mother Jenny. The postmark ('Zaroschitz/ Žarošice') indicated the bilingual character of the village. The first language of the family was German, but, as a growing number of Jews in Moravia did, especially after the collapse of the Habsburg monarchy and the proclam- ation of the Czecho-Slovak Republic in 1918, almost all of them were able to communicate in Czech, as well. When Ruth Maier spent summer vaca- tions there together with her parents and her sister Judith, the grocery store belonged already to the third son of Šimon Maier, Viktor. Before Šimon

Maier moved to Žarošice in 1880, he lived in neighbouring Dambořice.[10] There existed a Jewish graveyard and a Synagogue as well as a Catholic and a small Protestant church. Žarošice has been an important catholic pilgrimage site. Perhaps the annual pilgrimage with thousands of participants every September had been one of the reasons why Šimon Maier bought a house in this small village and opened a grocery store.

From the very start in 1933, Ruth's diary mentioned the summer vacations in Southern Moravia. In July 1936, when Ruth was 15 and Judith 14, the two girls first lived with their uncle Viktor in Žarošice for some time, after which they spent some weeks with the Rausch family, peasants in neighbouring Zdravá Voda (in German Rosenthal). Both sisters became fond of the two sons, Vena and Jenda, of the Rausch family who still lived with their parents. Although the family spoke German, they had given their children Czech names like Fanda (František), Vena (Václav) and Jenda (Jan). Ruth Maier did not write about the religious affiliation of her family members in Southern Moravia but was interested in how the Catholic Rausch family practiced their religion. In a diary entry of July 1936, she wrote: 'Yesterday I heard the father, the mother and the two sons praying. I imagine prayer to be something more beautiful. Prayer is beautiful, to thank a greater power for work, for the sun and everything! But they rattle through their prayer as if they'd been forced to do it. If they're not doing it because they really want to, then they shouldn't bother praying at all.'[11]

In the interwar period, ethnic affiliations in Czechoslovakia were fluid. A considerable part of the population was bilingual: Czech/German in the Czech lands (i.e. Bohemia and Moravia-Silesia) and Slovak/Hungarian in Slovakia. This eased the transition from the German (or Hungarian) ethnicity to 'Czecho-Slovak'. Especially members of the Jewish communities availed of the possibility to change ethnicity. However, they could also opt for 'Jewish'. The highest number of Jews who defined their ethnicity as

10   The property situation of the realties in Žarošice is described in Jaroslav Vlach, 'Žarošické grunty a chalupy 1650–1950' [Žarošice Realties and Farmsteads, 1650–1950], *Věstník Historicko-vlastivědného kroužku v Žarošicích* [Bulletin of the Association for Local History in Žarošice] 24 (2015), 222–63 (house number 20: 254–5). Šimon Maier is characterized as 'Israelite, language use: German'.
11   Ruth Maier's Diary, 21 (entry without date).

Jewish lived in the easternmost districts of the Czecho-Slovak Republic in Transcarpathia (in Czech: Podkarpatská Rus, since 1945 part of Ukraine), where they accounted for more than 14% of the population, according to the census of 1930. Most of them spoke Yiddish, and almost all of them declared their ethnicity as Jewish. In the western parts of the republic, during the census of 1930, only 1.1% had professed their Jewish faith, and a declining number among them opted for Jewish as ethnicity. In Moravia-Silesia, the number of members of the Jewish religion amounted to 41,000. Out of these, 17% declared their ethnicity Czecho-Slovak, 29% German and 52% Jewish.[12] In Vienna, the situation was completely different. The town had 1.9 million inhabitants. According to the census of 1934, 191,481 were of Jewish denomination.[13] Ruth Maier's family was not among them. Both the mansion, where Ruth spent her early childhood, and the municipal housing complex along the Gersthofer Straße, where the family moved in 1930, are situated in the so-called cottage quarter, a neighbourhood with rather well-off inhabitants.

There are hardly any diary entries which deal with religion. Neither Judaism nor Christianity played any role in her family life before 1938. However, Ruth's mother celebrated the traditional Catholic holidays with her daughters, especially Christmas. She even announced the Christmas gifts by telling them that 'the baby Jesus is coming'.[14] After her sixteenth birthday, Ruth realized with sadness that the enchantment of Christmas faded. In vain she tried to keep it: 'Come on, Christmas comes only once

12 Under the title 'Počítat a mapovat: statistika židovského obyvatelstva v českých zemích' [Count and Map: Statistics of the Jewish Population in the Czech Lands], in February 2014, the Jewish Museum in Prague and the Terezin Initiative Institute published a compilation of statistics about the development of the Jewish population on their common website 'Naši nebo cizí?/Židé v českém 20. století' [Ours or Someone else?/Jews in the Czech 20th Century]. The numbers follow these statistics, <http://www.nasinebocizi.cz/wp-content/uploads/2014/02/6-01_Pocitat_a_mapovat_statistika_zidovskeho_obyvatelstva_v_ceskych_zemich.pdf>, accessed 20 January 2022.

13 Jonny Moser, *Demographie der jüdischen Bevölkerung Österreichs 1938–1945* [Demography of the Jewish Population of Austria] (Dokumentationsarchiv des österreichischen Widerstandes: Vienna, 1999), 7.

14 Ruth Maier's Diary, 32.

a year. You've got to be jolly at Christmas. I'll pray to dear God, he'll make me happy again […] And for a moment, a tiny moment […] I'm full of joy and I want to sing a Christmas carol.' However, when she saw the Christmas tree with many candles, she felt 'so terribly empty. I want to lie under the Christmas tree and weep.'[15] Later, under the Nazi rule, Christmas became a nostalgic symbol for a lucky childhood. She detested the idea that Nazis also celebrated Christmas. On 23 December 1938, she remembered: 'There was a peaceful glow to those Christmas days. They've stolen that from us, too. Peaceful glow […] This time we're not celebrating Christmas. Dita wrote from England to say that she'd lit some Hanukah candles.'[16]

This is the only entry in the diary which refers to Hanukah. By the time Ruth wrote it, she, her mother and her grandmother had already moved to the Second district, where Catholic and Jewish children used to celebrate both Christmas ('Weihnachten' in German) and Hanukah together – they called it 'Weihnukka'. This was a new world for Ruth. But, as her diary shows, she was not really interested in Jewish culture. Nevertheless, after the 'Anschluss' in March 1938, engagement with Judaism became a crucial topic for her. In the beginning, she rejected Zionism as a nationalist aberrance. Gradually, she developed a 'we feeling' in response to the anti-semitism in her surroundings and eventually decided, for herself, to be part of a kind of shared destiny. In her diary, she started to question her identity, which she continued to do until her very last diary entries in the autumn of 1942. The more the persecutions intensified, the more she felt that – in one way or another – she belonged to this community. Some entries in her diary are very decisive in that respect – for instance, her descriptions of the scenes on 10 December 1938 when she and her mother said farewell to Judith at the railway station as she departed to England as part of the 'Kindertransport': ' "Mama", I said. "Mama, look. Those are our young people, young Jews." '[17] However, she still continued oscillating between 'us' and 'they' when she was writing about Jews.

15   Ruth Maier's Diary, 32–3.
16   Ruth Maier's Diary, 116.
17   Ruth Maier's Diary, 112 (entry of 11 December 1938).

An important role in Ruth's identification with Judaism was the new school she was forced to go to, although initially she rejected the Zionist policy of the director, Emil Eliezer Nohel, a teacher of physics who had been an assistant of Albert Einstein at the German university in Prague. Sunday, 2 October 1938, was Ruth's first day at the Jewish grammar school Chajes-Gymnasium. Her first assessment noted thus: 'This school is so wildly nationalistic'. The headmaster 'expressed his conviction that we would all end up in Palestine. He hoped that even those who were "christened and godless" would enter the Jewish community'.[18] And she continued: 'Yes, that's exactly what the danger is: "the Jewish community". My community used to be the human race; is Jewishness now suddenly supposed to replace humanity??'[19]

At the same time, she started to cast her doubts on assimilation, which had been an unquestioned matter of fact for her and her family: 'And yet, is there not something completely negative, unwholesome, about always wanting "assimilation"? One's own demise, the demise of one's individuality?'[20] A few days later, on Wednesday, 5 October 1938, she witnessed a harrowing scene:

> It's early, nobody on the streets. A Jewish man, young, well-dressed, comes round the corner. Two SS men appear. Both of them hit the Jew, he staggers […] holds up his head, moves on.

I, Ruth Maier, 18 years old, now pose the following question as a human being. As a human being I ask the world whether it should be like this […] I ask why it is allowed, why a German is permitted to hit a Jew for the simple reason that he is a German and the other man a Jew!
I'm not talking about pogroms, outrages against Jews. Window smashing, looting of homes […] These don't express so clearly the incalculable brutality.

18 This is the translation in the English edition of 2010. The German original runs 'hineinwachsen' which means 'to grow into'. Cf. the scan <https://media.digital arkivet.no/view/135774/7>, accessed 20 January 2022.
19 Ruth Maier's Diary, 92–3.
20 Ruth Maier's Diary, 93.

It's here, in this punch. If there is a God [...] I don't believe in one and I don't like to utter his name [...] but now I have to say it to Him up above[...] if there is a God: This punch, it must be [...] it must be paid for in blood!!!
And I want to tell you, all of you, you Aryans, Englishmen, Frenchmen who condone this: all of you must bear responsibility for this punch, for you have allowed it to happen.'[21]
On 16 October, she was still aghast: 'And you students, you sentimental do-gooders, socialists, communists, dreamers, enthusiasts with your white hands. Why do you let it happen? Why?'[22]
        But back to her entry of 5 October 1938. At the Chajes-Gymnasium, she had learnt that this was Yom Kippur 5699. But the Nazis knew the Jewish calendar, too: 'The SA have devised a joke for it. They've informed the Jews that they have to leave their homes within three days and leave Germany within one month. "Or you'll be beaten up." Is that the golden Viennese heart, or the apex of bestiality?' And she identifies herself with the Jews: 'We're used to being bullied.'[23] As being treated as a Jew, Ruth wrote about 'us' and 'we', when she described what Jews had to endure in those days (still quoting the entry of 5 October 1938):

> I think of an episode outside the tax office in Porzellangasse. It was raining. We Jews had been standing there in the rain, soaked to the bone and freezing cold, since seven o'clock that morning. A street sweeper appeared with his broom and bellowed at us, waved his hands in the air, shouted. He was foaming at the mouth: 'If you don't go away, you bastards, I'll drag you all away.' How delighted he was, the street sweeper, that he could take out all his fury on us, the inferior race. The street sweeper!

An Aryan woman went in before us, although we'd been standing in a queue for hours and she'd only just arrived at the last moment. When she tried to apologize, somebody said, 'But my dear lady, you do not need to apologize. We're second-class human beings.' 'He said it without any

21   Ruth Maier's Diary, 95.
22   Ruth Maier's Diary, 99.
23   Ruth Maier's Diary, 96.

pathos. It sounded so dreadful even though we're not second-class human beings, we are [...] what are we in fact?'[24]

Racism baffled her: 'In the past people used to believe in evil spirits, in masters. Now they believe in race. And us, are we not all martyrs of race? I could weep for the Jews now, for my childhood dreams of humanity and its redemption. I don't believe in this anymore. No, it's true, I've lost my faith.'[25]

In Vienna, the organized pogrom of 9 November 1938 had been foreshadowed by a series of violent assaults against Jews and Jewish institutions which had started in early autumn. On Sunday, 9 October 1938, Ruth wrote:

> 'I'm amazed that we can endure it. That in spite of everything, we don't turn on the gas tap or jump into the Danube.'[26]

Some people just cannot take any more! Frau Herr's mother killed herself! To be away from here![27]
(In German: 'Nur weg!!'[28])

The following Sunday, the harassment and bullying aggravated again. Ruth Maier's entry of 16 October 1938 started with 'Pogroms! They are beating up Jews and want to hang them from street lamps [...] They're tearing off the beards of old Jewish men, they're bashing the women. They're smashing windows.' Ruth reminded herself to document such encroachments: 'Make a note of this, Ruth.'[29]

In the same entry of 16 October 1938, she oscillated between identification and spectatorship:

> And I love the Jews, that's the one positive thing. I love them because they are suffering. I love them from the bottom of my heart. Yes, I almost love them physically. These intelligent faces [...] I am a Jew [...] What more do you want? Cut open my veins, so my Jewish blood flows.

---

24 Ruth Maier's Diary, 97.
25 Ruth Maier's Diary, 96.
26 Ruth Maier's Diary, 97.
27 Ruth Maier's Diary, 98.
28 <https://media.digitalarkivet.no/view/135774/13>, accessed 20 January 2022.
29 Ruth Maier's Diary, 98.

She concluded her entry of this day: 'And I'm consciously becoming a Jew, I can feel it. I cannot help it.' But in the same paragraph, she apologizes for accepting the imputation of being a Jew:

'[M]y mind is all over the place. My writing is so incoherent!'[30]

(In German: Alles ist so kreuz und quer in meinem Kopf. Ich schreibe so wirr.[31])

Ruth continued documenting the outrages she witnessed: 'It was yesterday that they attacked another Jewish home and there are many young Jewish boys in bandages. Beating up Jews is a sport. The director of the home said, "It is a peculiar morality to beat up Jews" and he's right. It is actually a peculiar morality [...] Yesterday I walked past a Jewish shop. The glass windows had been cracked. A tiny hole and sharp lines. It looked so wicked. I may go to England as a nanny.'[32]

And then, the climax of violence was imminent: it was on 8 November, the day after the assassination of the German ambassador in Paris by Herschel Grynszpan, whose family was among the thousands of Jews of Polish descent who were arrested and deported to the no-man's land between the German and Polish border on 27 and 28 October 1938. Ruth noted: 'A small, seventeen-year-old emigrant made an attempt on a German diplomat's life. He's a Polish Jew. My God! The mood of despondency has returned; the air is full of sadness. The Jews are sneaking along walls like baited animals. Now it's dead. No Jew goes outside. We're all scared that they'll beat us up because a Polish Jew wanted to kill a German.'[33]

On her eighteenth birthday, 10 November 1938, Ruth Maier had to witness the excesses of the November pogrom, which had started the night before. On 11 November, she wrote:

> We've been attacked! Yesterday was the most awful day of my life. Now I know what pogroms are, I know what human beings are capable of; human beings: made in the likeness of God. At school the headmaster told us they were burning temples,

30   Ruth Maier's Diary, 98–9.
31   <https://media.digitalarkivet.no/view/135774/15>, accessed 20 January 2022.
32   Ruth Maier's Diary, 99 (entry without date, between 16 October and 1 November 1938).
33   Ruth Maier's Diary, 102.

making arrests and beating people up. There's a lorry by the school gate […] they've arrested three teachers […] then we're called to the telephone in turn […] like in an abattoir, we didn't dare go out into the street, we laughed […] cracked jokes […] we were nervous […] Dita and I took a taxi home – it's a hundred metres. We raced through the streets; it was as if war had broken out.[34]

The more Ruth identified herself with the persecuted Jews around her, the closer she got to Zionism. On 27 November 1938, she wrote:

This evening – no, late afternoon – we said goodbye to Uncle Rudi, Papa's friend. I noticed his eyes suddenly welling with tears. I was brave. Mama wept. We gave each other a firm handshake, Goodbye! Uncle Rudi the socialist also says I ought to think about going to Palestine, because as a Jew it's the only place I'd feel at home. It's this feeling of being at home, secure, human – that's what I imagine the Promised Land to be. Because the life I'd lead in England, France, maybe even in America, would only be that of an 'emigrant'. How tragic, how distressing this 'emigrant life' is. We, the German Jews of 1938, we know it. No house, no home, me dependent on you, you dependent on me, united by our destiny, by our sorrow. It sounds melodramatic, but that's how it is. Through our sorrow we're all holding on to each other tightly.

Is it not understandable that we're looking at Palestine for the first time with tears in our eyes? Think about it: we who are outcast, pale, deathly tired and battered, will we not, as children do, finally find our way back to our mother? And this mother is Palestine: the 'Promised Land', Erez Israel. The land: Erez. And will you hold it against us that our eyes glint, that we shudder when we think of 'the Land'. Of our land where we are at home. Yes! It's true, Uncle Rudi has fortified my belief in this, he said it, said out loud what until now had been stifled within me: we Jews are only at home "in Palestine".[35]

And yet, she still hesitated, feeling that the Zionist nationalism contradicted her socialist, internationalist conviction: 'To that I'd like to add, "today". For tomorrow, tomorrow socialism will come. Then our home will be humanity, the world. Then we'll be able to live as human beings among human beings.'[36] And a few days later, on 9 December 1938, she

34 Ruth Maier's Diary, 102–3.
35 Ruth Maier's Diary, 106–7.
36 Ruth Maier's Diary, 107.

noted: 'I just know that Zionism is not compatible with socialism. I saw it today. I'm a socialist and I'm striving to conquer, develop this socialism I feel inside me.'[37]

Judith, who turned 17 in March 1939, was one of the oldest children in the 'Kindertransport'. She shared her fate with hundreds of Austrian Jewish emigres. A great number among them gathered in the organization 'Young Austria', whose political orientation was Austrian patriotism and support for the British warfare against Nazi Germany.[38] Ruth, being alone and without having contact with other refugees in Norway, was cut off from political discussions about socialism and Zionism. But she closely followed the events in Germany and the fate of the persecuted German (and Austrian) Jews.

On 2 October 1939, she wrote to her sister:

> And then you say that you're not a Zionist. Dittl, I don't believe you. Moreover, I sense Pippa's influence here.[39] I'm past wrestling with the ethics of whether socialism contradicts Zionism. No, Dittl, I'm absolutely convinced that the only home the Jews have today is in Palestine. I'm only 'assimilated' as long as people appreciate my assimilation and understand that I don't adapt out of cowardice but that – in proud recognition of my particularity and my Jewishness – I'm doing what I consider to be right. But if you want this acknowledgement of sacrifice that accompanies our assimilation, you can go and look for it on the moon. To put it harshly, it's undignified to talk of assimilation at present. Tragic, if you want to be old-fashioned. Today, at a time when racial hatred is flourishing in Germany – and to a tiny extent in Norway as well – you can't just close your eyes and say, 'I want to assimilate, even if others spit on me and curse me as a "Jew"', can you? You've got to understand that! To assimilate as quickly as possible, only so that I can finally stop being a Jew – I call that undignified.[40]

---

37   Ruth Maier's Diary, 111.
38   See Sonja Frank, *Young Austria: Austrians in British Exile 1938–1947. For a Free, Democratic and Independent Austria* (Verlag der Theodor Kramer Gesellschaft: Vienna, 2015).
39   Jan Erik Vold researched her identity: 'Pippa Sirotkova, a communist and Uncle Oscar's girlfriend in Prague, managed to escape to Britain from Czechoslovakia' (Caption of the photo on page 134). 'Uncle Oscar' is Oskar Grossmann (1903–1944), who, as a communist, rejected Zionism.
40   Ruth Maier's Diary, 186.

Maybe it was the experience that even in Norway she encountered anti-Semitism that reinforced her conviction that Zionism offered a 'solution to the Jewish problem', although she herself did not want to go to Palestine but rather to the US. On 22 January 1940, she wrote to Judith:

> The Norwegians are very friendly. How to put it? Yes, they are a democratic people. Debate takes up an inordinately large proportion of the newspapers.

> So, a 'democratic people'. Does this mean that anti-Semitism is unknown here? Sadly not! In Latin I sit further to the front, at a desk where another boy usually sits. He felt moved to write on the desk: 'Jews not wanted here.' So I went and sat somewhere else [...] Look, Dittl, here we are again. You refuse to grasp that Zionism is a moral solution to the Jewish problem. Your argument that socialism makes Zionism unnecessary does not hold any water. The first thing is that you could just as easily replace 'socialism' with 'democracy' here. Democracy also demands the equality of all citizens before the law, doesn't it? So mix in the socialism! Now I ask you: do you think that the situation of the Jews in a democratic state is acceptable? Do you think that the sacrifice the Jews make in trying to assimilate is recognized? Do you not think from a moral perspective that it is degrading to be thrown out once, join another cultural community, only to be thrown out again? Look, if we could be allowed to 'assimilate' in peace, it would be the simplest solution. But they torture us, they don't like us! You were German until '38, then they threw you out, they said, 'You're a Jew!' Listen, don't you feel something akin to pride, pride that you're Jewish? For myself, I know that to the very end I will be as conscious of my Jewishness as my Americanness.[41]

After a dispute with German soldiers ('so perverted by German propaganda'), she wrote to Judith: 'On my way home I just mumbled, "My poor people." This wasn't an affectation. I feel the same today: my poor people! And yet I'm forgetting that the Jews are my people.'[42]

In some of her letters, Ruth told Judith about her soul mate Gunvor, about the Labour Service and her considerations about Judaism and Zionism. However, she concealed the fact that she had had a nervous breakdown in one of the Labour Service camps and had sought help in Norway's most renowned psychiatric clinic, the Ullevål hospital in Oslo. Her stay there from 3 February to 27 March 1941 was a time of reflection

41   Ruth Maier's Diary, 209.
42   Ruth Maier's Diary, 247 (letter of 23 June 1940).

not only about her relationship with Gunvor but also about her stance as a Jewish refugee. She documented a dispute with a Jewish refugee who, as a member of a Jewish community somewhere in Eastern Europe, had no understanding of Ruth's uncertainty about her Jewish identity. This is the entry of 3 March 1941:

> There's now a Jewish woman on the ward. She's forty-three [...] We talk together. She speaks Yiddish. As her Norwegian is very poor, I ask her where she came from. She answers with a beaming smile, 'But I'm Jewish!'.
>
> She holds my hand in hers, explores my features with her gaze, as if she were looking for Jewish signs in my face.
>
> For her it's a matter of course that Jews can only feel comfortable in the company of other Jews, can only have Jewish friends.
>
> 'Do you have any friends?'
>
> 'Yes.'
>
> 'Jews?'
>
> 'No.'
>
> 'What do you mean "No"? I don't understand.' When she learns that I live with 'Christians' she shakes her head in astonishment.
>
> 'I don't understand. They're not Jews but they feed you, let you live with them. No! You have to go to the Jewish community. You must tell them that you don't have any parents, that you're alone in Oslo and ask them who you can live with who's Jewish. After all, it's better to live with Jews than Christians.'[43]

Of course, Ruth did not follow the advice. On the contrary, she tried to integrate herself into Norwegian society, she continued her education, learning stenography, attending a course at a business school and working as an artist's model, for the famous sculptor Gustav Vigeland among others. She went back to her host family in Lillestrøm, and she continued her relationship with Gunvor. In late 1941, the Strøm family started to 'treat Gunvor and Ruth as a couple and invite them together for birthday parties.'[44] Gunvor's family also accepted her as their daughter's partner.

---

43   Ruth Maier's Diary, 284.
44   Ruth Maier's Diary, 367 (introductory remarks of Jan Erik Vold).

Gunvor's father had even photographed the two in April 1942, after they had been swimming.[45] However, she could not suppress her sense of belonging: 'Sometimes I see Jewish people and they have this completely – how shall I put it? – erotic effect on me. They awaken a feeling of love within me. I feel myself drawn to them [...] I love Jewish people. I'd like to go up to them and say, "I love you." I'd like to kiss them.'[46]

After Ruth had filled out the 'Questionnaire for Jews in Norway' and sent it to the police in March 1942, she was registered as a 'Jew'. In June, she entered, for the first time, a synagogue:

> It was very strange. The Jews arrived, well dressed with hats on their heads. One, with a white scarf and black cap, was praying before a sort of altar. He prayed and sang. The Jews would frequently join in, half singing and half speaking. (It was like the inside of a beehive.) When I closed my eyes it was like being in the Orient. Occasionally I could make out 'Adonai'. That's Hebrew for 'God'. I didn't feel as if I belonged there. I was a stranger. The Jews had black hair, they were short and dark. I saw them as Jews and myself [...] as [...] a non-Jew. There was something inside me that held me back from them. It used to be different. I was very close to the Austrian soldiers again. I wanted to talk to them. My people, I want to be able to say. And yet they're not my people at all. Their language stirs deep in my soul. On the train, I consoled one of them. He was talking to a Norwegian girl. She asked him where he was from. From Austria, he said. It made me feel so good. Afterwards I saw lots of them with their green peaked caps. They were so familiar to me. Their language is like a lullaby. I've come to the remarkable conclusion that I don't know the Jews after all. It's very sad. I'd like to be with them again. To love them unconditionally. Like when I was with Dita in the Zionist Union. They sang Hebrew songs. Back then I had a sense of where I belonged.[47]

In late October 1942, Ruth felt that her existence as a Jewish refugee in Norway was no longer secure. Maybe in order to keep Strøm family out of trouble, she moved from Lillestrøm to a dormitory in Oslo, at Dalsbergstien. On 29 October 1942, she wrote:

---

45 Ruth Maier's Diary, 368 (caption to the photo by Erling T. Hofmo).
46 Ruth Maier's Diary, 373–4 (entry of 22 November 1941).
47 Ruth Maier's Diary, 393–4.

They're arresting Jews. All male Jews between the ages of 16 and 72. Jewish shops are closed. That doesn't surprise me. I just feel sick. I'm no longer 'proud' to be a Jew. I can walk past a Jewish face without going wild. But when I hear 'the Jewish question' I get a nasty taste in my mouth. I'm tired of hearing that Jews are being arrested again. I think: Why do they bother? Zionism, assimilation, nationalism, Jewish capitalism. Oh! Just leave us in peace! It's so horrible to hear about the yellow badges and the Jewish martyrs. It's so repulsive. It reminds me of disgusting worms, slippery, foul worms.

And still there was her complete lack of understanding of the racist rationale:

People oppress others because of their views. People kill other people to defend their fatherland. But you don't punish, you don't strike other people because they are what they are. Because they have Jewish grandparents. That's moronic, idiotic. That's madness. It runs counter to all reason.

I cannot understand that the Jews can withstand this. That they're not going insane. I no longer love them with the enthusiasm of a 17-year-old adolescent girl. But I will stand by them. Whatever happens.

This Jewish martyrdom creeps up on me like a repulsive worm. Eating away at my thoughts. There's something absurd about it. I thought I'd been more blunted. Why does it not affect me as much when they arrest Norwegians, shoot them by the dozen as happened recently in Trondheim? Am I too egotistical? Can I not see far enough? I think it's the absurdity that pains me so much. Norwegians are fighting for their country. They're socialists, Jøssinger [Norwegian patriots]. They torture us because we're Jews. I'd like to be able to destroy this boundary that makes Jews into Jews. I'd like to see Jews without wounds. Without any at all. They should not weep any more. They should walk upright.

Oh, my Muscherle [=mum]. It's now four years since Vienna. And still there's the same pain. The same inner turmoil. It's being Jewish. This continual beating of defenceless people disgusts me. It's like hitting into something soft. It's disgusting. Perhaps they'll fetch me too. Qui sait?[48]

They did fetch her. Four weeks later.

The vast majority of Jews who were deported to the extermination camps regarded themselves as Jewish. Many among them tried to find

---

48   Ruth Maier's Diary, 406–7.

religious explanations for the horrors of the Shoah. A certain number of mostly politically active people did not want to allow the Nazis to revoke a decision they had made for themselves (or their parents had made for them): not to be affiliated with Mosaic belief. Either because they had changed their religious confession and become Protestants or Catholics. Or, like Irma Maier and her brother Oskar Grossmann, because they did not want to belong to any religious denomination. They were a minority of those who had been deported and murdered. It is questionable as to whether their ascription as 'Holocaust victims' is correct. In Austria, they, too, count as victims of the Shoah – even if the Nazi authorities did not know that they were 'Jewish' according to their racist laws – like Ruth's uncle Oskar. Oskar Grossmann's name appears on Austria's Shoah Wall of Names, although he perished in the Gestapo dungeon of Lyon, murdered by Klaus Barbie, supposedly in June or July 1944, as a member of the French Résistance. His murder had no connection with the Holocaust.

Ruth Maier is a telling example for Holocaust victims who do not belong either to the first or to the second group. They were persecuted by the Nazis as 'Jews', and they accepted to a certain extent that they had been forced into a kind of community of destiny together with 'real' Jews. Ruth Maier's diary shows how painful and complicated this process of 'being made Jewish' had been for these persecuted people.

KATIE HOLMES

The Inspector, the Men and the Mallee: Establishing a Soldier Settlement in 1919–20[1]

February 1920 was a difficult month in the Mallee region of north-west Victoria. The soldier settlers who had recently taken up leases on the newly opened lands were anxiously awaiting rain. Crowns Land Bailiff George Frederick McIntyre was particularly concerned about 'the water question'. In his regular report to the Assistant Minister for Lands Sir Donald McKinnon, he observed that 'the promise to provide water has totally failed'. Settlers were carting water '6 and even 8 miles' on roads that were 'badly cut up'. Despite this grim picture, he expressed his satisfaction with the men under his care: 'On the whole the men are behaving well and considering the hardships thro [sic] the dry spell and water carting that they are enduring are taking things very philosophically and I hear very little complaint.'[2]

Such a situation was not to last. Within a month McIntyre forwarded a letter from the body representing the local soldier settlers. The letter called on the government to provide some form of sustenance for the men who had no means of earning an income while they waited for their yet-to-be-planted crops to be ready for harvest. McIntyre advocated their cause: 'the

---

1   My thanks to Karen Twigg for her invaluable research assistance, including the discovery of the 'Inspector' file and much more. Thanks also to the Melbourne Life Writers for their insightful suggestions and editorial advice.

2   Public Records Office Victoria (PROV), VPRS: 5357/P/0000; M23426. 'Soldiers Settled on Green Mallee'. Reports from G. F. McIntyre to Sir Donald McKinnon (MLA); Secretary of Lands; and Director of Soldier Settlement, 1919–20. Hereafter McIntyre to McKinnon; McIntyre to Sec; McIntyre to Dir; this quote is from McIntyre to Dir, 10 February 1920. All correspondence referred to in this chapter comes from this archive and file.

Department holds all the security. The men cannot get credit […] It seems to me absolutely necessary to provide some means whereby food and raiment could be obtained till at least their crops are put in. I would be glad if you would communicate your views to me on this all important matter.'[3]

There is no record of the director's response. Although the soldier settlement scheme was still in its infancy, the troubles that would plague it for the next two decades, and lead to its collapse, leaving the state of Victoria with a staggering debt of £45 million, were already evident in the reports McIntyre furnished to the director: settlers with no experience of farming in the challenging Mallee environment; their lack of financial resources and dependence on the state for everything; drought; farms – 'blocks' – too small to support a family; returned soldiers whose mental and physical wounds left them ill-equipped to cope with the demands of farming. In Australia, this narrative is now well known. In the history of Australia's various soldier settlement schemes, most of the attention has been on these settlers and their often heart-breaking struggles to make a living. In this chapter, I seek to shift the focus onto the men appointed to oversee the project of settlement: the Inspectors of the Closer Settlement Board, using George Frederick McIntyre as a 'from below' case study. I explore the micro-level impact of the land settlement policy devised in the aftermath of the First World War. McIntyre's reports provide a unique insight into the personal costs for a man involved with implementing public policy. Through his reports, I explore his interiorization of the cultural myths that underpinned the policy of soldier settlement and his personal confrontation with the realities of the Mallee environment and the failings of the settlement scheme. The conflicts McIntyre experienced as he struggled to reconcile the disparities between policy and reality reflected the contradictions within the policy itself. Both were captive to two myths of Australian settlement – that of Australia as an empty land, a wilderness, and the belief in the yeoman farmer as the foundation of the new nation.[4]

---

3   McIntyre to Dir, 15 March 1920.
4   In the late twentieth century, the terminology *terra nullius* was widely used for the idea that British colonists viewed Australia as a 'land of no-one' when in fact it was owned and peopled by over 250 Aboriginal nations. For a discussion about the

As McIntyre attempted to navigate the evolving boundaries between public official, community leader, advocate and judge within the newly established soldier settlement scheme, we see the private cost of trying to implement a doomed public policy.

Australia suffered heavy losses in the Great War. With a population of less than five million, nearly 417,000 enlisted voluntarily – 38.7% of the male population.[5] Of these, 62,000 were killed and a further 156,000 wounded, gassed or imprisoned. For Victoria, the figures are 89,000 serving overseas with 19,000 killed. The Australian casualty rate of 64.8% 'was among the highest of the war'.[6] The challenge of how to acknowledge and repay this sacrifice was one faced by federal and state governments alike. Soldier settlement schemes provided one such opportunity as they sought to make small blocks of newly released farmland available to returned servicemen. This would have the added benefit of removing such men from the cities where they were perceived to be at risk of becoming a public nuisance and placing them in rural settings where, it was hoped, they would aid in the project of the closer settlement of Australia's vast 'unsettled' lands.

While other Australian states introduced specific legislation for their soldier settlement schemes, Victoria adapted its existing Closer Settlement Acts. These had been developed and refined in the decades prior to the war, with the ambition of settling an independent yeomanry across the Victorian state, with very mixed success, especially in the Mallee region.[7] Detractors of the scheme, especially in Victoria, pointed to the failures of earlier settlement schemes and warned of the risks for both the state and

---

history of *terra nullius*, see Merete Borch, 'Rethinking the Origins of *Terra Nullius*', *Australian Historical Studies* 32/117 (2001), 222–39.

5   Australia did not have conscription for the First World War.

6   <https://www.awm.gov.au/articles/encyclopedia/enlistment/wwi>, accessed 13 January 2022.

7   For a discussion about Victorian land settlement, see J. M. Powell, *The Public Lands of Australia Felix: Settlement and Land Appraisal in Victoria 1834–91 with Special Reference to the Western Plains* (Melbourne, Vic.: Oxford University Press, 1970); on land settlement in the Mallee region of Victoria, see Richard Broome et al., *Mallee Country: Land, People, History* (Clayton, Vic.: Monash University Publishing, 2020), chs 5–6.

settlers alike.[8] The Victorian soldier settlement scheme removed the requirement that settlers possess any financial or material assets and increased the
amount they could be advanced. After two years of the scheme, for Mallee
settlers this was further increased to £1000, a recognition of the particular
hardships of this region. Settlers were not required to pay a deposit on
their selected block, no repayments were required for three years and cash
advances were charged at a lower interest rate than the government paid
to borrow it. In Victoria, approximately 11% of returned servicemen took
up allotments on dry land farms, with most blocks between 700 and 800
acres in size. The Closer Settlement Board was the agency tasked with the
implementation and management of the soldier settlement scheme.

The scheme tapped into two of the founding myths of Australia. First,
that the land in question was an empty wilderness just waiting to be rendered productive when it was in fact Aboriginal land stolen by previous
waves of settlers who had, in many cases, denuded and degraded the eco-
systems that had sustained Aboriginal people for millennia. The second
drew on pervasive ideas about the quintessential character of Australia,
one of which valorized the independent bushman as the Australian 'type'
and another of which envisaged the yeoman farmer as the foundation of
the new nation (despite a predominantly urban population). During the
First World War, the idea of the independent bushman became incorporated into the image of the classic Australian soldier: the Anzac. Originally
an acronym for the Australian and New Zealand Army Corps, the Anzac
became the embodiment of Australian masculinity, demonstrating the
qualities of courage, adaptability, endurance and mateship.[9] The qualities

8   Marilyn Lake, *The Limits of Hope: Soldier Settlement in Victoria, 1915–38*
     (Melbourne, Vic.: Oxford University Press, 1987), 38–9.
9   The identification and articulation of these qualities have been turbo-charged over
     the past few decades as the promotion of the Anzac legend as the defining myth-
     ology of the nation has received staggering levels of financial investment, especially
     surrounding the centenary of the campaign at Gallipoli, Australia's first military
     engagement in the war and a resounding defeat for the allies. See, for example,
     Marilyn Lake, *What's Wrong with Anzac?: The Militarisation of Australian History*
     (Sydney, NSW: New South, 2010); Bart Ziino, 'The First World War in Australian
     History', *Australian Historical Studies* 47/1 (2016), 118–34.

of the yeoman and the Anzac would be realized in the soldier settler. As Marilyn Lake noted in her ground-breaking study of soldier settlement in Victoria, 'the Bushman was "the stuff of which Anzacs were made"; so it was hoped the Anzac was the stuff of which successful settlers would be made.'[10] The Anzacs would succeed where other settlers had failed. In the process, the Anzacs would be offered the opportunity to serve their country once again by advancing land settlement and the agricultural future of the nation and, in the process, heal some of their scars of war. 'Soldier settlement promised to restore men, many of whom had been damaged physically and psychologically by war, to their "natural" status as breadwinners and providers.'[11] As Scates and Oppenheimer note, it was 'an intensely gendered discourse'.[12] It was also racialized: yeomen, bushmen, Anzacs, were all presumed to be white.

For soldier settlers who took up blocks in the Mallee region of Victoria, these ideas of masculinity would be overlaid with a further expectation of the qualities needed to succeed in this setting. As I have noted elsewhere, the ideal 'Mallee man' was tough and resilient, moulded by the punishing Mallee environment.[13] The Mallee region of north-west Victoria comprises 4.5 million acres or one-fifth of the state's landmass. Its climate is characterized by hot, dry summers, mild winters and highly variable rainfall: the average annual rainfall decreases as one travels north, from 356 mm to 254 mm. In a drought year, less than half these amounts might be recorded, whereas double in a year of high rainfall. The variability of the Mallee climate is one of its defining features. There are no permanent water sources in the Mallee as no rivers run through it to provide relief to a parched landscape and settlement. A further defining characteristic of the Mallee is its distinctive *eucalyptus dumosa* – or mallee, as the tree became commonly called. When Europeans first encountered the Mallee

10   Lake, *The Limits of Hope*, 37.
11   Bruce Scates and Melanie Oppenheimer, *The Last Battle: Soldier Settlement in Australia 1916–1939* (Melbourne, Vic.: Cambridge University Press, 2016), 4.
12   Scates and Oppenheimer, *The Last Battle*, 4.
13   Katie Holmes, 'The "Mallee-Made Man": Making Masculinity in the Mallee Lands of South Eastern Australia, 1890–1940', *Environment and History* 27/2 (2021), 251–75.

region, they considered it 'featureless' and hostile, a distinctive but forbidding landscape. The *eucalyptus dumosa* was regarded as a scrub rather than a tree, its form too 'stunted' to be 'dignified with the name of tree'.[14] The mallee reaches between five to eight metres in height and has a distinctive root structure: several stems grow from lignotubers beneath or just above the ground. The deep-reaching roots were a water source for Aboriginal people and enabled the tree to survive drought and fire. From the settlers' perspective, they were a formidable opponent: mallee roots not cleared would continue to sprout, making the task of 'clearing' particularly challenging. Settlement of the Mallee became possible with the invention of a plough designed to jump over the mallee roots. It was a combination of these characteristics that made farming in the Mallee so challenging. In the words of a local newspaper in 1912, it entailed 'one of the most strenuous and resolute battles with Nature', and the qualities needed for such work included 'wise judgements, great foresight, boundless resources and infinite adaptability'.[15] In the post-First World War context, another suite of qualities was added to those required of a good settler: he now needed to be a progressive modern farmer, implementing the latest scientific ideas about modern farming methods. And he needed to be a domesticated family man, not shy of the responsibilities such a role involved.[16]

For men such as George McIntyre, charged with over-seeing the settlers who sought to battle this particular stronghold of nature, the task before him was enormous. His duties as an inspector in the soldier settlement scheme were clearly delineated: he had general responsibility 'for all matters pertaining to land settlement in [his] districts'. This involved supervising and advising settlers on the working of their blocks; collecting and receiving payments for the Board; reporting on and making recommendations on applications for advances to settlers; advising them regarding the purchase of stock and equipment; supervising the vacant blocks; furnishing reports

---

14   Flora Shaw, 'Victoria: The Mallee Country, "Letters from Australia"', *London Times* (5 April 1893), 13.

15   *Mildura Cultivator* (6 January 1912), 4. See Holmes, 'The "Mallee-Made Man"', 257–8.

16   For further discussion, see Holmes, 'The "Mallee-Made Man"', 262–3.

'and keep[ing] such office records as may be laid down'.[17] If such a list captures some sense of the range of work involved, it only hints at the kind of authority and status that such a role brought. Inspectors effectively had oversight over all aspects of the settlers' finances and their work as farmers. They were the Board's men in situ responsible for implementing the policy of land settlement. As I have observed elsewhere, they were also the 'eyes and ears of the Closer Settlement Board'. They were required to pass judgement on the 'moral character of the farmers under their watch, on their sobriety and levels of ambition, honesty and desirability as farmers'.[18] This gave them considerable power within the soldier settler community but it was not unchecked. Inspectors were in turn overseen by supervisors and the files of most settlers indicate interactions with more than a range of different inspectors over the course of several years.[19]

George Frederick McIntyre was born in 1864 in the small farming district of Heywood in western Victoria. His birth certificate lists his Scottish father's occupation as sheep farmer; he had upgraded to 'grazier' by the time of George's wedding in 1890. George's English mother was 20 and George was her second child. McIntyre's first employment with the Victorian public service was in 1889 as a warder at Melbourne's Pentridge prison (although his marriage certificate lists him as a railway porter. Perhaps he viewed this as a more desirable occupation?). He worked at Pentridge for 20 years, where he was in 'charge of prisoners' and assisted in 'maintaining discipline'. It seems an unlikely background for a Crown Lands Bailiff, but in 1909, he moved to the Mallee town of Ouyen to assume that role. Perhaps it was his earlier experience on a farm that suggested he might have some background to equip him for the job. By the time the archival record begins to fill out our knowledge of McIntyre, he had been working at Ouyen for ten years gaining significant experience of Mallee country and

17 Royal Commission on Soldier Settlement, Victoria, *Report of the Royal Commission on Soldier Settlement: Together with Appendices*, Parliamentary Paper (Victoria Parliament) (1925), 10.

18 Holmes, 'The "Mallee-Made Man"', 266.

19 For a discussion of the ways inspectors operated within the settler community and relations between Inspectors and individual settlers, see Scates and Oppenheimer, *The Last Battle*, part 1.

the very different kind of farming from that of the much-wetter and more-undulating landscapes of his childhood. Part of his role as a Crown Lands Bailiff was to inspect and report on selections, and he thus had oversight of the closer settlement scheme on which the soldier settlement scheme was based. He had clearly proved himself capable. The Director of Soldier Settlement Donald McKinnon described him as 'an old and trusted officer who has been specially selected for handling returned soldiers'.[20]

The area over which McIntyre had authority when his reports in 1919 commenced was 'green mallee', meaning it had never been settled. It was available only to returned servicemen. His work in 'opening up' this area included the classification of the land, showing prospective settlers the available blocks and then guiding them in the process of clearing. He would also advise on the suitability or otherwise of locations for community buildings such as a school or community hall or arrangements for a bush nurse and a school teacher. It is clear from McIntyre's reports that he saw the progress and success of the settlement more broadly as part of his brief. Each report began with a variation of the theme 'Sir, I have the honour to report for your information that progress is being made with the Settlement', before outlining specific issues worthy of mention. The settlement was an entity, and the settlers likewise a body of men with a collective identity over whom McIntyre kept a watchful eye.

In the first year of the new settlement at Manangatang, McIntyre penned his reports regularly, often weekly, depending on the activities on the ground. These reports offer unusual insight into the perspective of a Lands Department inspector. Within the vast archive of the Lands Department and the soldier settlement scheme in particular, no other inspector reports appear to have been kept – a significant loss given the importance of their role in the implementation of the scheme. The reports were an important avenue through which McIntyre could raise concerns and provide updates on 'progress and success'; failure was not part of the brief. The reports were also a way for McIntyre to present himself as hardworking, conscientious and capable, always working towards the success of the broader settlement project and with the interests of the men and the settlement uppermost

20   McKinnon to H. V. McKay of Sunshine Harvester, 4 December 1919.

in his mind. Presumably other inspectors were writing similar reports and voicing comparable concerns to McIntyre, but the clarity of his voice as he pleads for assistance is even sharper in the absence of a background chorus.

There were two people to whom McIntyre reported. The first, Donald McKinnon, was the assistant minister for lands, and the two men appear to have known each other for some time. McKinnon responded to McIntyre's reports, often in detail and seeking further information from him. He took a keen interest in the development of the soldier settlement scheme and conditions of the settlement, in particular the presence or absence of rain and the state of the water supply. While the correspondence between them is not personal, there is the occasional hint of a more familiar tone that is missing from McIntyre's reports to the other man to whom he reported, Secretary for Lands (and later Director of Closer Settlement) McIver. To each he would sign off 'I have the honour to be, Sir, yours obediently, G. F. McIntyre'.

McIntyre's experience in the Mallee and his relationship with McKinnon gave him grounds to make suggestions for what he thought was needed to ensure the success of the settlement. In one of his early reports, he outlined his list of steps to success, reflecting his experience and understanding of the challenges of the settlement endeavour: land along the railway should be the first to be made available, thereby 'keeping the settlement together and not having it scattered over large areas'; advise settlers that schools will be built; advertise times for prospective settlers to view land; provide each settler with a pass book 'setting out the amount that may be advanced to him and a lien on mortgage taken on the land from the amount specified'. He was also concerned about the comfort of the families that men may bring with them into the settlement: 'It would be well to induce settlers *to make fairly comfortable homes for their wives and children so they could live decently during the first and most trying months of their occupation* [*sic*]; the houses could be standardised thereby making them as cheaply as possible.' McKinnon was an attentive and appreciative reader: the emphasis in this quote reflects underlining which appears to have been added by him rather than its writer. McIntyre concluded his 'short paper' by noting his commitment to the broader ambition of the soldier settlement scheme: 'to people these vast and fertile regions with a happy contented yeomanry'.[21] There was no questioning his adherence to the cause. Nor was there any doubt regarding his willingness to express his opinion on how things should proceed. Regarding the classification of land, McIntyre wrote, 'Sir I feel that we are at the forked roads and to take the wrong turn now would be fatal to the settlement or at least retard it for many years.' He felt that valuations should be done according to set criteria and by departmental valuers, not private operators. Precedent was important: 'Parliament wisely in the past put a small price on its Crown Lands to encourage the pioneers to go back into the Wilderness, to carve out homes, and in my opinion, this should not be departed from.' It is not clear what McIntyre saw as the relationship between land valuation and settler contribution; however, on this matter, the state had already declared its hand: encouraging returned servicemen into the 'Wilderness' would be best achieved by removing any expectation of deposit or down payment on their lease. The effect of this was that many settlers went to their block without cash or capital and thus had nothing to tide them over during lean years. They became dependent on the Closer Settlement Board for everything, including 'sustenance' payments.

The soldier settlement scheme was ambitious and implemented in haste. Thousands of predominantly young and single returning servicemen presented a challenge to the government. Increasing numbers of them were a threatening presence on the streets of Australia's capital cities, and skirmishes between police and returned soldiers were rising in number. Despite considerable concern about the failure of earlier land settlement schemes, the Victorian government pushed ahead with solider settlement, repeating many of the mistakes that had characterized earlier endeavours. For men like McIntyre, the lack of time to plan and prepare for all that was involved in establishing a new settlement had significant consequences. In August 1919, two months after his reports began, he asked for information about each settler he was required to oversee and other basics for the effective conduct of his work: 'I have not yet got any books, to put my system into operation I would like this as soon as possible; also my district defined

---

21   McIntyre to McKinnon, Ouyen, 21 June 1919; underlining in the original.

and powers outlined.'[22] Equally pressing was the fact that he had nowhere to live and no office from which to work. The local Manangatang Hotel provided the only source of accommodation. Despite raising these issues, no action was taken. By September, he reported 'I am working under very great difficulties and I am very busy I am scribbling this between interviews that is [*sic*] taking place the whole time, and have got to write piecemeal.'[23] The following week he returned to the issue of his working conditions: the men had 'many wants', and they were constantly interrupting him while he was trying to write. The need for his own workspace where he would write and keep proper records was urgent, leaving him 'greatly handicapped'. McIntyre became increasingly desperate about this issue, anticipating the consequences: 'I am overburdened now with so many things to attend to, I have to do any writing at or near midnight as I have a constant stream of inquirers, and without proper records one is apt to forget and the whole thing drift into chaos.'[24] The reports were an important vehicle through which McIntyre could articulate his concerns; they were also a record of the challenges he was dealing with and, in the event that things did not progress as planned, or did not *progress* at all, proof that he had done his best and had at all times kept his superiors informed of the challenges.

The lack of planning, forethought and support would have significant implications for the inspectors, the settlers and the settlement more broadly. Accommodating the inspector at the local hotel with 'no conveniences whatever' and an 'overflowing workload' might have been the only available option in an area where everything was in the process of construction, but it was far from ideal, as McIntyre explained: 'I am besieged night and day, many wait about the Hotel all day waiting for me when I am out and when I come in I am surrounded by many that are not in a fit state to do business with.' He declared it 'absolutely impossible to carry on much longer under such conditions [...] I have no time for inspecting or giving attention or supervision to the blocks that should be given, nor with the din and bustle can the correspondence be attended to'. He needed an office

22   McIntyre to McKinnon, Manangatang, 2 August 1919.
23   McIntyre to McKinnon, Manangatang, 13 September 1919.
24   McIntyre to McKinnon, Manangatang, 27 September 1919.

erected 'without a moment's delay' and a clerical assistant so he could attend
to the core tasks of his role.[25] Adding insult to injury, he revealed that he
had not received his full salary or reimbursement for expenses since 1 July,
over three months earlier. McIntyre repeated the plea of this report almost
word for word to the secretary of lands in a report written on the same
day. To McKinnon he apologized for mentioning his concerns: 'I have
hundreds of worries [...] but the ones mentioned are pressing.' McIntyre's
rising desperation was palpable.

His location at the hotel and his exposure to the behaviour of men
who had over-indulged in alcohol may have been a contributing factor
to McIntyre's strong opinions about the availability of alcohol across the
settlement areas. He certainly took the role of the public servant seriously
in giving frank advice, most especially on this topic. He first raised it with
McKinnon in November 1919. Rumours were circulating that some people
were applying for wine licences and he hoped that 'the Powers that be will
not inflict this abomination on the settlement. It would be a calamity for
the community if these licences were granted here and I would urge with
all my might to prevent it.'[26] His comment to the secretary for lands was
equally forceful: 'Our burdens and troubles are very real without having
an atrocious abomination like the wine licences.' McIntyre believed that
the 'hot thirsty climes' of the Mallee magnified the impact of alcohol. He
also believed that the availability of alcohol affected the settler's capacity
to make good farmers. Inspectors would regularly comment on whether
they believed a settler spent too much time in hotels, casting a harsh moral
judgement on their behaviour. McIntyre described one settler as 'a poor
type of settler & inclined to drink. He is a married man with two children
and has had the maximum amount allowed for sustenance'.[27] In the eyes
of many inspectors, settlers spending money on alcohol when being supported by the state through sustenance allowance was an inappropriate use
of government funds. For soldier settlers, many of whom would have spent

25   McIntyre to MacKinnon, Manangatang, 6 October 1919.
26   McIntyre to MacKinnon, Manangatang, 29 November 1919.
27   Balance of Advances, William George Bailey, 15 May 2020. PROV 749/
     P00000000010.

years in the army living in close proximity to their fellow soldiers, the local hotel would have provided one of the very few meeting places, a chance to break the gnawing isolation of farming on Mallee blocks.

McIntyre's disdain for alcohol most likely pre-dated his work as inspector for the Closer Settlement Board. He was successful in enlisting the support of McKinnon on the matter, who then referred it to the chief secretary. McKinnon wanted the areas that were exclusively being developed for soldier settlement to be free of wine shops.[28] The Chief Commissioner of Police Sir George Steward was also enlisted to the cause. He conducted a tour of the district, which happened to include a stop at Manangatang to talk with McIntyre, and reported his thoughts to McKinnon, adding 'a personal note to the correspondence for your information and consideration'. Of particular concern were a 'number of men' whom police had found 'in a condition of lunacy arising evidently out of wine drinking'. Steward was prompted to make 'exhaustive and discreet inquiries on the subject of wine licences in these hot areas'. He concluded that 'if there is one thing that might possibly affect the success of the settlement of returned soldiers in the Mallee, it is the facility for obtaining wine, or, as it is commonly known, "Pinkie"'. Steward was quick to note that he was not a teetotaller and 'therefore not bigoted' (unlike McIntyre perhaps), but he could not 'too strongly press this view' to McKinnon. Four months later, Steward dialled up his language, this time in a note to the under-secretary for lands: the 'many instances of insanity among young men' were 'unquestionably entirely due to the excessive use of wine [...] The bald plain fact is that the use of alcoholic liquor in the Mallee district, on account of the climate, is, in my opinion, the greatest conceivable menace to the success of the Settlement.'[29]

The focus on alcohol and climate as the scourge of settlement is striking. While governments might be able to regulate where and how many premises were granted licences, it was the individual who would succumb to alcohol's damaging effects. The settlers could not be trusted

28   McKinnon to Chief Secretary Honourable M. Baird, 4 December 1919.
29   Police Chief Commissioner George Steward to Under-Secretary for Lands, 8 April 1920.

to refrain from temptation, and the 'hot climes' of the Mallee could push them over the edge. The responsibility for any settlement failure, therefore, would not be due to lack of planning or inadequate support, or unviable block sizes, but it could be blamed on the combination of climate and individual weakness. Attributing such agency to climate was not new. As geographer Mike Hulme argues, early modern Europeans frequently understood tropical climates as morally degrading, and other 'problem climates' were regarded as detrimental to mental and physical health.[30] The heat of the Mallee was regarded as a problem for settlers, and the trope of the 'Mallee-made man' was in part a response to the challenge of the Mallee climate, described in early land sale advertisements as 'absolutely delightful […] for nine months of the year'. The temperatures of the remaining three months where they might reach between 38 and 42 degrees Celsius for days at a time were not mentioned.[31] For those overseeing the soldier settlement scheme, it was important to link climate with alcohol because if the climate alone could jeopardize the success of the settlement, then the wisdom of trying to establish the scheme in the Mallee would be called into question. Similarly, if it were alcohol alone, then the failure would lie with the individual settlers – all returned Anzacs and thus otherwise national heroes – who succumbed to its temptations.

The views of McIntyre, McKinnon and Steward about the evils of alcohol had broad support among large sections of the Victorian population. The temperance movement had achieved considerable success in Australia while Victoria joined South Australia, New South Wales and Tasmania in introducing six o'clock closing in 1916. Initially a wartime measure, it was made permanent in 1919 and not revoked until 1966, by which time the 'six o'clock swill', whereby hotel patrons would rush to buy drinks before the bar closed, was recognized as contributing to a culture of heavy drinking rather than allaying it. But not everyone in the Mallee agreed with McIntyre's assessment of the impact of wine licences on the settlement. A number of local police submitted reports to the chief commissioner of police, all of them supporting the granting of wine licences

30   Mike Hulme, *Weathered: Cultures of Climate* (Los Angeles, CA, 2017), 24–5.
31   'General Plan of Subdivision of Mallee Blocks, the Property of E. H. Lascelles & Co, County of Karkarooc', 1892.

because of the accommodation such premises offered. In the view of one police sergeant, they needed more rather than fewer such premises, especially for the 'travelling public': 'As I know them they are well conducted, supply good meals and beds, rank next to well run hotels, and are highly appreciated for the great service they render, especially in the Mallee where suitable or indeed any kind of accommodation at many places is hard to obtain.'[32] Despite the advocacy of the local constabulary, the chief commissioner of police chose to oppose wine licences 'on account of the climate'.

The 'problem' of the climate was very real. The heat was not the only worrying feature of the Mallee. Of far greater concern was the lack of rainfall. Anxiety about this emerged early in the correspondence between McIntyre and McKinnon. The year 1919 was proving to be a dry one and in July, McIntyre suggested that contingencies needed to be put in place for stock feed in the event that things deteriorated.[33] In August, he received a telegram from McKinnon asking if the water supply was sufficient to enable the rolling of the Mallee to continue.[34] By November, the situation was getting serious:

> We are handicapped greatly by the dry season and the lack of water. The tanks are nearly all dry, except the channel ones and water carting is the order of the day. This entails great hardship and worry to all; if rain does not come to fill the tanks before cropping time, I will be at my wits end to keep going, as teams [of horses] will be required for the work, the roads are churned up in a fearful state, and great difficulty is experienced in getting over them, even with light loads, I have great trouble in getting about, many places impossible with the car and to get over them with horses would be out of the question.[35]

Water was needed for domestic consumption, but equally importantly for stock. Teams of horses – essential for ploughing, seeding, cropping, transport – that carted water also needed to be fed and watered.[36] In the

32 Sergeant McLoughlin to Chief Commissioner of Police, 30 December 2019.
33 McIntyre to McKinnon, 29 July 1919.
34 McKinnon to McIntyre, 5 August 1919.
35 McIntyre to McKinnon, Manangatang, 29 November 1919.
36 For a discussion about the challenge of keeping horses during drought in the Mallee, see Rebecca Jones, *Slow Catastrophes: Living with Drought in Australia*, Australian History (Clayton, Victoria, 2017), 58–60.

early years of settlement, roads through the Mallee were very basic. None was paved, and the light, sandy soil made for a poor, readily gouged, surface. McIntyre spelt out the issue of the roads in more detail in a report of the same date to the secretary of lands. The carting of water over long distances in searing heat slowed progress in the settlement considerably and the situation was serious, for the settlement and for McIntyre himself: 'the wear and tear and cost of water carting over sandy roads and ridges is awful. I now have the greatest difficulty in getting about this district, and [it] entails a fearful bodily strain as well as the mental worry; it is nearly impossible with the car, and horses would be quite out of the question.'[37] McIntyre promised to wire McKinnon immediately if enough rain fell to replenish the tanks. A telegram sent in February 1920 reported that the 'tanks have given out' and called for water to be carried in by rail to the settlements.

It would be months before rain fell and even then it was barely adequate. Water carting continued and McIntyre reminded the director of soldier settlement that 'the promise to provide water has totally failed'. It was a pointed criticism. Mallee settlements had repeatedly run out of water in previous droughts, and the Victorian government had gone to consider lengths to construct a system of water channels that would bring water from another part of the state to the waterless areas. The Mallee's susceptibility to drought was also one of the points raised by those who had questioned the wisdom of the soldier settlement scheme and the suitability of the Mallee as an area for it.[38] Opening up land for settlement without a reliable water supply abrogated the responsibilities of the state.

McIntyre suggested that the railways should bring in water to the new areas and hoped that rain would soon bring water down the channels built for this purpose – a margin note in the report records 'this has been attended to 24.2.20'. McIntyre was conscious of the responsibility the Closer Settlement Board held toward the settlers. He interpreted his role as inspector to be one of overseeing the progress of the settlers as well as being their advocate when necessary. When he received and passed on

37   McIntyre to Sec, 29 November 1919.
38   See Lake, *The Limits of Hope*, chs 1 and 2.

a letter from the secretary of the Manangatang branch of the Soldiers and Sailors League, he recognized the validity of their claim. The secretary drew attention to the fact that the settlers had been supplied with fodder, seed, wheat and manure but had been 'granted no living allowance [...] In our district the time is not far ahead when our children will be crying for bread and clothes as some of the settlers have been here a considerable with time with poor results.'[39] McIntyre observed to the director that 'the position is critical seeing the Department holds all the security. These men cannot get credit [...] It seems to me absolutely necessary to provide some means whereby food and raiment could be obtained till at least their crops are put in.'[40] He named ten settlers most in need of support. The department was responsive to these requests, and presumably those of other settlers and inspectors. A document contained in the file lists the names of the 211 soldiers settled on 'Green Mallee'. Ninety-one of them applied for sustenance, some for three months and some six, with grants varying from a minimum of £3 to a maximum of £39.

It is evident from McIntyre's reports that the lack of rain added to the stress of his work as a Lands inspector. He knew that Mallee droughts could be devastating and he worried about the viability of the settlement, the welfare of the settlers and the management of the scheme more broadly. Towards the end of 1919, his regular reports suggest he was almost at breaking point. In late November, he wrote separately to report 'a very serious complaint' to the secretary of lands about an incident he believed threatened to undermine both himself and the settlement. One of the inspectors' responsibilities was to approve orders (and thus loans) for settlers wanting to purchase equipment. Companies would often send their agents into the settlement areas to promote their equipment and one such agent demanded an order for a piece of equipment for a settler, accusing McIntyre of only issuing orders for another company and getting a commission for sales. McIntyre denied such charges and took them as a personal insult. Furthermore, he claimed that the agent – Mr Rust – had been spreading

39 Secretary of the Manangatang Sub Branch of RSSILA to Minister of Lands per McIntyre, 15 March 1920.
40 McIntyre to Dir, Manangatang, 15 March 1920.

such claims among the settlers. 'Now one cannot protect himself from scandal mongering lying rascals such as this, when they are men of straw but in this case he represents an honorable and well known firm.'[41] The Closer Settlement Board took up these charges with Rust's firm, and Rust wrote a detailed rebuttal of the charges, believing their discussion 'was merely a difference' of opinion about the timing of orders for new equipment – 'No word passed me which could be construed to infer that Mr McIntyre was in any way influenced to favor any particular firm.'[42] The Board pursued the matter further and called Rust and his boss into their Melbourne offices where he was grilled about his side of the story. Again he denied making any insinuations about McIntyre being bribed: 'All I can say is that we both lost our tempers.'

McIntyre's response to the incident with Rust, elaborated upon over a number of reports, reveals much about the nature of the settlement and his role in it. This small, nascent community of returned soldiers struggling to establish themselves in the midst of a drought was vulnerable. McIntyre believed that the settlers were particularly vulnerable to the influence of rumour and innuendo that might undermine his own authority. He could not sit in judgement on men if his own moral standards and integrity could be called into question. His reports thus both protested his innocence and projected his unwavering commitment to the men and the settlement project more broadly. In denying any suggestion of favouritism toward any particular firm, he noted,

> I hold no brief or care for any implement makers or firm but I do hold a brief and I care for the men who brave these wilds to make a home and thereby doing good to all and they need all the protection that can be given them from unscrupulous agents such as this one proved to be.

McIntyre demanded proof of an apology: 'I must have this to clear myself or be discredited in the eyes of those whom I am here to help and protect.'[43] Two weeks later, responding to the news that the 'scandal mongering

41   McIntyre to MacKinnon, 6 December 1919.
42   F. Rust to H. V. McKay of Sunshine Harvester, 9 December 1919.
43   McIntyre to Sec, Manangatang, 29 November 1919.

mischief maker' Rust had booked a night at the hotel, McIntyre observed: 'One thing is certain, Manangatang is not large enough to hold us both.'[44] Rust agreed to the request for a 'full and free apology' which was forwarded to McIntyre.[45]

While McIntyre's years as Crown Lands Bailiff at Ouyen gave him considerable experience in the Mallee with regard to farming and the management of the closer settlement scheme, his new role at Manangatang in helping build a community from its foundations presented a fresh set of challenges. He knew the importance of an untarnished reputation for fairness and impartiality as well as of the authority he carried in the town and over the lives of the settlers under his watch. But the management of a collective of men who were often far from family, neighbours and, sometimes, even the basics such as water was new. The fact that these men were returned soldiers added a further challenge: they were used to acting as a collective, used to receiving instruction (if not always keen to take it), used to having many of their needs attended to by the army. McIntyre may have been selected for 'handling returned soldiers' presumably because of his experience as a prison warder, but returned soldiers were no longer subject to army discipline, and they were not prisoners. They were, of course, all men. Only two women featured in McIntyre's reports, and that too only in passing reference: the local shopkeeper and the nurse. Some men did have families but they seem to appear only in the yearly inspector reports on each settler, particularly if the settler's alcohol consumption suggested paternal neglect. Despite the intention of the scheme to be a family one, the settlement world constructed through McIntyre's reports to McKinnon and McIver was a homosocial one.

By December 1919, McIntyre was exhausted. He too was far from his family, all of whom appear to have been living in Melbourne, some 420 kilometres away. He was still awaiting news on his pay, the cost of living was high and he was 'having a struggle to make ends meet'. In requesting a week of leave prior to the Christmas holidays, he noted that he had only taken a few days of leave all year and he needed time to 'spend a

44 McIntyre to Sec, Manangatang, 15 December 1919.
45 Secretary of Closer Settlement Board to H. V. Mckay of Sunshine Harvester, 13 December 1919.

few days where I could not be found and leave all cares behind for a brief time and be with my family'.[46] In a subsequent report, he anticipated going on a short holiday over the Christmas period. 'I am working day and night to fix everything up so the Soldiers will want for nothing during the Xmas holidays as I want a few days complete rest and I would not be contented if I thought they would want anything while I was away. I must get away where I am not known for a complete rest.'[47] Always the loyal public servant, McIntyre seemed to carry the responsibility for the success or failure of settlement personally. He was a high-profile public servant in a small community where everyone looked to him to answer their needs and wants. The work was intense and unrelenting, poorly renumerated and supported, and without basic living and working arrangements. His reports reflect the high personal cost of changing public policy: complete mental, emotional and physical exhaustion.

When McIntyre returned from his Christmas break, he no doubt hoped that some of the challenges he had left behind might have been re-solved. Perhaps he managed to meet with the secretary of lands, as he had requested, in order to discuss the 'many urgent needs' of the settlement. However, in reality, some problems had only intensified. Worst of all were the lack of rain and the failure of the water supply. Increasingly men began abandoning their blocks. At the end of January 1920, he reported on the attrition: 'During the last few days a few of the settlers have got despondent and have abandoned but in every case these men in the first place were totally unfitted and seemed still shocked and not mentally normal.'[48] The problem was thus one of individual failing, nothing systemic. He named the individuals concerned. 'I have no confidence in them and am sure would not make good at any kind of farming.' McIntyre sought to reassure the director of soldier settlement, to whom he was now reporting rather than to the secretary of lands, that the majority of the settlers were 'contented' and 'doing good work'. They had 'settled down in earnest' and 'with a normal season' would 'make good'. He returned to the question of the well-being

46   McIntyre to Sec, Manangatang, 29/ November 1919.
47   McIntyre to Sec, n.d., December 1919.
48   McIntyre to Dir, Soldier Settlement, Manangatang, 30 January 2020.

of the men in his following report, noting that 'on the whole the men are behaving well', taking things 'philosophically' and not complaining much. McIntyre's continued reference to the men as a collective hints at a latent military mentality inclined to treat them as requiring care, instruction and a disciplining hand. His 20 years as a prison warder undoubtedly left an imprint on his management of the men under his charge.

Some of the men *were* totally unprepared and unfit for farming, and McIntyre would judge them harshly. In April 1921, one such settler, William Krog, informed McIntyre of his intention to surrender his block. The inspector paid him a visit and found his property in a 'delipidated [*sic*] condition'. The horses and other livestock were diseased, equipment 'neglected and ill-used' and 'no chance of saving but little from the standing crop'. McIntyre was 'unsurprised'. He believed Krog was 'mentally unfit for farming. He is very cruel [words missing] has a very sick wife and but for her I recommend that the Board be done with him for ever.'[49] McIntyre's letter, now badly torn and incomplete, nonetheless conveyed his intense disgust at this settler's behaviour. Krog's cruelty seemed to be inflicted on everything the inspector saw: animals, land, implements and his wife. Such 'a class of men', he believed, were 'unfit for pioneering'. They retarded the settlement (perhaps reflecting badly on the inspectors), consumed valuable time, wasted money and bred dissatisfaction. They were 'a menace and drawback to adjacent holders' and would be 'certain failures on the land anywhere and should never be in a position to control money or property, till such time as they have given proof of fitness by working under supervision for wages etc.'[50] McIntyre joined other inspectors in readily assessing the character of settlers – whether they were deserving or not and classifying them as good or bad farmers.[51]

As 'pioneers', McIntyre expected the soldier settlers to be worthy inheritors of a mythology well established by the First World War period.

49   McIntyre to Mr Curry, Bolton, 8 April 2021, VPRS 5714/P0 unit 2042, file 881/12; <https://prov.vic.gov.au/archive/EA180107-F912-11E9-AE98-25B5B0B5A4B7?image=16>

50   McIntyre to MacKinnon, Boulton, 25 June 1920.

51   See Scates and Oppenheimer, *The Last Battle*, ch. 1.

The classic settler of the pioneer legend battled against the land, tamed the wilderness and triumphed over the elements. He was endowed with the qualities of 'courage, enterprise, hard work and perseverance'.[52] A 1915 article from a Mallee newspaper the *Ultima and Chillingollah Star* celebrated the men who had sought to tame the Mallee and 'established themselves in the wilderness'. These men were 'no weaklings [...] but sturdy, willing, hardworking, brave-hearted, plodding pioneers'. They had an 'undaunted and an all-conquering spirit' and had 'made history'.[53] In drawing on the language and mythology of the pioneer, one which was closely aligned with the idea of the yeoman farmer, McIntyre was evoking a particular type of man and activity. History-making was white men's work (erasing an Indigenous past), and it was done by transforming nature, ensuring the success of the nation and the settlement of rural spaces. For McIntyre, men who were not endowed with the qualities of the pioneer or did not live up to his standards – whether because of excessive alcohol consumption, lack of application or mental strength – had no place in the Mallee. The stress was once again on the individual's characteristics and capacity. McIntyre acknowledged the failure of the state to supply water and the extreme difficulties of attempting to establish farms in drought conditions, but his attention to individual settlers' failures and his stress on the positive outlook of the majority of the men – 'hopeful and in good heart' – suggests his strong belief that success in the Mallee was a matter of individual perseverance combined with some appropriate state support. McIntyre himself was clearly a man of strong will and determination; he respected and expected such qualities in the men in his charge.

The year 1920 was an improvement on the previous year. Although good rain held off for many months, there was enough to enable the crops to grow and for McIntyre to report in June that if the season maintained its current trajectory until harvest time, 'the Settlement will be in a good position, and success will be assured'.[54] He was keen to encourage the settlers to take up 'outside work, to bring in some ready cash to keep down store

---

52   J. B. Hirst, 'The Pioneer Legend', *Historical Studies* 18/71 (1978), 316.
53   *Ultima & Chillingollah Star* (10 September 1915), 354.
54   McIntyre to MacKinnon, Boulton, 25 June 20.

bills', and to contribute to the success of the district by working on the roads and channels that were desperately needed for transport and water. McIntyre himself seemed less stressed than before. Early in the year, he was given a clerical assistant and by March they had an office – but no furniture – at the nearby township of Boulton – some distance from the Manangatang Hotel, although not far enough to stop him declaring the public house 'a great hindrance and a terrible menace to the whole settlement'. By November 1920, the season was looking good, and the settlers were 'in good heart'. McIntyre seemed to share their mood: 'The season continues all that could be desired, and a record harvest for the Mallee is assured [...] We are getting a good number of new settlers and many are still coming, and we are working at high pressure to get the rolling down and scrub cleared.'[55] His upbeat tone belies the problems that would continue to challenge the soldier settlement scheme, not least being the environmental devastation caused by the widespread rolling down and clearing of scrub so celebrated here.

McIntyre's November report was the last one filed in the 'Green Mallee' soldier settlement file; he slipped quietly out of the archive. He stayed on at Manangatang until he resigned in September 1921 for reasons unknown.[56] He was 56. He died in 1933 in the Melbourne suburb of Coburg, aged 67. His death certificate indicates he had been suffering from gallbladder trouble for years and died after surgery to remove it.

When George Frederick McIntyre took on the role of inspector for the soldier settlement scheme, he was determined that both the men and the settlement itself would succeed. Evident throughout his reports, however, are the tensions between the new settlement as an imagined enterprise and the realities of establishing small farms in the challenging Mallee environment. McIntyre's determination and will were not enough to counter the personal challenges he faced or the problems encountered by the fledging settlement. As he worked to bring a new settlement into being, to help the settlers clear the mallee scrub, sow crops and establish farms, he looked to the ideals of the settlement scheme and the legendary status of those who

55   McIntyre to Dir, Bolton, 12 November 1920.
56   *Victorian Government Gazette* (Wednesday, 5 October 1921), 3452.

had gone before. Like the government, he clung to the belief of a settled yeomanry populating Australia's rural spaces. Although McIntyre had a more realistic understanding of the challenges of the Mallee environment than the designers of the soldier settlement scheme, even he believed that the men could 'carve out homes' in the wilderness and transform this drought-prone land into viable farms. But as his reports reveal, the signs of trouble were evident at the very beginning of the scheme and McIntyre exposed the problems that would plague the soldier settlement scheme through to its abandonment in the 1930s. They also reveal the power of ideology in the face of alternate environmental realities. As we now know, much personal, social, environmental and economic damage could have been avoided if adherence to the ideals of rural settlement had not muted detractors of the scheme and rendered invisible the characteristics of the distinctive Mallee environment and the realities of farming the region.

Bibliography

Broome, Richard, Charles Fahey, Andrea Gaynor, and Katie Holmes, *Mallee Country: Land, People, History* (Clayton, Vic: Monash University Publishing, 2020).

Hirst, J. B. 'The Pioneer Legend.' *Historical Studies* 18, no. 71 (1978): 316–37.

Holmes, Katie, 'The "Mallee-Made Man": Making Masculinity in the Mallee Lands of South Eastern Australia, 1890–1940.' *Environment and History* 27, no. 2 (May 1, 2021): 251–75.

Hulme, Mike, *Weathered: Cultures of Climate* (Los Angeles, California: Sage, 2017).

Jones, Rebecca, *Slow Catastrophes: Living with Drought in Australia* (Clayton, Victoria: Monash University Publishing, 2017).

Lake, Marilyn, *The Limits of Hope: Soldier Settlement in Victoria, 1915–38* (Melbourne: Oxford University Press, 1987).

Lake, Marilyn, *What's Wrong with Anzac?: The Militarisation of Australian History* (Sydney, NSW: New South, 2010).

Powell, J. M., *The Public Lands of Australia Felix: Settlement and Land Appraisal in Victoria 1834–91 with Special Reference to the Western Plains* (Melbourne, Victoria: Oxford University Press, 1970).

Royal Commission on Soldier Settlement, Victoria, *Report of the Royal Commission on Soldier Settlement: Together with Appendices*, Parliamentary Paper (Victoria. Parliament; H. J. Green, Government Printer, 1925).

Scates, Bruce, and Melanie Oppenheimer, *The Last Battle: Soldier Settlement in Australia 1916–1939* (Melbourne, Australia: Cambridge University Press, 2016).

Shaw, Flora. 'Victoria: The Mallee Country, "Letters from Australia."' *London Times*, April 5, 1893.

Ziino, Bart. 'The First World War in Australian History.' *Australian Historical Studies* 47, no. 1 (January 2, 2016): 118–34.

MARKUS WURZER

Colonial Wars, Dis/Loyalty and Discourses of Belonging at Italy's Margins

In Südtirol/Alto Adige,[1] an autonomous province in Northern Italy, the twentieth-century past regularly causes a stir. Debates over its interpretation threaten to destabilize the painstakingly negotiated coexistence between the German and Ladin language groups, on the one hand, and the Italian, on the other. For example, when, on 2 November 2015 to commemorate the end of the First World War, the municipal council of the city of Brixen/Bressanone together with the Assoziazione Nazionale Alpini (ANA), representing the Italian mountain troops, laid a wreath at the grave of Heinrich Sader, a German-speaking local who was killed in 1931 during the 'pacification' of Italy's colony Libya.[2] Hartmuth Staffler, a spokesman for the Südtiroler Freiheit (Südtiroler Freedom) Party, sharply criticized this.[3] This right-wing party pursues the goal of 'a Süd-Tirol independent of Italy';[4] from its point of view, the province's

1 Behind the terms 'Südtirol' and 'Alto Adige' are German and Italian nationalist claims to power, respectively, because they emphasize either belonging to the Austrian Tirol or to the Italian catchment area of the Adriatic, into which the Adige drains. In order to take these opposing perspectives into account, I leave these terms untranslated in direct quotations. In the body text, I include both variants.

2 'Heinrich Sader', *Alpenzeitung* (1 May 1936), 4.

3 Harthmuth Staffler, 'Brixen: Imperialismus noch aktuell – Kritik an Kranzniederlegung', <https://suedtiroler-freiheit.com/2015/11/03/brixen-imperialismus-noch-aktuell-kritik-an-kranzniederlegung/>, accessed 4 September 2023.

4 'Das sind wir', <https://suedtiroler-freiheit.com/bewegung/>, accessed 4 September 2023; 'ein von Italien unabhängiges Süd-Tirol'; all translations are my own unless otherwise noted.

population should be able to decide in a plebiscite whether it wants to remain with Italy, be its own state or merge with the Austrian Tyrol.

Staffler took particular offence at the site of the commemoration: Sader's grave, which had been erected in 1936 at the instigation of the local fascist authorities, is not considered neutral but rather as an 'imperialist monument', given its aesthetic and inscription, which reads 'Errico Sader / heroic son of Bressanone / fell on African soil / for the greater Italy / 1909–1931'.[5] Consequently, this right-wing spokesperson condemned the instrumentalization of the German-speaking dead man and local politicians' lack of distance from the fascist memorial;[6] at the same time, however, he seized this occasion to challenge Südtirol/Alto Adige's political belonging to Italy and lent weight to his party's desire to change the state borders in favour of its independence.

Although the debate about Südtirol/Alto Adige's political belonging is centuries old, it really took off in the nineteenth century with the rise of nationalism. Back then, nationalist players from both sides started to draw borders, create identities and thus lay claim to the mountainous borderscape. While the Italians began insisting that the Brenner/Brennero Pass in the Central Alps was the 'natural' border, the Germans were arguing for an imagined border further south between the language groups. Later, in 1920, when the area was finally seized by Italy after the First World War as a result of the Peace Treaty of Saint-Germain-en-Laye, the German-speaking group inhabiting the area perceived this as a shock and still remember it as a Zeitenwende.[7] For centuries, they had been part of the Habsburg Empire and its dominant language group. Now, within the Italian state, however, they formed a politically marginalized and oppressed language minority. A debate about the legitimacy of the new state border immediately began and lasted throughout the interwar period. At its centre, among others,

5   Staffler, 'Brixen'; 'Errico Sader/Figlio eroico di Bressanone/caduto in terra d'Africa/
     per la più grande Italia/1909–1931'; 'Errico' is the Italian version of the German
     name 'Heinrich'.
6   Staffler, 'Brixen'.
7   For instance, see Georg Grote, *Im Schatten der Zeitenwende. Leben in Tirol 1900–
     1918* (Bozen: Athesia, 2019).

were men like Sader. As German-speaking soldiers, they were involved in the fascist regime's colonial expansion because the fascist dictatorship relied on conscription and military service – besides other well-researched measures[8] – in order to legitimize its rule and enforce state sovereignty over the region's German-speaking majority. On the one hand, the regime tried to sell the service, especially deployments in the colonial wars that Italy fought in North and East Africa in the 1920s and 1930s, as a statement of loyalty. On the other hand, German secessionists, who believed that Südtirol/ Alto Adige was unrightfully part of Italy, instrumentalized the conscripts in order to challenge the legitimacy of the state border.

Only recently have historians begun to recognize that colonial expansion had been central to Italy's nation-building project.[9] In the case of Südtirol/Alto Adige, the integration of German speakers into Italy's colonial wars also provided the setting for arguing about the region's political affiliation. Therefore, this chapter examines the social constructions and (re-)negotiations of borders and identities in the alpine borderscape of Südtirol/Alto Adige in the interwar period. In the second section of the chapter, I address discourses of belonging by drawing on newspaper reports published in Italy, Germany and Austria. The third section contrasts these identity politics from 'above' with an analysis of ego documents such as diaries and photographs to analyse how German speakers articulated feelings of belonging from 'below'. Before launching into the analysis, in the following section I provide some historical context on the integration of Südtirol/Alto Adige into the Italian 'nation-empire'.[10]

8   For instance, see Sabrina Michielli and Hannes Obermair (eds), *BZ '18–'45: ein Denkmal, eine Stadt, zwei Diktaturen. Begleitband zur Dokumentations-Ausstellung im Bozener Siegesdenkmal* (Vienna: Folio, 2016), 52.

9   Roberta Pergher, 'Impero immaginario, impero vissuto. Recenti sviluppi nella storiografia del colonialismo italiano', *Ricerche di storia politica* 10/1 (2007), 53– 66, 58; Nicola Labanca, 'L'Impero del fascismo. Lo stato degli studi', in Riccardo Bottoni (ed.), *L'Impero fascista. Italia ed Etiopia (1935–1941)* (Bologna: Mulino, 2008), 35–62, 42; Valeria Deplano and Alessandro Pes, 'Introduzione', in Valeria Deplano and Alessandro Pes (eds), *Quel che resta dell'Impero. La cultura coloniale degli italiani* (Milan: Mimesis, 2014), 9–16, 11.

10   Roberta Pergher, *Mussolini's Nation-Empire: Sovereignty and Settlement in Italy's Borderlands, 1922–1943* (Cambridge: Cambridge University Press, 2018).

Südtirol/Alto Adige as an 'internal colony' of the
Italian Empire

When Italy took possession of Südtirol/Alto Adige following the First
World War in 1920, the young kingdom had already been participating
in the European 'race for Africa' for at least 38 years. The colonial late-
comer had seized swathes of land by purchase and military occupation
in the 1880s and established colonies in Eritrea (1882) and Somalia
(1889). Further colonial efforts in East Africa, however, failed. In 1896,
Emperor Menelik II succeeded in putting a (temporary) end to Italy's
colonial dreams in the Battle of Adwa. In 1911–12, Italy took advantage
of the Ottoman Empire's weakness and, in addition to the Dodecanese
Islands in the Aegean Sea, occupied the two provinces of Cyrenaica and
Tripolitania on the North African coast.[11] By referring to the geographical extent of the Ancient Roman Empire, nationalists revealed that they
considered both provinces as 'natural' Italian possessions.

To legitimize the seizure of Trentino, Istra/Istria and Südtirol/Alto
Adige along Italy's north-eastern border after the First World War, nationalists fell back on the same narrative: since ancient times, the watersheds
of the Adriatic Sea had been considered as Italy's 'natural' border, and
now, in 1920, its Italian-speaking inhabitants had finally been 'redeemed'.
However, these new provinces were also home to around 500,000 people
who spoke Slovenian, German and Ladin – but not Italian – as their mother
tongues.[12] While the Italian authorities initially treated them quite liber-
ally, this changed when fascists took power in 1922.[13] The enforcement
of state sovereignty in the border regions was of great importance to the
regime – this was especially true in the province of Bozen/Bolzano where

11   Nicola Labanca, 'Erinnerungskultur, Forschung und Historiografie zum
      Abessinienkrieg', in Gerald Steinacher (ed.), *Zwischen Duce und Negus.
      Abessinienkrieg und Südtirol 1935–1941* (Bolzano: Athesia, 2006), 33–57, 38–9.
12   Pergher, *Mussolini's Nation-Empire*, 12–14.
13   Rolf Steininger, *Südtirol. Vom Ersten Weltkrieg bis zur Gegenwart*
      (Innsbruck: Haymon, 2012), 19.

its rule was vigorously questioned due to disparities in size between the language groups: around 90% of the locals spoke either German or Ladin. The nationalists' argument of 'redemption' was therefore a weak one.[14] Consequently, fascists began to assert their claim to rule over the province and to affirm its 'Italian' character, so vehemently claimed by propaganda, through various measures. Indeed, anti-Italians were to be ousted, '*Allogeni*'[15] were to be assimilated through a repressive denationalization and Italianization policy while 'real' Italians from the old provinces were to be settled.[16] Furthermore, German and Ladin were forbidden in the public sphere, and topographical names were Italianized.[17] The '*Allogeni*' also lost their political representation. The only party, the Deutsche Verbund (German Association), was dissolved in 1926.[18] Through all these measures, 'not just a colonisation of the land – an ethnic filling-in up to the border – but a radical erasure of [German and Ladin] Otherness' was set in motion.[19] According to Mia Fuller, 'the campaign of cultural cleansing that Italy waged in Alto Adige/Südtirol [...] was far more detailed, and certainly had an even greater impact, than its equivalent in Libya or any other external colony'.[20] Therefore, along with Sicily, Fuller describes the province of Bozen/Bolzano as one of Italy's 'internal' colonies.[21] This is a historical interpretation that seems to correspond with contemporary perceptions: Hake, a correspondent for the Swedish daily *Svenska Dagbladet*, reported about the situation in the province in June 1928 that 'the Südtiroler are outlaws, they no longer have any rights. Young fascists can allow themselves every

14   Pergher, *Mussolini's Nation-Empire*, 15.
15   Fascists created this term to express that non-Italian speakers of the new provinces were native but foreign. They only had to be 'reminded' of their forgotten 'Italian' heritage; see Pergher, *Mussolini's Nation-Empire*, 56–7, 182, 246.
16   Pergher, *Mussolini's Nation-Empire*, 56–7.
17   Mia Fuller, 'Laying Claim: Italy's Internal and External Colonies', in Marco Ferrari, Andrea Bagnato and Elisa Pasqual (eds), *A Moving Border: Alpine Cartographies of Climate Change* (Irvington: Columbia Books on Architecture and the City, 2019), 98–111, 109–11.
18   Pergher, *Mussolini's Nation-Empire*, 64.
19   Fuller, 'Laying Claim', 111.
20   Fuller, 'Laying Claim', 109.
21   Fuller, 'Laying Claim', 98–111.

kind of assault against the inhabitants; they [the fascists] are acting worse than in a colony.'[22]

By 1939, the proportion of Italian speakers in the province was already 24%.[23] Twelve years earlier, Benito Mussolini had told the province's prefect that he believed that the assimilation of the '*Allogeni*' adult population was hardly possible, but at the same time presented himself as convinced that their children could still be moulded into 'real' fascists.[24] Schools, fascist youth associations and the fascist militia became important organizations in this attempt to indoctrinate children and young people.[25] Another was the military. Conscription had already been reintroduced in Italy in 1921.[26] Protests by German-speaking men who did not want to serve in the army their fathers had fought against in the First World War went unheeded.[27] During the 12 to 18 months of service, the German speakers were mostly ordered to the old provinces, where the Italian-speaking group domin-ated. According to Martha Verdorfer, most German speakers considered military service as a civic duty, the fulfilment of which, however, could not be equated with a loyal commitment to the state, which was perceived as 'foreign'.[28] Rather, it may have been a strategy of 'minimal loyalty',[29] so that

22   ' "Bei den 200.000 Vogelfreien in Südtirol". Feststellungen eines Neutralen',
      Innsbrucker Nachrichten (21 June 1928), 3; 'Die Südtiroler sind vogelfrei, irgend
      ein Recht besteht nicht mehr. Junge Faschisten können sich gegen die Einwohner
      Uebergriffe jeder Art erlauben. Man geht schlimmer vor als in einer Kolonie'.

23   Fuller, 'Laying Claim', 108–9; Pergher, *Mussolini's Nation-Empire*, 69; in Venezia
      Giulia, by comparison, around 40% of the inhabitants were Italian-speaking.

24   Pergher, *Mussolini's Nation-Empire*, 64–5.

25   The structures and activities of these organizations in Südtirol/Alto Adige form
      major desiderata, the investigation of which seems extremely worthwhile, especially
      with regard to the attempted 'Italianization' of the province.

26   Gerald Steinacher, 'Vom Amba Alagi nach Bozen. Spurensuche in Südtirol', in
      Steinacher, *Zwischen Duce und Negus*, 13–32, 16.

27   Martha Verdorfer, *Zweierlei Faschismen. Alltagserfahrungen in Südtirol 1918–1945*
      (Vienna: Verlag für Gesellschaftskritik, 1990), 83.

28   Verdorfer, *Zweierlei Faschismen*.

29   Oswald Überegger, 'Minderheiten-Soldaten. Staat, Militär und Minderheiten im
      Ersten Weltkrieg – eine Einführung', in Oswald Überegger (ed.), *Minderheiten-
      Soldaten. Ethnizität und Identität in den Armeen des Ersten Weltkriegs*
      (Paderborn: Schöningh, 2018), 9–24, 17.

although they fulfilled their soldierly duties without complaint, they did not enlist with patriotic enthusiasm. However, what German speakers experienced in the Italian army was sometimes very different: the spectrum ranged from nationalistically motivated humiliation and harassment by superiors and comrades to men who were promoted and who made careers due to their supposed 'German' qualities, such as loyalty and discipline, which were appreciated and rewarded by some superiors.[30]

This demonstrates that military service had a double thrust: it not only represented a state gesture of submission but was also to be understood as an offer of integration. This was not only the practice under fascist rule but dated back to the liberal era and the *Risorgimento*: when Sicily and Lombardy became part of the kingdom in 1860 and Veneto in 1866, their young men were also obliged to serve in the armed forces. Political leaders hoped that fighting together against external aggressors, such as the Habsburg Empire, or against 'Others' on African soil, would ensure that a sense of national belonging developed among the soldiers.[31] Fascist leaders relied on something similar when they called men from the military

30   Markus Wurzer, '*Nachts hörten wir Hyänen und Schakale heulen*'. *Das Tagebuch eines Südtirolers aus dem Italienisch-Abessinischen Krieg 1935–1936* (Innsbruck: Universitätsverlag Wagner, 2016), 34–9; Markus Wurzer, 'Die sozialen Leben kolonialer Bilder. Italienischer Kolonialismus in visuellen Alltagskulturen und Familiengedächtnissen in Südtirol/Alto Adige 1935–2015', PhD dissertation, University of Graz, 2020, 106.

31   Antonio Baldissera, for instance, who was general of the Italian army and governor of Eritrea, was one of Italy's leading figures of colonialism in the 1890s. He started his military career in the Habsburg army since he was born in the Veneto, which, at that time, still belonged to Austria-Hungary. In the Third War of Independence in 1866, he still fought in the Habsburg army. When Veneto subsequently became part of Italy, he joined the Italian ranks and made a career for himself there; see Piero Pieri, 'Baldissera, Antonio', Dizionario biografico degli italiani (1963), <https://www.treccani.it/enciclopedia/antonio-baldissera_(Dizionario-Biografico)>, accessed 4 September 2023. In Comelico Superiore, the northernmost municipality of the Veneto, local war memorials still commemorate the four locals who lost their lives in colonial wars in Eritrea in 1885–96 and in Libya in 1911–12; see 'I caduti di Comelico Superiore', <http://www.comelicocultura.it/Pdf/Gruppi/La_Stua/Stua_19/art3.pdf>, accessed 4 September 2023.

district of Bozen/Bolzano to arms to 'pacify' Libya (1922–32) and subjugate Ethiopia (1935–41). In any case, they wanted to instrumentalize the deployed '*Allogeni*' to legitimize the nation-empire's northern state borders.

Colonial wars and metropolitan claims of loyalty

In the years after the First World War, Italian and Austrian daily newspapers fought a war of words over the situation in Südtirol/Alto Adige. While the latter denounced the oppression and Italianization of the German-speaking population and tried to attract international attention, the former sought to play down reports as misinformation and in return prove the loyalty of the '*Allogeni*' to their new state.

When Siegfried/Sigfredo Wackernell (born in 1903) from Meran/Merano, the first German speaker to lose his life in one of Italy's colonial wars, was killed in Libya in 1928,[32] this also provided an occasion for the daily newspapers on both sides of the Brenner/Brennero Pass to either affirm or question the border region's new state affiliation. Wackernell was one of five 'white' officers who died in action during Italy's attack on Senussi positions in February 1928. While the dead '*Ascari*'[33] received hardly any recognition, the fascist regime endeavoured to honour the five officers. They were declared heroes and were awarded the silver medal for bravery.[34] Furthermore, their bodies were transported from Tripoli to Rome, where a great funeral ceremony was held in the presence of Benito

---

32 'Ein Südtiroler in Tripolis gefallen', *Innsbrucker Nachrichten* (5 March 1928), 3; 'Ein Südtiroler als italienischer Kolonialsoldat gefallen', (*Neuigkeits*) *Welt-Blatt* (8 March 1928), 6.

33 This term originated in colonial practice and referred to men from the colony of Eritrea who were recruited for military service by the Italian colonial regime. Furthermore, the term bears an inherent essentializing intention. Therefore, I put inverted commas around it to draw attention to its construction.

34 'Die silberne Tapferkeitsmedaille für Leutnant Wackernell', *Alpenzeitung* (10 March 1928), 1.

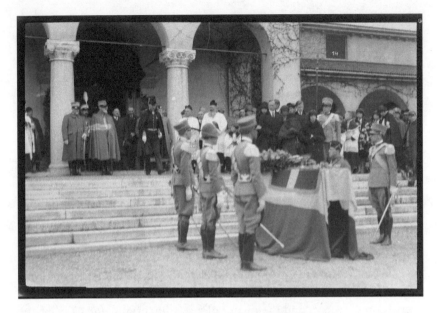

Figure 3. The local fascist authorities turned Wackernell's funeral into a propaganda spectacle to prove the province's loyalty to the state. Source: 'Begräbnis von Leutnant Siegfried Wackernell' [Funeral of Lieutenant Siegfried Wackernell], *Autonomous Province of Bolzano-South Tyrol*, Virtual Catalogue of the Cultural Heritage in South Tyrol, *Palais Mamming Museum*, Meran/Merano, inventory number: 11200/1371.

Mussolini and the king, Vittorio Emanuele III. Subsequently, Wackernell's corpse was further transported via Bozen/Bolzano to Meran/Merano at the state's expense, where comprehensive ceremonies were held by the local fascist elites (see Figure 3).[35]

Since Wackernell represented the new province's first war death, his figure was of particular importance to the fascist regime on both a local

35   'Das Programm des heutigen Tages', *Alpenzeitung* (23 March 1928), 2; 'Der Unterleutnant Siegfried Wackernell', *(Neuigkeits) Welt-Blatt* (29 March 1928), 7. The propaganda film of the Istituto Nazionale Luce is accessible online: 'Le onoranze funebri ai militari italiani caduti in Africa', <https://patrimonio.archivioluce.com/luce-web/detail/IL3000052091/1/le-onoranze-funebri-ai-militari-italiani-caduti>, accessed 4 September 2023.

and international level. In the province, he was intended to serve as a role model of assimilation particularly for children and young people, inspiring them to follow his example: to be dutiful and loyal to the fascist state and to behave like 'good' Italians. Accordingly, the obituary printed in the fascist provincial press stated, for instance, that Wackernell had 'taken pleasure in service, in fighting for the greatness of his new fatherland, which he had learned to love and for which he had given his young life'.[36] 'With the heroic death of one of their own in the distant colonial war theatre', as the newspaper had already stated a couple of days before, 'the youth of Alto Adige have now also sealed their loyalty to the new fatherland for all eternity'.[37] To anchor Wackernell's status as a role model in the local sphere, soon a street, the city's Balilla[38] legion as well as local school rooms and the barracks of the 231st Infantry Regiment, where Wackernell had also served, were named in his honour.[39]

But the regime also exploited Wackernell's death on the international stage. When Mussolini gave an interview to Lord Harold Rothermere – a British press tycoon and the owner of the influential *Daily Mail*, at the end of March 1928, only a few days after the funeral ceremonies in Rome, in discussing the legality of the Brenner/Brennero border – the dictator referred to Wackernell. He argued that Wackernell's death was proof of the province's loyalty to the fascist state and, therefore, rejected foreign accusations concerning the compulsive Italianization of Austrian citizens

---

36   'Sigfrido Wackernell', *Alpenzeitung* (23 March 1928), 3; 'Freude am Dienst, am Kampf für die Größe seines neuen Vaterlandes, das er lieben gelernt und für das er sein junges Leben in die Schanze geschlagen hatte'.

37   'Zum Heldentod Wackernells', *Alpenzeitung* (8 March 1928), 1; 'Mit dem Heldentode eines der Ihrigen auf dem fernen Kriegsschauplatz […] hat nunmehr auch die Jugend des Alto Adige ihre Treue zum neuen Vaterlande […] für alle Ewigkeit besiegelt'.

38   Opera Nazionale Balilla (ONB) is the youth organization of the Italian Fascist Party, founded in 1926.

39   'Balilla-Legion "Sigfrido Wackernell"', *Alpenzeitung* (2 June 1928), 5; 'Die Feier des 21. April in Merano', *Alpenzeitung* (20 April 1934), 4; 'Die Feier des 21. April in Merano', *Alpenzeitung* (24 April 1934), 4.

as 'completely unfounded'.[40] An unknown editor of the *Freie Stimmen*, a German nationalist newspaper, remarked how this statement that 'the Germans south of the Brenner would not be forced to become Italians, borders on morbid cynicism'.[41]

The interview had been preceded by a month-long skirmish over the significance of Wackernell's death between Italian and Austrian dailies. While the fascist local newspaper *Alpenzeitung* argued that Wackernell formed 'the most splendid and noble example of the devotion of the youth of the Alto Adige to the new fatherland',[42] Austrian dailies such as the *Innsbrucker Nachrichten* considered this juvenile patriotic enthusiasm to be a propaganda lie[43] and interpreted the glorification of Wackernell as an 'Italian' colonial war hero as a 'large-scale humiliation of the Germans in Südtirol'.[44] What also particularly provoked the Austrian press was the idea of the Roman newspaper *Tevere* to name a mountain on the border between Austria and Italy after Wackernell, 'so that the name of the German Südtiroler who fell for Italy's glory would be permanently held up to his compatriots on the other side of the Brenner'.[45] Furthermore, the Austrian press vehemently defended itself against the prediction of the Milanese

40 'Mussolini leugnet alles ab', *Innsbrucker Nachrichten* (28 March 1928), 1; 'völlig unbegründet'; see also 'Rothermere bei Mussolini. Italien und die Brennergrenze', *Neues Wiener Journal* (28 March 1928), 1; 'Für die Ungarn nationale Freiheit – für die Südtiroler Unterdrückung. Mussolini neuerdings zur Südtiroler Frage', *Freie Stimmen* (30 March 1928), 1.

41 'Für die Ungarn nationale Freiheit', 1; 'die Deutschen südlich des Brenners [...] nicht mit Gewalt zu Italienern gepreßt [würden], grenzt an krankhaften Zynismus'.

42 'Zum Heldentod Wackernells', 1; 'das herrlichste und edelste Beispiel der Anhänglichkeit der Jugend des Alto Adige an das neue Vaterland'.

43 'Lügnerische Folgerungen', *Innsbrucker Nachrichten* (9 March 1928), 6.

44 'Die Ueberführung des gefallenen Wackernell als Mittel der faschistischen Propaganda', *Innsbrucker Nachrichten* (23 March 1928), 3; 'Demütigung der Deutschen in Südtirol in ganz großem Stile'.

45 'Ein deutscher Südtiroler als Offizier in Lybien gefallen' (*Linzer*) *Tages-Post* (15 March 1928), 16; 'um so den Namen des für Italiens Ruhm gefallenen deutschen Südtirolers seinen Landsleuten jenseits des Brenners dauernd entgegenzuhalten'; see also 'Das Panorama von der "Wackernell-Spitze"', *Alpenzeitung* (10 March 1928), 1.

Corriere della Sera, which wrote that those who are convinced of Südtirol/ Alto Adige's 'Germanness' would now probably brand Wackernell as a 'traitor to German folklore'.[46]

Nevertheless, the Austrian (and soon also German) press tried to make sense of the incident on their own, because, as the *Südtiroler Heimat*, a monthly newspaper that commented on events in the province from abroad, wrote, 'the cult that fascist Italy has created around the fallen Südtiroler German Siegfried Wackernell must not go unchallenged'.[47] The press tried to come up with explanations regarding why a German speaker would volunteer to be deployed in fascist Italy's colonial theatre of war. The *Badische Presse*, for example, wrote that it had gathered 'information from absolutely reliable sources' that the fascist regime had caused the Wackernell family economic distress; thus, Siegfried saw colonial service as the only way out, since the 'military stationed in the colonies is much better paid'. Thus, concludes the unknown author, it was not the 'enthusiasm for Italy, but the harassment of the Germans in Südtirol and the hardship this created that forced his decision to go to Africa'.[48] The *Tages-Post* took the same line, arguing that the fact 'that Wackernell saw his career as an officer in the Italian colonial service did not prevent him from remaining German [...] Every Südtiroler knows to distinguish between duties towards the state and those towards the people'.[49] Likewise, the *Südtiroler Heimat* believed it recognized

46   'Ein deutscher Südtiroler als Offizier in Lybien gefallen', 16; 'Verräter am deutschen Volkstum'; see also 'Ein Südtiroler in Lybien gefallen', *Innsbrucker Nachrichten* (22 March 1928), 4.

47   'Tunichtgut oder Held?', *Südtiroler Heimat* (1 April 1928), 1; 'der Kult, den das faschistische Italien [...] mit dem gefallenen Südtiroler Deutschen Siegfried Wackernell treibt, darf nicht unwidersprochen bleiben'.

48   'Wie Mussolini die Wahrheit verdreht', *Badische Presse (Morgen-Ausgabe)* (5 April 1928), 2; 'Auskünfte von unbedingt verläßlicher Seite'; 'in den Kolonien stationierte Militär wesentlich besser bezahlt ist'; 'Begeisterung für Italien, sondern die Drangsalierung der Deutschen in Südtirol und die dadurch geschaffene Notlage [die] seinen Entschluß, nach Afrika zu gehen zur Reife gebracht [hat].

49   'Ein deutscher Südtiroler als Offizier in Lybien gefallen', 16; 'daß Wackernell in der Offizierslaufbahn im italienischen Kolonialdienst seinen Beruf sah, hinderte ihn nicht, Deutscher zu bleiben [...] Denn jeder Südtiroler weiß zwischen den Pflichten gegen den Staat und denen gegen das Volk zu unterscheiden'.

in Wackernell a desperate man who, like 'so many wayward sons'[50] before him who had emigrated to the Americas, was trying to make a new life in the Libyan colony. An unknown author in the *Innsbrucker Nachrichten*, however, came up with a different explanation. He stated that Wackernell had been 'adventurous, the problem child of his mother, a poor widow'. The author continued by explaining that Wackernell had been dismissed from his position as a post clerk due to irregularities. When he was drafted into military service, Wackernell 'made friends with Italians and separated himself from the Germans, so that he was promoted rather quickly'.[51] The unknown author insinuated that due to the path Wackernell had taken in life he might no longer have been altogether 'German'.

In turn, the Italian press responded to the German reports by accusing the 'irresponsible journalists across the Brennero'[52] of a 'campaign of lies'[53] – which they of course rejected.[54] In his speech at Wackernell's funeral in Meran/Merano, Secretary of the Fascist Party Augusto Turati said that 'one should not worry about the cries of the people [the journalists] on the other side of the border who have realized that they have lost the game'.[55] He highlighted that because the youth were being educated in the Balilla, and were thus the future of the province, they belonged to the fascists.[56]

50 'Tunichtgut oder Held?', 1; 'so viele ungeratene Söhne'.
51 'Ein Südtiroler in Lybien gefallen', *Innsbrucker Nachrichten* (22 March 1928), 4; 'abenteuerlustig, das Sorgenkind seiner Mutter, einer armen Witwe'; 'freundete sich mit Italienern an und sonderte sich von den Deutschen ab, sodaß er ziemlich rasch befördert wurde'.
52 'Das Panorama von der "Wackernell-Spitze"', 1; 'unverantwortlichen Journalisten jenseits des Brenneros'.
53 'Zum Heldentod Wackernells', 1; 'Lügenkampagne'.
54 'Tunichtgut oder Held?', 1.
55 'Totenfeier in Bozen und Meran', *Deutsche Allgemeine Zeitung* (24 March 1928), 1; 'man solle sich nicht um das Geschrei der Leute jenseits der Grenze kümmern, die gemerkt hätten, daß ihr Spiel verloren sei'.
56 'Turati über die Politik in Südtirol', *Deutsche Allgemeine Zeitung* (27 March 1928), 1.

In-between: Self-positioning in the colonial theatre of war

While the German speakers who participated in the 'pacification' of
Libya in the 1920s were mainly volunteers, the situation in 1935, when
Italy invaded Ethiopia, was different: the fascist state not only called for
volunteers but also drafted those born between 1911 and 1913, as well as
specialists of older and younger age groups, for military service. In the
military district of Bozen/Bolzano, at least 1,259 German speakers were
inducted, of which 196 of them deserted and fled across the northern borders to Austria, Switzerland and Germany.[57] Even though the Austrian
press reported on the call-up, its tone had significantly changed in comparison to the Wackernell media campaign. This was because the political situation had altered. The Dollfuß-Schuschnigg regime, which took
power in Austria in 1934, sought Mussolini's support in order to be able
to meet Nazi Germany's expansionist desires. Therefore, Austrian journalists mostly wrote sober reports about German speakers who had met
their 'soldier's death'[58] in East Africa. There were no emotional accusations of fascist instrumentalization as before.

Meanwhile, the Italian press continued its campaign. In particular, it
framed the dead German speakers as proof beyond all doubt of the loyalty of the province's youth to the fascist state. A telling example is Mario
Warner, who died in Ethiopia in June 1936.[59] In the obituary, which was
distributed through the fascist provincial daily *Alpenzeitung*, he was, of
course, represented not as a 'Südtiroler' but as a seemingly completely assimilated 'Alto Atesino'

---

57   Thomas Ohnewein, 'Südtiroler in Abessinien – Statistisches Datenmaterial', in
     Steinacher, *Zwischen Duce und Negus*, 269–72, 269–70.

58   For instance, see 'Die in Abessinien gefallenen Südtiroler', *Allgemeiner Tiroler
     Anzeiger* (28 April 1936), 5; 'Soldatentod'; see also 'Wieder ein Südtiroler im Kriege
     gefallen', *Freie Stimmen* (13 May 1936), 3; '15 Südtiroler im abessinischen Krieg
     gefallen', *Freie Stimmen* (10 March 1937), 3.

59   'In Ausübung seiner Soldatenpflicht in Ostafrika gestorben', *Dolomiten* (17 June
     1936), 2.

who, in the fulfilment of his soldierly duty, laid down his life on the soil of the new empire.[60] Mario Warner, who lived with his family in Bolzano, was part of the fascist youth's Group Commando's Fanfare before his departure for East Africa and was one of the most eager, one of those young people who, having grown up with fascist discipline, inspired by inner conviction, spares no effort, no danger, when it comes to fulfilling their duty to the fascist fatherland and serving the Duce.[61]

Warner, however, does not seem to have been as loyal to the state as the fascist press would have had provincial society believe. In the private collections of several German-speaking veterans, which have been handed down in families to this day, there is a song that contemporaries attribute to Mario Warner.[62] According to a German-speaking soldier, Warner wrote the song, entitled 'Tiroler Fighter Song'[63] because 'his comrade had fallen next to him in Abyssinia.'[64] In the song, the lyrical I mourns a fallen German speaker whose 'young Südtiroler blood' lies under 'the weight and heat of the sun in hot foreign soil'. He had bowed to Italy's 'foreign force' 'in order to remain loyal to his homeland'. The lyrical further denounces that the unknown soldier had died 'not for his homeland', but

60 After the conquest of the Ethiopian capital city of Addis Ababa in May 1936, Mussolini announced the proclamation of a new empire. In doing so, he made a clear reference to the ancient Imperium Romanum, which the fascist state saw itself as inheriting.

61 'Im Dienste des Vaterlandes gestorben', *Alpenzeitung* (17 June 1936), 5; 'der in Erfüllung seiner Soldatenpflicht das Leben auf dem Boden des neuen Imperiums gelassen hat. Mario Warner, der bei seiner Familie in Bolzano wohnte, gehörte vor seiner Abfahrt nach Ostafrika der Fanfare des Verbandskommandos der Jugendfasci an und war einer der Eifrigsten, einer jener jungen Leute, die, in faschistischer Disziplin herangewachsen, von innerer Ueberzeugung beseelt, keine Mühe, keine Gefahr scheuen, wenn es sich darum handelt, die eigene Pflicht für das faschistische Vaterland zu erfüllen und dem Duce zu dienen'.

62 Franz Piazzi, *Die Reisse nach Afrika und Zurück* (unpublished war diary, 1935–7), 48–9 [spelling according to the original].

63 Piazzi, *Die Reisse nach Afrika und Zurück*; 'Tiroler Kämpfer Lied'.

64 *Abbessienien-Lied. Das Grab in der Steppe – Abbessienien in Ostafrika* (unpublished copy from Alois Bacher, 1986), South Tyrolean Folklore Museum, Collection Bacher, U/5797; 'sein Kamerad neben Ihm in Abbessienien gefallen war' [spelling according to the original].

'for a foreign desire for glory', wherefore the dead had put a curse on die 'Others' – meaning the Italians.[65]

Figure 4. 'Memory of the war / in Africa / Debrì, on 7 February 1936 / Here in the far distance, under / the weight and heat of the sun / in hot foreign soil / lies young Südtiroler blood' ['Erinerung am Krüge / in Africa / Debrì am 7.2.36 / Stil in weiter Ferne unter / Sone last und Glut ligt / in Heiser fremder Erde / Junges Südtiroler Blut' (spelling according to the original)]. Source: Collection Winkler, Lüsen/Lusone, Photo 47.

This poem makes the figure of Warner an ambivalent one. While fascists instrumentalized it in order to support the idea of the province's loyalty, some German speakers referred to him in order to reiterate their feelings of belonging towards the German-speaking group even if they were far away from it in the East African theatre of war. Both this poem, that so firmly condemned Italian imperialism, and the story of Warner, who succumbed to illness in a field hospital a short time later, circulated among soldiers who wanted to counter the fascist pressure to assimilate and identify themselves as 'Südtiroler'.[66] These men incorporated photographs

65 *Abbessienien-Lied. Das Grab in der Steppe*; 'junges Südtiroler Blut'; 'Sonnenglast und Glut [...] in heißer fremder Erde'; 'fremden Zwang'; 'um seiner Heimat Treu zu halten'; 'nicht für seine Heimat'; 'für fremde Ruhmessucht'; 'Anderen' [spellings according to the original].

66 Through my dissertation project (already completed in 2020), I surveyed the private collections of 56 veterans in Südtirol/Alto Adige. In 10% of the collections, either Warner's song or pictures of his funeral and grave have survived; see Wurzer, 'Leben', 216.

of Warner's funeral and grave into their visual collections,[67] wrote the six-verse poem in whole or in part in their diaries[68] or – as, for instance, did Eduard Winkler from Lüsen/Lusone – on the back of a photograph (see Figure 4). Winkler used the verses to subversively undermine the meaning suggested by the motif, namely the successful subjugation of the 'foreign' – symbolized by the camel – by 'Italian' colonial soldiers (who were visually marked as such by their uniforms), and to identify those depicted, whose ethnicity remained invisible, as 'German'.

While there were, of course, German-speaking soldiers who retreated to a position of 'minimal loyalty' in their war service (enforced by the state),[69] like Mario Warner, at the same time as criticizing the colonial enterprise – in self-testimonies or perhaps behind closed doors – there were also a few who were actively disloyal and were sanctioned by the state as a result. Matthias Gapp, for instance, was deprived of his Italian citizenship, sentenced to ten years in prison and ordered to pay court costs because he had deliberately not rushed to the aid of an Italian soldier during an attack by Abyssinian soldiers.[70]

Equally, however, there were German speakers who hoped to improve their social position by avowing their loyalty to the state by volunteering for colonial deployment.[71] Wilhelm Conci, for instance, who in his civilian profession had worked in the municipal administration of St Andrä/Sant'Andrea near Brixen/Bressanone, probably volunteered for military service in the colony. Since he had completed the reserve officer course in 1930 following his 1927–8 military service, he took command of an '*Ascari*' company in the colony and was deployed in counter-guerrilla warfare in 1939–40.[72] The pictures he took with his own camera and sent to his wife

67 Private Collection Volgger, Rodeneck/Rodengo, photo 28; private collection Winkler, Lüsen/Lusone, photos 37, 47.

68 Piazzi, *Reisse*, 48–9.

69 Ohnewein, 'Südtiroler', 269–70.

70 Leopold Steurer, 'Südtirol und der Abessinienkrieg', in Steinacher, *Zwischen Duce und Negus*, 195–239, 236.

71 Wurzer, 'Leben', 102, 112, 212.

72 Markus Wurzer, '(Re-)Produktion von Differenzen im kolonialen Gewaltregime. Private Fotopraxis aus dem Italienisch-Abessinischen Krieg 1934–1941', *Zeitgeschichte* 45/2 (2018), 177–200, 181–3.

Figure 5. 'Addis-Abeba, on 17 December 1939. / Visit to the camp of the Battalion of Mr and Mrs Podestà. The latter with long men's trousers. The other two are your husband's "lovely" secretaries' [Addis-Abeba, am 17. Dezember 1939. / Besuch im Zeltlager des / Bataillons des Herrn und Frau Podestà (title of the fascist major). Letztere mit lange Herrenhos- / sen. Die anderen zwei sind Ihres Mannes "reizende" Sekräterinnen' (spelling according to the original)]. Source: Tyrolean Archive of Photographic Documentations and Art (TAP), Lienz, Collection Wilhelm Conci, L60054, L60054-RS.

and daughter at home, however, recount his long-term dream of building a new life for himself and his family as farmers in the colony. In Figure 5, for instance, Conci presents himself to his wife in his officer's uniform on the far right together with the colonial elite – and thus also as one of them. According to the caption, the photograph was taken during a visit to the tent camp of the battalion of the *podestà* (fascist mayor) of Addis Ababa.[73]

Margarete, Wilhelm's wife, was apparently not convinced by the idea of moving to East Africa. Therefore, her husband tried to make the colony and above all the possibility of social advancement as comprehensible to her as possible through his photographic production: he documented vegetables he grew himself as well as newly built roads and cars, staging the colony as a fertile and modern land.[74] In this regard, as shown in Figure 5, he drew his wife's attention in particular to the fact that the *podestà*'s wife

73 Tyrolean Archive of Photographic Documentation and Art (TAP), Lienz, Collection Wilhelm Conci, L60054-RS.
74 TAP, Collection Wilhelm Conci, L60048-RS, L60052-RS, L60058-RS.

wears long trousers. He thus presented the colony as a place of modernity where the fascist promise of social revolution would be fulfilled.[75] The implicit assumption behind the trousers is that his wife could only participate in this enterprise in situ. The prospect of being able to dress like the most socially respected women as well as to have 'black' servants like them was supposed to promise Margarete social advancement. This was a wish that Wilhelm already saw fulfilled for himself: after all, as he wrote on another photograph, he felt like a 'little king' in the colony, since 'all the subordinates would grovel at his feet'.[76]

However, all these arguments do not seem to have changed Margarete's mind. When the so-called Option forced Wilhelm to decide between Italian and German citizenship, he chose the latter while he was still in the colony in June 1940. Apparently, he had come to the conclusion that he would find a more promising future for his family in National Socialist Germany than in Italy or its colonies. However, he was not able to emigrate; Conci's path through the Suez Canal back to Europe was blocked due to the war. He became a prisoner of war in Eritrea but was moved to Canada for the duration of his internment. In 1947, he returned to his family in Südtirol/Alto Adige.[77]

Conclusion

The First World War changed both the world's political landscape and the national borders in the Alps-Adriatic region. Even if, as the Italian leaders

---

75   Ruth Ben-Ghiat, *Fascist Modernities: Italy, 1922–1945* (Berkeley: University of California Press, 2001); Ruth Ben-Ghiat, 'Modernity Is Just Over There: Colonialism and the Dilemmas of Italian National Identity', *Interventions* 8/3 (2006), 380–93; for the representations of women in Italian fascism, see Victoria De Grazia, *Le donne nel regime fascista* (Venice: Marsilio, 1993).

76   TAP, Collection Wilhelm Conci, L60048-RS; 'kleiner König'; 'alle Untergebenen kriechen ihm zu Füssen' [spellings according to the original].

77   Wurzer, '(Re-)Produktion von Differenzen im kolonialen Gewaltregime', 183.

had hoped, they were not granted the German colonies, in the north they were able to shift the border from Lake Garda to Italy's seemingly 'natural' border, the Brenner/Brennero Pass. This 1920 border demarcation, however, remained controversial well into the twentieth century. After all, around 200,000 German speakers now lived in Italy, the majority of whom disliked the idea of Italian nationalist propagandists that they had been 'redeemed' by Rome.

Italy, especially when the fascists took power in 1922, tried to make the *Italianness* of the province – so vehemently claimed in their propaganda – a reality through a variety of measures. Military service and war deployment represented important parts of this policy to further the assimilation and the loyalty of German-speaking young men, respectively. National integration through military service in colonial wars was already a widely used integration practice in liberal Italy, dating back to the *Risorgimento*. Against this background, the two colonial wars that Italy fought in Libya (1922–32) and Ethiopia (1935–41) became moments in which the national belonging of the province of Bozen/Bolzano and its '*Allogeni*' population was negotiated. While Italy's fascist leaders instrumentalized the conscripted German speakers – and especially those who lost their lives in action – to affirm the asserted loyalty and enthusiasm of the province's youth for their new 'fatherland', the foreign (especially the Austrian) press challenged these narratives, accusing the regime of suppressing its German-speaking citizens.

Discourses of nationhood were not limited to the media sphere. German-speaking soldiers serving in the colonies negotiated their quite contradictory feelings of belonging in cultural practices, such as writing diaries and songs or in their photographic practices. While the collective memory of the province's German-speaking society today is dominated by the idea that 'Südtiroler' were exclusively forced to serve in the colonial wars and thus were more distanced observers of the fascist wars than their protagonists,[78] an analysis of ego documents gives a more differentiated

---

78 The veterans thus successfully integrated their colonial experience into the victimization narrative of German-speaking society after 1945; see Sebastian De Pretto, *Im Kampf um Geschichte(n). Erinnerungsorte des Abessinienkriegs in Südtirol* (Göttingen, Vandenhoeck & Ruprecht, 2020), 274–86, 300–12.

impression. Admittedly, the majority were forced into military service in the colonies, many of whom adopted a position of 'minimal loyalty', meaning they fulfilled the expectations that their superiors placed on them as dockworkers, bakers, telegraphists, artillerymen, machine-gunners or officers, but did not go beyond them. Other German speakers, however, willingly integrated themselves into the fascist narrative of the loyal 'Alto Atesini' and volunteered for the colonial war because they hoped that this declaration of loyalty would improve their economic and social situation.

Bibliography

'15 Südtiroler im abessinischen Krieg gefallen', *Freie Stimmen* (10 March 1937), 3.

Abbessienien-Lied. Das Grab in der Steppe – Abbessienien in Ostafrika (unpublished copy from Alois Bacher, 1986), South Tyrolean Folklore Museum, Dietenheim/ Teodone, Collection Bacher, U/5797.

'Balilla-Legion "Sigfrido Wackernell"', *Alpenzeitung* (2 June 1928), 5.

'"Bei den 200.000 Vogelfreien in Südtirol". Feststellungen eines Neutralen', *Innsbrucker Nachrichten* (21 June 1928), 3.

Ben-Ghiat, Ruth, *Fascist Modernities: Italy, 1922–1945* (Berkeley: University of California Press, 2001).

——— , 'Modernity Is Just Over There: Colonialism and the Dilemmas of Italian National Identity', *Interventions* 8/3 (2006), 380–93.

'Das Panorama von der "Wackernell-Spitze"', *Alpenzeitung* (10 March 1928), 1.

'Das Programm des heutigen Tages', *Alpenzeitung* (23 March 1928), 2.

'Das sind wir', <https://suedtiroler-freiheit.com/bewegung/>, accessed 4 September 2023.

De Grazia, Victoria, *Le donne nel regime fascista* (Venice: Marsilio, 1993).

Deplano, Valeria, and Alessandro Pes, 'Introduzione', in Valeria Deplano and Alessandro Pes (eds), *Quel che resta dell'Impero. La cultura coloniale degli italiani* (Milan: Mimesis, 2014), 9–16.

De Pretto, Sebastian, *Im Kampf um Geschichte(n). Erinnerungsorte des Abessinienkriegs in Südtirol* (Göttingen: Vandenhoeck & Ruprecht, 2020).

'Der Unterleutnant Siegfried Wackernell', *(Neuigkeits)Welt-Blatt* (29 March 1928), 7.

'Die Feier des 21. April in Merano', *Alpenzeitung* (20 April 1934), 4.

'Die Feier des 21. April in Merano', *Alpenzeitung* (24 April 1934), 4.

'Die in Abessinien gefallenen Südtiroler', *Allgemeiner Tiroler Anzeiger* (28 April 1936), 5.

'Die silberne Tapferkeitsmedaille für Leutnant Wackernell', *Alpenzeitung* (10 March 1928), 1.

'Die Ueberführung des gefallenen Wackernell als Mittel der faschistischen Propaganda', *Innsbrucker Nachrichten* (23 March 1928), 3.

'Ein deutscher Südtiroler als Offizier in Lybien gefallen', *(Linzer) Tages-Post* (15 March 1928), 16.

'Ein Südtiroler als italienischer Kolonialsoldat gefallen', *(Neuigkeits)Welt-Blatt* (8 March 1928), 6.

'Ein Südtiroler in Lybien gefallen', *Innsbrucker Nachrichten* (22 March 1928), 4.

'Ein Südtiroler in Tripolis gefallen', *Innsbrucker Nachrichten* (5 March 1928), 3.

Fuller, Mia, 'Laying Claim: Italy's Internal and External Colonies', in Marco Ferrari, Andrea Bagnato and Elisa Pasqual (eds), *A Moving Border: Alpine Cartographies of Climate Change* (Irvington: Columbia Books on Architecture and the City, 2019), 98–111.

'Funeral of Lieutenant Siegfried Wackernell', *Palais Mamming Museum*, Meran/ Merano, Inventory number: 11200/1371.

'Für die Ungarn nationale Freiheit – für die Südtiroler Unterdrückung. Mussolini neuerdings zur Südtiroler Frage', *Freie Stimmen* (30 March 1928), 1.

Grote, Georg, *Im Schatten der Zeitenwende. Leben in Tirol 1900–1918* (Bozen: Athesia, 2019).

'Heinrich Sader', *Alpenzeitung* (1 May 1936), 4.

'I caduti di Comelico Superiore', <http://www.comelicocultura.it/Pdf/Gruppi/La_ Stua/Stua_19/art3.pdf>, accessed 4 September 2023.

'Im Dienste des Vaterlandes gestorben', *Alpenzeitung* (17 June 1936), 5.

'In Ausübung seiner Soldatenpflicht in Ostafrika gestorben', *Dolomiten* (17 June 1936), 2.

Labanca, Nicola, 'Erinnerungskultur, Forschung und Historiografie zum Abessinienkrieg', in Gerald Steinacher (ed.), *Zwischen Duce und Negus. Abessinienkrieg und Südtirol 1935–1941* (Bolzano: Athesia, 2006), 33–57.

——— , 'L'Impero del fascismo. Lo stato degli studi', in Riccardo Bottoni (ed.), *L'Impero fascista. Italia ed Etiopia (1935–1941)* (Bologna: Mulino, 2008), 35–62.

'Le onoranze funebri ai militari italiani caduti in Africa', <https://patrimonio.archi violuce.com/luce-web/detail/IL3000052091/1/le-onoranze-funebri-ai-milit ari-italiani-caduti-africa.html?startPage=0&jsonVal={%22jsonVal%22:{%22qu ery%22:[%22tegrift%22],%22fieldDate%22:%22dataNormal%22,%22_perP age%22:20}}>, accessed 4 September 2023.

'Lügnerische Folgerungen', *Innsbrucker Nachrichten* (9 March 1928), 6.

Michielli, Sabrina and Obermair, Hannes (eds), *BZ '18–'45: ein Denkmal, eine Stadt, zwei Diktaturen. Begleitband zur Dokumentations-Ausstellung im Bozener Siegesdenkmal* (Vienna: Folio, 2016).

'Mussolini leugnet alles ab', *Innsbrucker Nachrichten* (28 March 1928), 1.

Ohnewein, Thomas, 'Südtiroler in Abessinien – Statistisches Datenmaterial', in Gerald Steinacher (ed.), *Zwischen Duce und Negus. Abessinienkrieg und Südtirol 1935–1941* (Bolzano: Athesia, 2006), 269–72.

Pergher, Roberta, 'Impero immaginario, impero vissuto. Recenti sviluppi nella storiografia del colonialismo italiano', *Ricerche di storia politica* 10/1 (2007), 53–66.

——, *Mussolini's Nation-Empire: Sovereignty and Settlement in Italy's Borderlands, 1922–1943* (Cambridge: Cambridge University Press, 2018).

Piazzi, Franz, *Die Reisse nach Afrika und Zurück* (Unpublished war diary, 1935–7), 48–9.

Pieri, Piero, 'Baldissera, Antonio', *Dizionario biografico degli italiani* (1963), <https://www.treccani.it/enciclopedia/antonio-baldissera_(Dizionario-Biografico)>, accessed 4 September 2023.

Private Collection Volgger, Rodeneck/Rodengo, photo 28.

Private Collection Winkler, Lüsen/Lusone, photos 37, 47.

'Rothermere bei Mussolini. Italien und die Brennergrenze', *Neues Wiener Journal* (28 March 1928), 1.

'Sigfrido Wackernell', *Alpenzeitung* (23 March 1928), 3.

Staffler, Harthmuth, 'Brixen: Imperialismus noch aktuell – Kritik an Kranzniederlegung', <https://suedtiroler-freiheit.com/2015/11/03/brixen-imperialismus-noch-aktuell-kritik-an-kranzniederlegung/>, accessed 4 September 2023.

Steinacher, Gerald, 'Vom Amba Alagi nach Bozen. Spurensuche in Südtirol', in Gerald Steinacher (ed.), *Zwischen Duce und Negus. Abessinienkrieg und Südtirol 1935–1941* (Bolzano: Athesia, 2006), 13–32.

Steininger, Rolf, *Südtirol. Vom Ersten Weltkrieg bis zur Gegenwart* (Innsbruck: Haymon, 2012).

Steurer, Leopold, 'Südtirol und der Abessinienkrieg', in Gerald Steinacher (ed.), *Zwischen Duce und Negus. Abessinienkrieg und Südtirol 1935–1941* (Bolzano: Athesia, 2006), 195–239.

'Totenfeier in Bozen und Meran', *Deutsche Allgemeine Zeitung* (24 March 1928), 1.

'Tunichtgut oder Held?', *Südtiroler Heimat* (1 April 1928), 1.

'Turati über die Politik in Südtirol', *Deutsche Allgemeine Zeitung* (27 March 1928), 1.

Tyrolean Archive of Photographic Documentation and Art (TAP), Lienz, Collection Wilhelm Conci, L60054, L60054-RS, L60048-RS, L60052-RS, L60058-RS.

Überegger, Oswald, 'Minderheiten-Soldaten. Staat, Militär und Minderheiten im Ersten Weltkrieg – eine Einführung', in Oswald Überegger (ed.), *Minderheiten-Soldaten. Ethnizität und Identität in den Armeen des Ersten Weltkriegs* (Paderborn: Schöningh, 2018), 9–24.

Verdorfer, Martha, *Zweierlei Faschismen. Alltagserfahrungen in Südtirol 1918–1945* (Vienna: Verlag für Gesellschaftskritik, 1990).

'Wie Mussolini die Wahrheit verdreht', *Badische Presse (Morgen-Ausgabe)* (5 April 1928), 2.

'Wieder ein Südtiroler im Kriege gefallen', *Freie Stimmen* (13 May 1936), 3.

Wurzer, Markus, 'Die sozialen Leben kolonialer Bilder. Italienischer Kolonialismus in visuellen Alltagskulturen und Familiengedächtnissen in Südtirol/Alto Adige 1935–2015', PhD dissertation, University of Graz, 2020.

——, *'Nachts hörten wir Hyänen und Schakale heulen.' Das Tagebuch eines Südtirolers aus dem Italienisch-Abessinischen Krieg 1935–1936* (Innsbruck: Universitätsverlag Wagner, 2016).

——, '(Re-)Produktion von Differenzen im kolonialen Gewaltregime. Private Fotopraxis aus dem Italienisch-Abessinischen Krieg 1934–1941', *Zeitgeschichte* 45/2 (2018), 177–200.

'Zum Heldentod Wackernells', *Alpenzeitung* (8 March 1928), 1.

GEORG GROTE

'Siblings are being torn apart, brothers may shoot each other …': The Hitler-Mussolini Agreement of 1939 and the Fate of One South Tyrolean Family

One of the most drastic examples demonstrating the impact of changing borders on a people's sense of belonging is the case of South Tyrol in Northern Italy at the end of the 1930s. Italy annexed the southern part of the Austrian Crownland of Tyrol in 1918, today's South Tyrol and Trentino, in accordance with the 1915 Secret Treaty of London between the kingdom and the Western Allies.[1] Italy had thus gained an almost pyrrhic victory in its struggle to become a European Great Power. According to international post-First World War law, the acquired territory with its predominantly German-speaking population in the North and the bilingual population in the South, became an integral part of Italy and completed the *Risorgimento* aspirations which had begun in 1866.[2] In fact, with this acquisition Italy went beyond the *Risorgimento* idea by incorporating an area that was 'a German land'[3] – its population being Austrian in its cultural traditions and almost exclusively German-speaking. However, gaining access to South Tyrol's water resources, which Italy required to transform its north into an

---

1   Antony Evelyn Alcock, *Short History of Europe* (Basingstoke: Palgrave Macmillan, 1998), 221.

2   Rudolf Lill, *Südtirol in der Zeit des Nationalismus* (Konstanz: Universitätsverlag Konstanz, 2002), 26.

3   Hans Kinzl, 'Die Forderung Italiens nach der Brennergrenze', in Franz Huter (ed.), *Südtirol. Eine Frage des politischen Gewissens* (Munich: Oldenbourg, 1965), 236–53, 240.

industrial powerhouse for the 'nation',[4] came at a high price, because the native South Tyroleans rejected Italian citizenship embarking on a campaign of resistance.

After the initial shock and a period of war fatigue, dissatisfaction with the new regime emerged in South Tyrol.[5] In 1923, the by-then fascist Italy did not endear itself to its new conquest by introducing far-reaching measures to suppress the German language and the Austrian traditions of South Tyrol. Indeed, much of this was symbolized by the renaming of the region Alto Adige. In accordance with his plan to form a homogeneous Italian nation-state, Mussolini intended to turn the province into a fully Italianized part of the Kingdom of Italy and South Tyroleans into proper Italian citizens.[6] In effect, Ettore Tolomei's '32 Provvedimenti per l'Alto Adige' were an assault on the collective and individual identity of South Tyrol[7] and were met with civic disobedience and international protest. Bavaria, which had become a safe haven for South Tyrolean emigres after 1918, took on the role of an advocate for this new suppressed minority in Italy. The engagement of the Bavarian government in the mid-1920s was strong, and Mussolini's rebuttal of any foreign influence in Italy's domestic issues was even more forceful. The row between Munich and Rome prompted the German foreign minister, Gustav Stresemann, to enter the fray and focus on the South Tyrol issue to highlight the difference between the freedom provided by democratic political systems in Europe and the suppression of fascist ideology.[8] Not surprisingly, and in keeping with its anti-Semitic propaganda, Adolf Hitler's new National Socialist movement, which also rejected parliamentary democracy, took an opposed stance to

4   Georg Grote, *I bin a Südtiroler. Kollektive Identität zwischen Nation und Region im 20. Jahrhundert* (Bozen: Athesia 2009), 34.

5   Rolf Steininger, *Südtirol im 20. Jahrhundert: Vom Leben und Überleben einer Minderheit* (Innsbruck: Studienverlag, 1997), 36.

6   Montserrat Guibernau, *Nationalisms* (Cambridge, MA: Polity, 1996), 47.

7   Grote, *Südtiroler*, 73.

8   See Georg Grote, *The South Tyrol Question 1866–2010, From National Rage to Regional State* (Paris: Peter Lang, 2012), 44–51.

Stresemann and made the case of South Tyrol's strive for freedom from Italy part of the much-quoted Jewish conspiracy.[9]

However, upon gaining power in 1933, Hitler's pan-German 'Heim ins Reich' policy, which was in effect a version of Italy's *Risorgimento* for German peoples, meant South Tyrol took on a heightened significance. Both the Saar referendum of 1935,[10] in which 90.7% of the population voted in favour of a return to the Reich, and the 'Austrian Anschluss' of March 1938[11] were generally regarded as steps towards bringing the Reich to all German populations – the idea of a pan-German Empire took on greater force and focus. However, in the South Tyrolean case, the implications of this policy were extremely problematic for the Reich as it would inevitably lead to a confrontation with Mussolini and fascist Italy. This was out of the question – Italian fascism was National Socialist's ideological blueprint, Italy a potential war ally and Mussolini enjoyed Hitler's lifelong personal adoration.

Instead of bringing the Reich to Bozen, the Hitler-Mussolini agreement of 1939 enabled South Tyroleans to choose between remaining in their homeland and becoming Italian citizens or leaving and joining the ranks of citizens of the Reich. In effect, this agreement transformed Hitler's 'Blut und Boden' doctrine to 'Blut oder Boden'. German-speaking South Tyroleans were obliged to make this extraordinary choice by 31 December 1939. The implications for families and individuals were immense – to retain their German-Austrian identity they had to renounce their ancestral homes, however, the price of retaining their home was Italianization.

It was an existential dilemma for a society which, since medieval times, had identified as the last outpost of the Germanic world in the south of Europe. Inevitably, following the publication of the 'Option' conditions,

---

9   Adolf Hitler, *Mein Kampf* (Munich: Franz Eher, 1926), 520.
10 It had been part of the Treaty of Versailles to let the people on the Saar decide after 25 years as to whether they wanted to remain with France or return to Germany. The overwhelming majority voted for Germany, and despite this referendum being an integral part of the Versailles Treaty, Hitler's National Socialists interpreted the outcome as a validation of their policies.
11 The Wehrmacht marched into Austria on 13 March 1938, and thus Hitler united both German-speaking countries to form the Greater German Empire.

passions ran high as the society split between those advocating for a Yes
vote for Germany and those who favoured remaining in South Tyrol. The
fact is that the Option – as the resettlement programme was cynically
called – divided the German-speaking minority in Italy deeply. The debate
and fallout from the Option resulted in a shattering of the social and cultural cohesiveness which had endured the partition of Tyrol in 1918 and
the Italianization of the 1920s and 1930s.

Irrespective of the enormity of the decision, every adult of the German-
speaking population was obliged to declare allegiance to either Italy or
Germany by the deadline. The details of the resettlement agreement became
known only gradually throughout the late summer and early autumn of
1939, and many South Tyroleans lacked detailed knowledge of the special
compensation packages and the conditions of the actual resettlement plans
until late in the autumn of 1939. As the flow of information remained sparse,
those who were not currently in the province could not even rely on hearsay
and the grapevine to find out what lay in store for them.

Relatively little historical attention has been paid to the emotional
impact on the community that constituted the German-speaking population. This chapter adopts a 'history from below' approach and the history of
emotions to explore through various sources of everyday life the emotional
and psychological ramifications of the Option. It focuses on ego documents
such as letters and diaries in order to reveal the impact on the emotional
community of South Tyrol and give voice to the micro-individual impact
of macro-political choices.

The following exchange of letters between three brothers and two sisters is an outstanding and rare example of this process as it unfolded within
one family, and it demonstrates the devastating effect of the bilateral agreement between fascist Italy and the National Socialist German Reich on the
German-speaking minority in Italy, both on a collective and individual level.
The members of the Schuler[12] family from the Unterland, an area south
of Bozen, exemplify the confusion among the German-speaking South

---

12   Adhering to the private archive's owner desire for anonymity, the names of the pro-
      tagonists have been changed and their geographical details have been kept vague in
      order for them to remain unidentifiable. All sources are under the author's custody.

Tyrolean people at this time of great existential uncertainty. Comprising some three dozen letters, in their exchange[13] in the run-up to 31 December 1939, and beyond, the five orphaned siblings discussed the pros and cons of the Option agreement and the likelihood of deciding in favour of or against Germany.

On 22 November 1939, Ludwig, the oldest of the five, who was serving in the Alpini regiment of the Italian army in Turin, wrote to his brother Richard, who was running a small carpentry shop near Meran: 'I have no inner peace being so far away from home in this tough time. Berta has written to me yesterday that almost everybody intends to go [to Germany] and that our relatives are still very brave. I myself have no great desire to go, but when they all leave, will I then stay back?'[14]

These lines express the turmoil and lack of a sense of orientation Ludwig was going through, far away from home and stuck within an all-Italian all-male environment – no place for contemplation and reflection of a possible future.

13   These letters are part of the digital archive titled 'South Tyrolean Correspondences' which the author has been collecting for the past several years. The archive is located in the EURAC, South Tyrol's vivid research hub in Bozen/Bolzano. More than 15,000 ego documents – private letters, military postcards and photographs – have already been contributed by ordinary citizens of the region, and the numbers are growing. This developing database forms the backbone of a 'history from below' publication project in German, which is currently been realized in co-operation with Athesia publishers in Bozen/Bolzano. Vol. I: *Im Schatten der Zeitenwende. Tirol 1900–1918* (2019) and Vol. II: *Die zerrissene Generation, Südtiroler Schicksale zwischen Faschismus und Nationalsozialismus* (2021) have been published and a third volume focusing on the period between 1943 and the post-war era in South Tyrol is in preparation.

14   These letters are obviously written in German and they are in a strong vernacular which comprises numerous orthographical and semantic errors. My translations cannot pay tribute to these very personal stylistic means, and I have therefore printed the original quotations from the siblings' letters as well, containing all of their peculiarities.
'es läst mir keine Ruhe, sofern der Heimat in diesen so harten Tagen weilen zu müssen. Berta hat mir gestern geschrieben, das fast alle gehe und das unsere Verwandtschaft so tapfer ist. Ich nach meiner Ansicht habe nicht ein groses Verlangen zu gehen, doch wenn die meinen alle gehen sol ich dann zurückbleiben??'

However, being physically removed from South Tyrol also allowed him
to take a more distanced view of the German propaganda advocating the
move to Germany. He remarked sceptically: 'I think that not everything in
Germany is as good as it is being reported with all those conditions existing
out there, and only God knows how long they are going to endure: please
consider that religion plays its part as well. It is the only consolation and
the only possession worth having in this world. God will make sure it will
all turn out well.'[15] His trust in God was an expression of hope but appears
to be no more than a thin veil over his anxiety for all of them. On top of
this, Ludwig felt great pain that he was separated from his siblings at this
crucial time, but the physical distance made him try all the more harder to
remain part of their decision-making. Ending his letter, he pleaded: 'Please
tell me about your views and decisions. Good bye – Heil – Heil – Heil.'[16]

On 4 December 1939, he had to learn that his siblings tended towards
leaving South Tyrol, and he responded to his brother with a desperate
plea: 'Forgive me, dearest Richard when I write like that, but I have to be
honest that I am not satisfied with your decision, even if you took it for
the best of reasons. Forgive me again but I cannot hold back and have to
be open as my chest is overly full. Your news, in which you told me about
your and brother Hermann's signing off, has struck me like lightning, and
since that moment I haven't had a peaceful moment, no other thought dis-
perses this one. I am fighting with myself with a violent force. If I consider
staying I am overwhelmed by desperation and exclusion from my dearest.
If I consider leaving [...] – I cannot express myself properly. Forgive me
but I had to let it out. Why do we go??? To follow our sentiment to search
for a good life now.'[17] His inability to express his desperation in writing is

15   'Mir kommt vor, in Deutschland ist nicht alles gar so gut wie es vorgemacht wird,
      bei den Verhältnissen wie sie drausen gegenwärtig sind und nur Gott weis wie lange
      sie noch dauern werden: dan bedenkt das auch die Religion [...] fest gefordert ist.
      Den einzigen Trost und das einzige Gut das wir auf dies Welt haben. Doch Gott
      wird alles zum besten Lenken.'
16   'Bitte schreibe mir deine Entschüsse und Deine Meinungen. Auf Wiedersehen –
      Heil – Heil – Heil.'
17   'Verzeihe mir liebster Richard wen ich so schreibe, doch wen ich will aufrichtig
      sein war ich mit eurem Entschluss, wenn Ihrs auch zum besten gemeint habt gar
      nicht zufrieden. Verzeihe mir nochmals doch ich vermags nicht mer zu halten ich

obvious in these lines, and his anxiety appears to have been multiplied by being alone in Turin, some 300 kilometres away from the rest of his family. After receiving letters from his siblings in which they convince him to leave Italy with them, Ludwig finally seeks clarification himself and travels to Bozen to garner as much information as possible about the Option details. On the day of the deadline, 31 December 1939, Ludwig wrote another letter to his brother Richard:

> I know you have been waiting for my news, but I have to apologize, because I know that I disappoint you and maybe even offend you. I urge you to understand me, it's simply not in my nature to go, I have considered and considered but there has always been a black fog before my conscience whenever I have considered going, I simply cannot act against my nature, it feels like something is moving inside me. I feel it strongly, in such a way that my brother will not succeed to put on paper, and my heart is overfull and struggles for words but I cannot find any.
>
> Yesterday I went to Bozen to enquire, but I could not come clear: now I have decided to remain here. I will face my future with a strong will and an iron strength and will share fate with reality. I am not worried about myself, I will find my way. The future prospects are certainly not as bad as you make them out to be. Yesterday I talked to Paula [who was living in a home for people with special needs], and her first question was as to whether I was going to leave as well. Hermann is here too and has been accepted [by the German army], I hope he will be fine, I wish him all the best, and the same to you. Even if national boundaries may separate us in the future, nobody will be able to take away our mental proximity.[18]

---

muss mich ausletun meine Brust ist übervol. Deine Nachricht in welcher du dein Abmelden sowie auch von [Bruder] Hermann mittgeteilt hast hat mich wie ein Blitz getroffen, und seid dieser Stunde hatt ich kein friedlichen Augenblick mer; kein anderer Gedanke vermag mir diesen zu vertreiben. Ich kämpfe mitt mir sebst mitt einer verbitterten Gewalt. Wen ich an das hierbleiben denke überfällt mich eine trostlose Verlassenheit und Ausgeschlossenheit meiner Lieben. Wen ich an das gehen denke dan ... - ich kann mich nicht klar genug Auslegen. Verzeihe mir doch es muss heraus. Warum gehen wir??? Um unserem Gefühl zu folgen und das zeitliche Wohlsein zu suchen.'

18 'Ich weiss das du auf meine Nachricht wartest, doch verzeih mir, ich weis ganz genau das dich enttäuschen werde und vielleicht auch beleidigen. Ich bitte dich suche mich zu verstehen es liegt einfach nicht in meiner Natur hinaus zu gehen ich hab überlegt und überlegt doch immer ist mir ein schwarzer Nebel vor das Gewissen gegangen so oft ich an das gehen dachte ich kann einfach nicht gegen

Berta responded to his letter and stated her own views to him and the other siblings: 'Dearest brother. My very best wishes for the new year. I have finally decided as well. [Cousin] Otto stays here, and therefore I will remain as well, I beg you forgiveness but I cannot do otherwise in these times, I have prayed a lot […] yet there was no other decision than to stay; God will leave nobody who remains here and neither those who leave and place their trust in God as ever. Berta, Faithful to our Heimat.'[19]

Hermann's decision to opt for Germany was closely related to the fact that he had been rejected by the Italian army, but instantly accepted by the German Wehrmacht. On 4 January 1940, four days after the Option deadline, he wrote to his brother Richard expressing his regret that they had chosen different paths and that their relationship had deteriorated as a result:

> I report that Ludwig and Berta opted for Italy, which you may know already. It is sad and regrettable that siblings have to be torn apart in such a manner, and it may actually happen that brothers will have to shoot one another, but there is very little to be done about it if he thinks he cannot exist among the Germans. Yet it is even sadder that sister decided for Italy as well, if Ludwig had not been here on holidays then

---

meiner Natur handeln, es ist als ob mir etwas vorginge. Ich fühle es auch hart, ja in einem Masse das es meinem Bruder nie gelingen wird, dies aufs Papier zu setzen und das Herz ist übervoll und fragt nach Worten doch ich kann keine finden.

Ich war gestern in Bozen um mich einigermassen zu erkundigen, bin aber nicht übereingekommen; und nun bin ich fest entschlossen hier zu bleiben. Mitt festem Willen und eiserner Kraft werde ich meiner Zukunft entgegenschauen und das Schicksal mit der Gegenwart teilen. Bin mir nicht besorgt um mich ich werde mir schon einen Weg banen. Die Aussichten sind gewiss nicht so schlecht wie "Ihr" sie anschaut. Habe gestern mit der Paula gesprochen das erste Wort war von ihr gehst du auch hinaus? […] Hermann ist auch hier hat auch schon den Annameschein bekommen, wenn es ihm nur recht gut geht ich gönne es ihm von ganzem Herzen wie auch dir. Sollen uns auch später Staatsgrenzen trennen unsere geistige Nähe wird niemand trennen können.'

19 'Liebster Bruder. Wünsche dir alles gute zum Jahreswechsel. Endlich habe ich mich entschlossen. Otto bleibt hier so will auch ich bleiben, verzeih mir ich kann einfach nicht anders habe in dieser Zeit viel gebetet […] ich kam auf keinen anderen Entschluss als hier zu bleiben; Gott wird keine verlassen welche hier bleiben und die welche gehen nur auf Gott vetrauen da geht es immer. Berta, Treu der Heimat.'

Berta would most certainly have opted for Germany, Ludwig is guilty, not only that Berta decided that way, but both of them changed Otto's mind. This is sad because Otto is not a real man, as the saying goes; one man one word. Cousin Anna cried for a good while when she heard that and said: she doesn't care so much about Ludwig, but she does mind Berta's decision because she [Berta] had always remembered her, when she needed anything she could use her, but now that it's done it's done.[20]

Nevertheless, Hermann remained steadfast and intended to leave the country soon: 'Dear brother. You may know that I will have to leave soon, I do not know quite when, maybe at the end of this month or early in February, but I do not care, the sooner the better.'[21]

In the meantime, Ludwig was still serving in the Italian army. He expressed both sadness and helplessness in a letter to some friends. He wrote to them from Turin on 7 January 1940:

My eyes are staring over the sea of houses into the distance. Yet my thoughts travel further, they fly over mountains and valleys towards the lands that our forefathers turned into a paradise, towards those families who have remained faithful to that paradise: those who are facing fate with a strong will and an iron strength and who are prepared to share with their Heimat whatever comes their way. Yet, how few are they! Never had I thought that Tyroleans would be so faithless towards their Heimat, and yet. My heart is overly full with this thought and I am struggling for words, but

20 'Berichte dier das der Ludwig und die Berta für Italien gestimt haben wie du vielleicht schon weist. Das ist Traurig – Traurig das Geschwister so auseinander gerissen werden es kann soweit kommen das Brüder aufeinander schiesen müssen aber da kan man nichtz machen wen er glaubt das er bei den Deutschen nicht exischtieren kan.
Aber noch trauriger ist das auch die Schwester italienisch gestimt hat wen der Ludwig nicht in Urlaub gekommen were dan hät die Berta ganz sicher Deutsch gestimmt der Ludwig ist schuld daran nicht nur das die erta. sonder beide mitteinand habn sis so weit gebracht das auch der Otto umgestimt hat das ist traurig der Otto ist kein Man den das Sprichwort sagt: Ein Man ein Wort. Die Basl Anna hat recht Geweind als si es gehört hat und hat gesagt: Wegen den Ludwig ists Ihr noch gleich aber wögen der Berta nicht den sie hat Ihr immer gedacht wen mal was fehlt kan man si hernemen aber geschehen ist geschehen.'

21 'Lieber Bruder. Wie Du wielleicht schon weist das ich bald Abreisen mus weis noch nicht genau wen vielleicht ende dieses Monats oder anfang Februar das ist mier gleich wie früher wie liber.'

there are none in this case to describe. One wants to rage and quarrel with them, but alas, now the deed has been done! All of this might insult me and make me sad, but no, the thought is consoling: Not everybody goes! We leave it to God's divine plan. He will abandon nobody, if he is not abandoned by human beings. We wish and we hope that they will find happiness even elsewhere.[22]

Ludwig attempted to bridge both the geographical and ideological divide between himself and his brother Richard in several touching letters, for example, on 17 January 1940, he wrote from Turin:

Dear brother. For several days I have been yearning for news from you, but in vain. Have I offended you? I ask you, be upfront and tell me, I will certainly understand. Let us remain brothers to each other even as fate has cast its dice [...] Indeed, I had never asked for this, and neither had you, I know that without even asking you. You will probably blame me, and according to your and many other's point of view I will probably be to blame. I am very sorry, but I could not do otherwise, I hope you will understand and do not consider me stubborn [...] I want to continue, but all the letters double up through the tears in my eyes. The deepest pain has no words, as the saying goes.[23] Nevertheless, Ludwig remained convinced that his decision to opt for

22   'Mein Blick starrt über das Häusermeer in die Ferne hinaus. Die Gedanken aber gehen weiter, sie fliegen über Berge und Täler hinauf zu jener Landschaft, die von unseren Ahnen zu einem Paradies umgewandelt worden ist, zu jenen Familien, die ihr treu geblieben sind: die Pflichtbewusst mit starkem Willen und eiserner Kraft dem Schicksal entgegen schauen und bereit sind, alles wie es kommen mag mit ihrer Heimat zu teilen. Wie wenig aber sind solche! Nie hätt man die Tiroler so treulos gegen ihre eigene Heimat gehalten und doch. Mein Herz ist übervoll von diesen Gedanken und ringt in Worte, doch es kann der Sache keine geben, dies zu beschreiben. Man möchte sich darüber zürnen und mit ihnen hadern, doch es wäre unnütz; nun ist es geschehen. Dies alles möchte mich kränken und in Traurigkeit setzen; aber nein, der Gedanke tröstet mich: Es gehen nicht alle! Überlassen wir alles der Vorsehung Gottes! Er wird niemand verlassen, wenn ihn nur die Menschen nicht verlassen. Wünschen und hoffen wir, das es ihnen auch anderswo recht gut gehe.'

23   'Lieber Bruder. Schon seit mehrere Tage wartete ich mit Sehnsucht auf eine Nachricht von dir, aber vergebens. Habe ich dich beleidigt? Ich bitte Dich sei nur aufrichtig und rede, ich werde Dich gewiss verstehen. Bleiben wir doch Brüder füreinander auch wenn das Schicksalslos so gefallen ist [...] Ja gewiss ich hatte mir das nie erhofft und Du auch nicht, das weis ich ohne Dich zu fragen. Du wirst die Schuld vielleicht auf mich schieben, und nach Deiner Ansicht sowie vieler andern werde ich sie auch haben. Verzeih mir, aber ich konnte nichts anderes, ich hoffe du

Italy, was the right one: 'Not that I regret not to have opted to leave, on the contrary. It is just so painful that all of you are leaving me behind.'[24]

Ludwig's pain clearly indicates that the Nazis' 'Blut und Boden', which had been turned into 'Blut oder Boden' for the desperate South Tyroleans, was rendered completely meaningless to these siblings, as blood and soil were now being torn apart, and everything meaningful was falling to pieces in the process. The Option made a complete mockery of those 'building blocks' of nationalism the Nazis were claiming to be the foundation of their philosophy. Ludwig's outcry discloses Hitler's raw and brutal power politics that defenceless individuals had to endure.

By the end of February 1940, the painful consequences of their decisions became obvious: Hermann was by then conscripted into the German Wehrmacht and moved to the Reich, while Ludwig wrote to Richard who had declared he was leaving for Germany too but, due to the slow pace of the Option resettlement, still remained in South Tyrol until 1943: 'I have received a card from Hermann before he left our Heimat. Where is he now? How long will it be before I see him again? Terrible thoughts! […] I apologize if I keep creating these stirs, I cannot help myself, these events have hit me too deeply.'[25]

His pain of separation was shared by those of his siblings who remained in South Tyrol. All they had was hope for a better future. On 5 May 1940, Ludwig wrote to Richard: 'Dear brother! I noticed there was a lot of hard pain in your letter and I have had a lot of sympathy, especially one sentence however moved my heart deeply: 'Hermann has been the first to tear apart what is left of our little family!' Dear Ludwig, you wrote you did not want

---

wirst mich verstehen und mich nicht als stützköpfig abschauen […] Ich möchte weiterfahren, sehe aber alles doppelt, die Buchstabe spiegeln sich in den trene meiner Augen. Der tiefste Schmerz hatt keine Worte, sagt ein Sprichwort.'

24 'Nicht etwa das es mich reut, nicht hinaus gewählt zu haben, im gegenteil. Es schmerzt mich nur, da ihr mich alle verlasst.'

25 'Habe von Hermann eine Karte bekommen vor seiner Abreise aus der Heimat. Wo ist er den jetzt? Wie lange werde ich diesen nicht mehr sehen? Schreckliche Gedanken! […] Verzeihe mir wenn ich immer wieder diese Aufrürung bringe, ich kan nicht anders; diese Ereignisse haben mich zu schwer getroffen.'

to make my heart even heavier, but I beg you to console only yourself and do not take things to heart too much; now this has happened, and then, our dear Father knows why he allowed all this to happen. Be brave and do not give up, life goes on and everything will be fine in the end.'[26]

The geographical separation between the siblings became more permanent as the war continued: Ludwig returned to South Tyrol and worked in the Italian administration, and once the German army occupied South Tyrol in 1943 and turned it into the so-called Operations zone Alpenvorland, Richard was conscripted into the Waffen-SS and remained there until the end of the war in 1945.[27] Hermann served on nearly all European fronts and kept writing letters which exude homesickness and a great worry that his 1939 decision to opt for Germany may have negatively influenced the relationship between the siblings in the long run. Many of his letters to his brothers contain sentences such as: 'Have I offended you? What is missing in my letter that you do not respond?'[28] The degree of alienation between the siblings is obvious at this stage as they all lived with the consequences of their respective decisions. They all survived the war, but there is no indication whether or not the Option led to a long-lasting rift between them.

The effects on the South Tyrolean population, however, have been well-documented: The chasm between the Dableiber, those who intended to stay, and the Optanten, who were willing to resettle into the Reich, often turned into hate and persistent mutual resentment, which survived the war

26 'Lieber Bruder! Habe in Dein Schreiben man hartes Leid von Dir gesehen und gleichzeitig auch mitgefühlt hauptsächlich der Satz ist mir tief zu Herzen gegangen: "Hermann hat den Anfang gemacht unser bischen Familie was noch ist zu zerreisen!" Lieber Richard, Du Schreibst, Du willst mir das Herz nicht noch schwärer machen doch ich bitte Dich tröste nur Du Dich und lass es Dir nicht ganz zu Herzen gehen; nun ist es geschehen und dan, der lb. Gott wird schon wissen, warum er es so zugelassen hat, nur Mut und nicht verzagen es wird schon wieder gehen und alles gut werden!'

27 The conscription of foreign nationals living in occupied territories was a breach of international law, but it was widespread Wehrmacht practice in South Tyrol. Serving in the SS Divisions was at that stage no longer a voluntary decision by the young soldiers; instead they were forced to fight in these elite troops.

28 'Habe ich dich beleidigt? oder was fehlt? das du mir nicht geantwortet hast?'

by a long shot. Despite the unifying policies adopted by the ethno-regional Südtiroler Volkspartei (South Tyrolean People's Party, which became the voice of German-speaking South Tyrol after 1945), as late as the 1980s successive generations of people in towns and villages of the province were still able to point out where the Optanten and the Dableiber had lived.

After 1945, the allegiance to Germany cost the Optanten their initial moral high ground: in 1939, they described themselves as the true Germans among the South Tyroleans, but after 1945, they were associated with Nazi policy and the atrocities committed by soldiers on all fronts, including genocides and the Holocaust. While in global public perception, after 1945 all South Tyroleans were tarnished for simply 'being German', the Optanten lost out twice: they were seen as German, and they had lost their *Heimat*. Those among them who attempted to resettle in the old *Heimat* after the war were often shunned and ostracized by their fellow people. After 1945, the Optanten were judged harshly for their declaration of allegiance with the Reich – a judgement based on the benefit of hindsight.

Those who opted to leave were made to feel that they had made the wrong decision after the war. They had, undoubtedly, backed the wrong horse in 1939. This was clear to see in 1945, but who was to predict in 1939 that the Third Reich was to last no longer than another six years? To judge the Optanten in this way was the luxury of a post-war generation that could judge only with the benefit of hindsight. Contemporaries had no looking glass. In 1939, nobody could guess that Hitler was going to be gone in six years and that the Third Reich, which was to last 1,000 years, was going to disappear with him. Decisions to stay or go were taken against the backdrop of a prolonged Italianization campaign in South Tyrol in the 1920s and 1930s and based on the hope that Hitler symbolized the reunification with the German-speaking world. The agony and torment expressed in the exchange between the five Schuler siblings may hopefully help understand the situation of the German-speaking minority in Italy in the autumn of 1939.

The numbers: by the deadline of 31 December 1939, 86% of the 200,000 German-speaking South Tyroleans had decided to leave their Heimat and follow the call to resettle in the German Reich, including Austria. However, no more than 75,000 actually moved physically as the resettlement scheme started slowly and came to a grinding halt once the German advancement had been stopped in Stalingrad in the winter of 1942–3. A total of 20,000 to 25,000 of those who had left returned to South Tyrol after the war, and they faced a society that no longer welcomed them with open arms. Many elderly South Tyrolean citizens never forgot which of their fellow villagers or town neighbours opted to go and who stayed. Furthermore, losing 50,000 fellow citizens meant a significant numerical weakening of the German-speaking minority in Italy, which was now – in post-Second World War Italy – facing a very difficult period characterized by Italian proto-fascist legislation, protest and violence, policies and responses which brought the region to near-civil war conditions in the early 1960s. While the German-speaking minority reunited somewhat under this perceived pressure, its pre-Option homogeneity was never regained. Sources such as the one presented here elucidate the enormity of the psychological impact of the Option decision on families, villages and communities, and therefore complement the anonymous numerical toll by adding the human condition and the personal impact, which is often totally lost to historical research and often not even considered in tables and tallies of going and leaving, living and dying.

Notes on Contributors

ANDREA CARLÀ is a senior researcher at the Institute for Minority Rights, Eurac Research, Bozen/Bolzano, Italy. He received his PhD in politics from the New School for Social Research, New York, and has completed his postgraduate studies in diplomacy and international relations at the University of Bologna, Italy. His research explores the interplay among ethnic politics/minority protection, migration studies and security issues, focusing in particular on the concepts of (de)securitization and human security and their application to minority issues. He is the co-editor of *Migration in Autonomous Territories. The Case of South Tyrol and Catalonia* (Boston: Brill-Nijhoff, 2015). He is currently a network member and part of the network board of the Erasmus+ project called 'The Securitization of Migrants and Ethnic Minorities and the Rise of Xenophobia in the EU' (SECUREU) (November 2020 to November 2023).

ENIKŐ DÁCZ is a research associate at the Institute for German Culture and History in South-East Europe (Institut für deutsche Kultur und Geschichte Südosteuropas; IKGS) at Ludwig Maximilian University of Munich. She received her PhD from the University of Szeged (Hungary) and her research areas include German-language literature in Central Europe, spatial and postimperial discourses in German-language literature in Central Europe, inter-ethnic relations in Transylvania in the twentieth century, the reception of the *Nibelungenlied* as well as the reception of Romanian and Hungarian literature in German-speaking countries. Her most relevant publications are as follows: 'Colonizing a Central European City: Transnational Perspectives on Kronstadt/Brașov/Brassó in the First Half of the Twentieth Century', in Jenny Watson, Michel Mallet and Hanna E. Schumacher (eds), *Tracing German Visions of Eastern Europe in the Twentieth Century* (Edinburgh German Yearbook 15) (Rochester, NY: Camden House, 2022). She has co-edited (with Raluca Cernahoschi) special issues titled "Transnationale

Karpaten" of *Spiegelungen. Zeitschrift für deutsche Kultur und Geschichte Südosteuropas* 16/1&2 (2021), and (with Réka Jakabházi), *Literarische Rauminszenierungen in Zentraleuropa. Kronstadt/Brașov/Brassó. Veröffentlichungen des IKGS*, Band 141 (Regensburg: Pustet Verlag, 2020).

WINFRIED R. GARSCHA worked at the Documentation Centre of Austrian Resistance/DÖW, Vienna, as a senior historian (retired). He is also the co-director of the Austrian Research Agency for Post-War Justice and the spokesperson for the consortium of associations of Austrian Nazi victims and resistance fighters. He received his PhD from the University of Vienna and his research interests are persecution and resistance during the Nazi era as well as how Austria has dealt with its Nazi past in judiciary, historiography and the arts. He is the author of studies about the Deportation of Austrian Jews to Nisko (1939), the General Governorate (1941) and Minsk/Maly Trostenets (1941–42), in the DÖW Yearbooks 2018–2020 and the co-author of 'Verfahren vor den österreichischen Volksgerichten', in *DÖW Yearbook* (2021). He has also published a chapter titled ' "Violation of Human Dignity" and Other Crimes against Humanity in Austrian War Crimes Trials', in Beth Griech-Polelle (ed.), *The Nuremberg War Crimes Trials and Their Policy Consequences Today* (Nomos: Baden-Baden [2009] 2020).

GEORG GROTE is a senior researcher at the Institute for Minority Rights, Eurac Research, Bozen/Bolzano, Italy. He has previously worked as an associate professor at University College Dublin. In his academic work, he has focused on collective emancipation movements in Europe (past and present) and the role of history and historiography in peoples' self-definition. He has published on Irish cultural nationalism in the late nineteenth and early twentieth centuries and on the German process of coming to terms with its Nazi past. He has also written extensively on the South Tyrol question between historical nationalism and European regionalism. His most recent publications comprise a three-volume social history of South Tyrol based exclusively on private archives employing letters, postcards, diaries and photographs from the late nineteenth and the twentieth centuries titled *Im Schatten der Zeitenwende. Leben in Tirol,*

1900–1918; *Die zerrissene Generation. Südtiroler Schicksale im Faschismus und Nationalsozialismus, 1922–1942* and *Das bittere Ende. Südtiroler Erfahrungen im Zweiten Weltkrieg und in der Nachkriegszeit, 1943–1956* (Athesia: Bozen, 2019–22).

KATIE HOLMES is a professor of history and director of the Centre for the Study of the Inland at La Trobe University, Melbourne, Australia. She lives on unceded Wurundjeri country. Her work integrates environmental, gender, oral and cultural histories, and she has a particular interest in the interplay between an individual, their culture and environment. Her recent research is on the cultures of drought in regional Victoria, and on water cultures and conflicts in Australia's Murray Darling Basin. Her books include *Spaces in Her Day: Women's Diaries of the 1920s–1930s* (1995) and *Between the Leaves: Stories of Women, Writing and Gardens* (2011). She has also co-authored *Reading the Garden: The Settlement of Australia* (2008), *Mallee Country: Land, People, History* (Clayton, Vic.: Monash University Publishing, 2020) and *Failed Ambitions: Kew Cottages and Changing Ideas of Intellectual Disabilities* (Clayton, Vic.: Monash University Publishing, 2023). Holmes is a Fellow of the Academy of Social Science Australia in addition to the Gough Whitlam and Malcolm Fraser Visiting Chair in Australian Studies at Harvard University (2023–4).

KARL KÖSSLER is a research group leader at the Institute for Comparative Federalism, Eurac Research, Bolzano/Bozen, Italy. Due to his background in both comparative public law and political science, Kössler's research adopts a multi-disciplinary perspective regarding the following principal fields of expertise: comparative federalism, local government, intergovernmental relations and institutional design in divided societies. He is the author of over 50 academic publications with prestigious publishers such as Routledge, Palgrave Macmillan, Edward Elgar, Hart and Oxford University Press. In 2018, Kössler was appointed as a member of the Council of Europe's Group of Independent Experts on the European Charter of Local Self-Government. His work has obtained third-party funding from private foundations and the EU. Since 2019, he has been the scientific coordinator of the five-year EU

Horizon 2020 project called 'Local Government and the Changing Urban-Rural Interplay' (LoGov), which brings together 18 partner institutions from around the world.

JUSSI P. LAINE is a professor of multi-disciplinary border studies at the Karelian Institute of the University of Eastern Finland and holds the title of Docent of Human Geography at the University of Oulu, Finland. He served as the president of the Association for Borderlands Studies and is currently the president of the World Social Science Association. He has also been a member of the Steering Committee of the International Geographical Union's Commission on Political Geography. He acts as the project coordinator for the H2020 Research and Innovation Action titled 'Migration Impact Assessment to Enhance Integration and Local Development in European Rural and Mountain Areas' (MATILDE). Within border studies, he seeks to explore the multi-scalar production of borders and bring a critical perspective to bear on the relationship between state, territory, citizenship and identity construction.

ROBERTA MEDDA-WINDISCHER, LLM (Essex), PhD (Graz), is Senior Researcher and Group Leader of Equality and Diversity in Integrated Societies at the Institute for Minority Rights, Eurac Research, Bolzano/Bozen, Italy. She is an international lawyer specializing in migration issues, human rights and minority protection. Medda-Windischer worked as a legal officer for various international organizations, including the European Court of Human Rights (CoE/ECHR, Strasbourg); the UN High Commissioner for Refugees (UNHCR, BiH; the Organisation for Security and Co-operation in Europe (OSCE/ODIHR, Albania); and the UN Centre for Human Rights (OHCHR, Geneva). At Eurac Research, her research focuses on the protection of minorities in international law as well as on new minorities stemming from migration. She has authored and edited monographs and multi-authored volumes as well as published numerous articles and chapters in edited volumes in Italy and abroad on her research areas.

ALEXANDRA TOMASELLI is a senior researcher at the Institute for Minority Rights, Eurac Research, Bolzano/Bozen, Italy. Her recent research foci include human and Indigenous Peoples' rights, anthropology of law, linguistic and national minorities, stateless nations, gender and intersectionality. She has authored a monograph, titled *Indigenous Peoples and Their Right to Political Participation: International Law Standards and Their Application in Latin America* (Baden-Baden: Nomos, 2016); co-edited a bilingual book, *Challenges to Indigenous Political and Socio-Economic Participation: Natural Resources, Gender, Education and Intellectual Property/Desafíos de los pueblos indígenas en su participación política y socio-económica: Recursos Naturales, Género, Educación y Propiedad Intelectual* (Bolzano-Bozen: Eurac Research, 2017); co-edited an anthology entitled *The Prior Consultation of Indigenous Peoples in Latin America: Inside the Implementation Gap* (London: Routledge, 2019); and published several scientific articles on this subject.

TOBIAS WEGER, PD, is a senior researcher at the Institute of German History and Culture in South-East Europe (Institut für deutsche Kultur und Geschichte Südosteuropas; IKGS), Munich, Germany, since 2018. After studying history and European ethnology at LMU Munich, he worked at the Munich Municipal Archives (1997–2002), the Silesian Museum at Görlitz (2002–4) and the Federal Institute for Culture and History of the Germans of Eastern Europe (BKGE) at Oldenburg (2004–18). His research interests include the history and culture of Central and South-Eastern Europe; history of the German academic research on Eastern Europe; cultural and political history; and the history of stereotypes. He is the author of *Temeswar/Timişoara. Kleine Stadtgeschichte* (Regensburg: Verlag Friedrich Pustet, 2023) (with Konrad Gündisch); *Großschlesisch? Großfriesisch? Großdeutsch! Ethnoregionalismus in Schlesien und Friesland, 1918–45* (Munich: De Gruyter/Oldenbourg, 2017); and *'Volkstumskampf' ohne Ende? Sudetendeutsche Organisationen, 1945–55* (Frankfurt am Main: Peter Lang, 2008).

LEAH SIMMONS WOOD is a fundraising and communications officer for Sponsored Arts for Education (SAFE), a Kenyan NGO, and working for The Launchpad Collective, a UK community interest company that help refugees get jobs in the UK. She graduated from the University of Bristol with an MSc in migration and mobility studies in 2021, where she focused on questions of citizenship, identity and belonging in refugee communities mostly in East Africa and the Mediterranean. Beyond migration, she is also interested in issues around climate change, land rights, African literature, Female Genital Mutilation/ Cutting (FGM/C) and the four-day week campaign, in addition to all the intersections between them. She has written two blog posts to date that have been published by Eurac's Mobile People and Diverse Societies page (<https://www.eurac.edu/en/blogs/mobile-people-and-diverse-societies/migrant-journeys-and-the-re-formation-of-diasporic>; <https://www.eurac.edu/en/blogs/mobile-people-and-diverse-societies/project-failed-abolish-frontex-s-week-of-action>).

MARKUS WURZER is a lecturer at the Department of History, University of Graz. His research interests focus on fascism, colonialism, collective memory, visual history and postcolonial studies. His publications include *Der lange Atem kolonialer Bilder. Visuelle Praktiken von (Ex-)Soldaten und ihren Familien in Südtirol/Alto Adige 1935–2015* (Visual History. Bilder und Bildpraxen in der Geschichte 9) (Wallstein: Göttingen, 2023); 'The Social Lives of Mass-Produced Images of the 1935–41 Italo-Ethiopian War', *Modern Italy* 27/4 (2022), 351–73; and 'Kolonialkrieg im visuellen Familiengedächtnis. Erinnerungsproduktion durch transgenerationale Albumpraktiken in Südtirol/Alto Adige', *Zeitgeschichte* 49/2 (2022), 209–35.

Printed by
CPI books GmbH, Leck